3—

THINKING
ABOUT WINE

Elin McCoy

John Frederick Walker

SIMON AND SCHUSTER

NEW YORK · LONDON · TORONTO · SYDNEY · TOKYO

SIMON AND SCHUSTER
Simon & Schuster Building
Rockefeller Center
1230 Avenue of the Americas
New York, New York 10020

Designed by Edith Fowler
Manufactured in the United States of America

10 9 8 7 6 5 4 3 2 1

Library of Congress Cataloging-in-Publication Data

McCoy, Elin.
    Thinking about wine / Elin McCoy,
John Frederick Walker.
        p.   cm.
    Includes index.
    1. Wine and wine making.
I. Walker, John Frederick.   II. Title.
TP548.M467   1989   89-31256
641.2'2—dc20   CIP
ISBN: 0-671-66303-8

TO THE MEMORY OF MARGARET WENDELL MCCOY

CONTENTS

ACKNOWLEDGMENTS

What we owe to the kindness and sagacity of others involved with wine—producers, fellow writers, enologists, shippers and merchants, generous hosts and indulgent friends—can hardly be overstated. Some of them make brief appearances in the following pages; many more, to whom we are equally indebted, do not.

We owe a very special debt to four people, without whom this book would not have come to be: to William Rice, who first asked us to write for *Food & Wine,* where much of this material originally appeared in a somewhat different form; to Ila Stanger, the magazine's current editor in chief, who wanted more; to Carole Lalli, our patient and understanding editor, for seeing the book the way we did; and to Theron Raines, wise friend and literary agent, for keeping faith.

PREFACE

Kitchen scene, our house, early evening. A duck is roasting. One of us selects a wine from the cellar, keeps it under wraps. We're playing "mystery wine"—just to stay in practice. Two glasses are poured.

"Well, what do you think?"

"It's wet and it's red. What more could one want?"

"Be serious."

"It's very nice, but I don't think you raided the special-occasion rack."

"True. Give me a description."

"Okay, Cabernet . . . or to play it safe, Cabernet or associated grapes. It's lighter, somehow, more open. We could have Merlot here."

"You're getting warm. Any thoughts on origin?"

"Doesn't seem weighty enough to be California . . . perhaps Italy . . . or the Loire . . . I'll say Bordeaux."

"Very good. But more to the point, what do you think of it?"

"It's young, fresh, very drinkable, tender-textured . . . not elegant or ravishing, but right now, I'm liking it a lot."

"Any last guesses?"

[13]

"*Petit château.* It's not telling me more, or maybe I'm just not getting the message. What are we drinking?"

"Château du Beau Vallon, 1985. St.-Emilion."

"Never heard of it."

"Neither had I, but I found it listed in Féret."

"Let's check on the bird."

Later, at dinner. One of us takes a brief note on the wine, looks up.

"Now let's get precise. What score would you give it?"

(*The other replies with thumbs-up gesture.*)

"My rating exactly. Think it's worth mentioning in print?"

"Possibly. But a lot of people wouldn't find this a big-deal wine. It doesn't have the muscles of a California Cabernet. Or the distinction of a *cru classé*. On the other hand, it was highly satisfactory with the duck, and it hasn't been difficult to drink." (*Points to level of wine in bottle.*)

"Hmmm . . . 'the modest charms of modest wine.' Is there an idea for an essay there?"

That scene, and its endless variations, has been the real source of this book. For us, writing about wine is an extension of talking about it. The setting could have been a restaurant banquet or a lakeside picnic, our own dining room or a château's. The meal could have been cracked crab on newspaper, *carré d'agneau,* or chicken pot pie. The wine could have been *grand cru* or generic jug, singled out for undivided attention or culled from a blind tasting of a dozen bottles to be further discussed over dinner. As always the dialogue would have taken its own direction. And sometimes the ideas it inspired would have found their way into print.

For us, wine has been the ideal subject for coauthorship. The research, for the most part, is a very pleasant chore, and we find the writing, like the particular conversations that sparked it, a matter of tossing the idea back and forth in draft form until we concur on the conclusions and the expression, at which point it's no longer possible to say who wrote what. We don't always agree, but that can be useful. When comparing notes after tasting, we feel confident when we concur, and when we don't, that we ought to retaste. Always having a second opinion is an advantage in curbing exaggerated enthusiasms and guarding against standing prejudices. Then, too, deciding between us how good a wine is at dinner has become a simple matter: We know if we pour a second glass from the same bottle, it's a decent wine; if we finish the bottle off, it's clearly splendid stuff; if, while doing so, we quibble over who got an extra serving or even stoop to squinting at the levels in our glasses, we know we're in the presence of greatness.

Our first insights that there might be something special about wine came, curiously, in similar ways, in the form of bottles of white Graves and Pouilly-Fuissé respectively, served to us in our teens by our fathers, who thought we ought to know such things existed. Later, there were other experiences, separate, but similar—quaffing Beaujolais with fellow students in Paris, being startled by the remarkable taste of the Champagne poured on a boat in the Bahamas from a funny squat bottle much later recognized as Dom Pérignon. When we met, a 1964 St.-Emilion, the château long forgotten, was the wine of the moment. But it was a visit to the Napa Valley in 1971 that first opened the world of wine to us, from vineyard to cellar to bottles that made us realize that fine wine is as close as you can get to potable poetry. Wine, we saw at once, is one subject where beginners have as much fun as experts.

What began then as a personal passion grew into something we wanted to write about. From the start we thought wine was worth discussing intelligently, so long as one kept a sense of proportion—if not humor. The subject is, after all, only wine, and most people's interest in it goes no further than finding something good to drink with dinner. It's understandable, therefore, that most wine writing comes down to tasters' tales and their choice of bottles, and much of ours has been no different.

But beyond the timely list of recommendations lies the writer's challenge of conveying the fascination of fine wine, wine that transcends simple drink the way fine food transcends mere sustenance, wine that excites the senses and inspires comment. Wine that is distinctive enough to be individual is, on that score alone, intellectually intriguing. If complex enough to challenge analysis and elude description, it rightly evokes a sense of wonder. Although always in evolution and ultimately perishable, it can, to a limited degree, offer a repeatable experience, allowing the pleasure of recognition and the stirring of memory. But wine cannot be fully enjoyed alone. Its deepest appreciation is essentially social in nature—anyone who prefers not to share it simply doesn't understand it.

It's partly for that reason that we've come to believe that wine's best stage is the table. It's there, over the span of a meal, that most of us are prepared to enjoy it, dropping for a moment deeper topics and weightier concerns to pause over a beverage curiously worth savoring. With like-minded friends, wine serves as tabletop entertainment, a focus for whimsy and the display of trivial learning, a sort of five-finger exercise for the mind and senses. Surely half the fun of wine lies in forming opinions, nosing out nuances, and determining favorites. But too many people, we think, confuse sophistication in wine with the kind of stuffiness that ultimately stifles enjoyment. We've long noticed that those of our friends who seem to enjoy wine the most manage to be both casual and analytical about it. True connoisseurship as it's usually described resides in the ability to tell finesse from flash, pronounce a wine true to type, and discover greatness in a glass without a peek at the label. But an easygoing expertise requires something more: a sense of perspective, an open-mindedness, and a nose that wrinkles at nonsense.

Hence this book.

Over the past fifteen years and in the course of writing some 250 wine articles and columns as well as several books on gastronomic subjects, we've frequently found ourselves taking a second look at many of the ideas, attitudes, and trends that seem to be undermining the simple enjoyment of wine. We're concerned that there's a growing reliance on scores and ratings instead of trusting one's own taste buds, a misplaced idolatry of old wines, a mad scramble for fashionable labels, an ominous trend toward taste-alike wines. Such fashionable foolishness befuddles the credulous wine drinker and threatens to turn wine appreciation into an arcane hobby at best or a kind of tulipomania at worst.

In the pages that follow, we've taken a critical look at the world of wine, tried to decide what's worth pursuing and what's not, pondered the role it should play on the table, considered the occasions it can grace, and reflected on the innocent pleasures it can provide. Not everyone will agree with what we have to say. But that's just as it should be.

Many of the things said in the following pages we've said before; they are collected here because we think they're worth saying again. The themes are grouped but crisscross in various ways because all the perennial issues about wine—great growths versus little local wines, longevity versus drinkability, classics versus challengers, and so forth—recur in various guises from situation to situation.

Although we've often found ourselves taking a contrary, revisionist point of view on various fashions and issues over the past decade and a half, we share many of the same vinous passions that most wine lovers have (a wine critic who didn't would be a highly suspect guide to the pleasures of the palate). We're fascinated by the subtle differences among fine Bordeaux, impressed with the depth of California's rich reds and fleshy whites, and stand ready to be seduced by the sensual glories of Burgundy, the romance of Port, the pure dancing elegance of Champagne, and the soul-warming satisfactions of authentic country wines. . . . But we're getting ahead of ourselves.

These notes and essays are offered to the reader for the same reasons we like to serve unusual wines to friends at dinner: we think our tastes will be shared, perhaps our selections will spark some controversy—and because someone might find them amusing.

1

The Critical Palate

THE NUMBERS RACKET

"Let's all take a vote and find out which was the best," the taster to our right said to the host. We groaned inwardly. More often than not at the wine tastings we attend, someone will suggest totaling scores. We had detailed notes, and had been especially impressed with several bottlings, but said we'd find it hard to rank the dozen top-flight Cabernets (each a superb wine in its own way) 1 through 12. The advocate of voting later told us our objection to assigning numbers was an indication we hadn't really come to grips with the wines.

Another incident: Recently at dinner in a restaurant with another couple, we selected one of our current favorites, 1980 Château Pichon-Lalande. Our guests found it as delicious as we did, and the husband was determined to buy a case. The next day, however, he called with some second thoughts. He'd discovered that the vintage charts he consulted gave the 1980 Bordeaux a low rating—5 points out of 10—and so he began to think that perhaps the wine he'd liked so much the night before wasn't so great after all. Despite our reassurances that the wine was ex-

ceptionally good for the year, he had more confidence in the
numbers on his pocket chart than in his taste buds and decided
not to buy it.

And still another: A couple came up to us after a wine tasting
to say how upset they were to discover that a wine they had enjoyed immensely had only been given a middling score by a critic
whose pronouncements they took as gospel. They seemed convinced that, because the wine had been given a mere 14 out of
20 points, they couldn't have had more than a 14/20 experience.

In all three of these instances, the people seemed to have forgotten that they were drinking wine, not numbers. Sadly, their
attitude isn't unusual. We've begun to realize that an amazing
number of wine lovers are overly impressed, even mesmerized,
by the seemingly precise numerical ratings and rankings bestowed
on wines by critics and tasting panels—so much so that these enthusiasts appear to let their enjoyment be dictated by numbers
instead of taste.

It's as if these wine lovers believe that every wine is bottled
with some preordained ranking in some imaginary ultimate wine
list and that experts exist whose palates can infallibly register
this magic number. This sort of wine enthusiast is distressed when
experts disagree over wines and asks himself which one is right.
Actually, the fact that acknowledged experts disagree is evidence
that no great degree of precision is possible in these matters and
that placing too much stock in any one set of wine ratings is un-
wise.

The fact is that how wines stack up in a given tasting or are
viewed by a certain critic is partly dependent on the circumstances
of the tasting. In many instances the results would be quite different if the tasting were repeated, with the same judges. That's
not to say there's no such thing as consistency of results, but
merely that wine tasting is far from an exact science, and that it
takes more than one tasting to develop a meaningful consensus
about a given vintage or a given wine.

Of course, everyone wants a simple answer to the question
"What's the best?"—whether it's wine, automobiles, movies, or

first novels. But the truth is that there's no pat answer—unless there are a lot of pat assumptions about what constitutes "the best."

Certainly, wine ratings have their place. It's natural for those beginning to develop a taste and passion for wine to rely on ratings and the results of wine competitions. Even among experienced wine lovers, who can make their own choices with confidence, few conduct extensive tastings to select a bottle for Sunday's dinner or a case to lay away. They, too, take ratings seriously. But both novices and veterans alike often fail to recognize the limited usefulness of wine ratings. Number scorings and comparative rankings—as opposed to tasting notes that seek to describe wines in their own terms—can be especially misleading. In fact, it's safe to say that the better the wine, the more pointless the score—and the more meaningful the description. Consider some examples.

When it comes to inexpensive jug wines, just about everyone is looking for the same thing: a clean, fresh wine with some flavor interest. Since such tastings are largely elimination procedures, a scoring system such as the Davis 20-point scale (which gives points for color, aroma, body, etc.) is appropriate and useful in weeding out the poorest examples. The lowest-scoring wines invariably lack something or suffer some fault. We'd regard the top-scoring wines of a well-conducted Davis-scored tasting of current jugs as good bets. But it's just this sort of point-scoring approach that can be so misleading when it comes to fine wines.

That's because barring the odd poor bottle, tasting any of the world's finer wines is largely a matter of assessing good, better, and best. Any attempt to rate, say, fine California Chardonnays or classified-growth Bordeaux from a good vintage results in many scores bunched toward the top. But a wine tasting isn't a horse race; in many cases the also-rans are just as interesting as the "winners." Minute differences in scoring—for example, the difference between a 17.5/20 and a 17.75/20 wine—are actually inconsequential in tasting terms. Attempting to rank truly fine,

subtly different wines is largely an exercise in artificially assigning numbers to something that can't really be quantified but only
described: individual character and style.

We're not saying that it makes no sense to rank highly individual fine wines—the *crus classés* of Bordeaux, for example. In every
vintage some properties excel, others disappoint, but it often
makes more sense to measure them against their own stylistic
standards than against each other, in which case all must be assessed in terms of a single model. And depending on what that
ideal standard is, some wines will measure up better than others.
These days, the results of scoring stylistically different wines of
equal quality are often weighted toward the most powerful and
concentrated wines, not only because elegance and finesse are far
subtler qualities than sheer intensity and richness and more difficult to detect in a comparative tasting, but because big wines are
currently more fashionable than delicate ones. A weighty Château
Léoville-Las-Cases will typically score higher in comparative tastings of St.-Juliens than the lighter Château Beychevelle. To most
people, that implies that the Beychevelle is inferior, when in fact
the real point is that it is quite different in style. And that difference isn't something that can be conveyed by a simple numerical
score.

Take the situation we found ourselves in a couple of years ago
at the fifth annual Bordeaux dinner at The Four Seasons in New
York. We were faced with a stunning array of great wines, including glasses of Lafite, Latour, Haut-Brion, Margaux, Mouton,
and Pétrus, all from the much-talked-about '82 vintage. All are
markedly individual wines, and all appeared to be magnificent
examples. We took copious notes on each. To be sure, there were
differences in how well they showed—the Mouton and the Lafite
were brilliant, and the Margaux was impressive; and on the other
hand, the Latour was very closed, the Haut-Brion very quiet, and
the Pétrus curiously duller than when we'd tasted it from the barrel at the château. Should we have concluded that the first three
are "the best"? Clearly, they were in their infancy, and the track
record of all these properties suggests that snap judgments about
the wines in their extreme youth (and predictions about which

ones will look the most impressive in ten or twenty years' time) are very risky, if not irrelevant. After all, as a great Bordeaux matures, it changes considerably.

What, really, would scoring these wines have added to the notes we took? To have reduced our impressions to a set of numbers would have been to concede that the evident variations in style in the wines were of little interest. And what value would a premature conclusion be about which wines were "the best"?

In brief, when it comes to jug wines, it makes sense to save breath and prose—and deliver the scores. When it comes to rating the middle-range bottles, we think a taster's reactions should be grouped into categories from "forgettable" to "super"—with some individual descriptions for the latter. The really great wines, however, deserve an intelligent paragraph—a portrait in miniature, so to speak.

But hold the numbers, please.

IN DEFENSE OF WINETALK

Let's face it. Winetalk is an easy target for ridicule. After all, many of those to whom wine is just a drink that happens to be made from grapes find the whole idea of someone furrowing their brow over a glass of red or white, sniffing, savoring, and trying to come up with *les mots justes* downright laughable, and the resulting jargon even sillier.

Take this wine description we overheard at a dinner party: "It's got body and legs but no soul." We laughed, of course, but not *that* loud because we know how difficult it is to put the evanescent impressions a wine makes into words.

But that it's worthwhile to try and convey through language

the experience of wine is tacitly acknowledged by every wine lover who's ever tried to explain the attractions of one wine over another. Wine writers take this a step further and try to share with others an experienced palate's reactions to various wines and some insight into the connoisseurship of the subject. Ideally, wine writing enlarges a reader's powers of discrimination, enhancing his appreciation of the next wine he comes across. In reality, many wine lovers find a lot of winetalk more exasperating than enlightening.

The wilder excesses of winetalk have rarely been criticized by wine professionals and enthusiasts, which is understandable since some of them are the worst offenders. Lately, however, several California enologists have been trying to reform winetalk. They want to develop an objective vocabulary for describing the odors and flavors of wine, which—no argument from us—would be a useful tool in laboratory situations. In fact, terms such as acidity, tannin, and sweetness, which are linked to some measurable component of a wine, have always been the bedrock of sensible winetalk. Sensible winetalk also includes less obviously objective terms, such as "grassiness" to describe the perceptible flavor characteristic of Sauvignon Blanc or "oaky" to indicate that the wine has been in contact with oak barrels—terms that can be used with precision, given enough experience.

But how far can sensible winetalk go before it becomes preposterous? What about when free association reigns and the terms used to describe the scents, flavors, and textures are limited only by the taster's imagination: licorice, butterscotch, mangoes, cough drops, every known variety of berry, cigar boxes, iron fists in velvet gloves, and all the rest?

There's often a fine line between sensible and silly. If such freewheeling comparisons help capture the impression a wine makes, they're all to the good. Saying that a sip of a delicious young Mosel is like biting into a tart, juicy apple certainly characterizes the wine better than merely stating that it has a high level of malic acid. But this approach can easily be overdone. Some wine pundits seem overly eager to demonstrate their ability to nose out a startling variety of nuances from a given wine, finding a veritable fruit salad, for example, in Chardonnays where others discern only "ripe, full flavors." Problems arise when wine lovers take such descriptions in print literally. No one should think he has a wooden palate if he can't find the whiff of "sweaty saddles" in Pinot Noir; an association that is a useful *aide-mémoire* for one taster may be highly misleading to another.

Anthropomorphic wine terms—those that refer to wines as if they were people—are even more problematic. It might seem that calling wines "charming," "seductive," "honest," "teasing," "foursquare," "boring," and so forth is clearly the lunatic fringe of winetalk and ought to be stamped out, as some enologists think. But we'd argue that not all of these personifications are silly.

Can a wine be "seductive"? It's not an objective term, because there's nothing to measure. But it's not totally devoid of sense either. We think the average wine lover can figure out that a seductive wine doesn't make you grimace when you drink it; in fact, it's the kind of wine that is hard to keep your hands off of. And who hasn't found some wines "boring"? (Either someone who's awfully easy to please or whose cellar is a lot better than ours, that's for sure.)

Just about the only terms that don't cause confusion are purely judgmental expressions ("dreadful," "divine," "delightful," etc.) because it's quite clear that someone is either giving the wine a rave or a pan. What causes the most problems is the shorthand winespeak that critics commonly use to convey their impressions and opinions of what's in their wineglasses. What should have been an intelligible paragraph on a wine becomes, typically, a dense mix of the factual ("some volatile acidity," "a trace of residual sugar") and the fanciful ("wisps of woodsmoke," "cascading loganberries"), topped off with a snappy summation ("contrived thrills, but not worth a detour"). The compression leaves the neophyte confused if not cross-eyed. When penning a wine description, we find it helps to imagine what someone might think if that passage were their first encounter with winetalk. Phraseology that defies translation into English may be good for a laugh, but it won't shed light on its chosen subject.

Wouldn't a vocabulary list of sensible wine descriptors, if widely adopted, help keep such jargon under control and make winetalk easier to follow? We doubt it. Who would it help but the enologists? Permanently retiring the more farfetched wine phrases to where old clichés go may sound like a laudable goal, but we're against limiting winetalk to the strict description of measurable, perceptible components of the beverage. That kind of truncated vocabulary may suffice for analysis, but not for appreciation. As we see it, it takes every resource of language to talk meaningfully about wine. Wine lovers—and that includes wine writers—need to be able to convey, however inadequately, that a wine gives (or doesn't give) a particular kind of pleasure. Drinking wine isn't entirely an objective experience, and wine description that eschews imagination and subjective impressions is flat, clinical, and, frankly, no fun.

THE TROUBLE WITH "BLIND" TASTINGS

Not long ago, we found ourselves at a dinner where an unidentified Vintage Port was served. Guests were invited to guess the year. Lacking inspiration, we fell back on deduction and decided, given its evident maturity, '55 would be about right. Several other guests came to the same conclusion, including someone who looked as if he'd passed a few decanters in his day. It turned out to be a '48. The connoisseur shook his head. "Don't know how I missed it," he muttered aloud. "It had '48 written all over it." The remark made us think of Peter M. F. Sichel's oft-expressed reminder that "one look at the label is worth decades of experience."

Knowing what the wine is tends to influence one's perception of it, of course, which is why hiding the labels is the only way a taster can make assessments on what's in the glass in an unprejudiced manner. In fact, it's the only way one can honestly compare a classic and a contender (say a Chambertin versus a California Pinot Noir) unfettered by preconceived ideas. Blind tastings keep the palate honed, the mind open, and the match fair.

But we've come to realize that blind tasting has definite limitations—more than most people think.

Situation #1—Blind Ranking: We, along with several other tasters, were asked to rank a series of red wines served blind. They were all under $6. We ended up with several favorites but found their styles too different to compare. One we liked was criticized by some as thin and woody. It turned out to be a Rioja, which is supposed to be light, lean, and dry. Another we found attractive was disliked by others because of its obvious fruitiness. It was revealed to be a Beaujolais, which is supposed to be grapy and direct.

It's one thing to compare inexpensive jug wines blind to determine the most appealing examples because they aren't very distinctive, but to compare wines with markedly different styles on the same basis will yield mixed results because the premise of the tasting isn't clear. In mixed-bag blind tastings, some wines will inevitably be faulted for showing the characteristics they are normally praised for having.

The moral: If you're comparing apples to oranges, don't do it blind.

Situation #2—Vertical Tasting: We had been invited to a vertical tasting of a dozen vintages of Château d'Yquem, from 1977 back to 1928. The tasting was blind, which sounded sensible, but in the end, tasting blind made detailed analysis difficult and defeated part of the purpose of the tasting—tracing the style of the wine through successive vintages. Why? You don't look for the same things in old and young wines, but in a blind tasting, you're forced to judge all the wines on the same basis. If we had known which vintage was which, we could have decided, for

example, whether a young wine was aging prematurely or an old
one was remarkably well preserved. There are other questions
you might want to ask of a wine if you know what it is. For
example, how well is it showing, given the reputation of the
vintage.

Though it was a format that allowed us to discover—uninflu-
enced by the modest reputation of the vintage in Sauternes—that
'66 was excellent for Yquem, in this particular instance we felt
our judgments would have been more complete if we'd known
in advance what the wines were.

The moral: Although it's instructive to taste several vintages
blind, assessment becomes confused if the vintages span too
many years.

Situation #3—Mystery Wine: We suppose it's one of the
hazards of writing about wine, but dinner hosts will sometimes
invite us to guess the identity of a mystery wine. We recall a
dinner party at which we were asked to follow up our praise for
the main-course red with an identification. Our lack of enthusiasm for this was not, as some might suppose, because we're
poor sports, but because, in our view, the connoisseurship of
wine shouldn't be confused with the parlor trick of putting a
name to it. It's quite possible to do a fair job of assessing a wine
and yet have no idea what it is or from where it originates. In
fact, very few of the world's wines are so individual that they can
readily be identified even under the best conditions; and lacking
a context or a category to circumscribe the almost endless possibilities the world's wines offer, even world-famous palates are
liable to read the signals wrong and mistake Bordeaux for Burgundy. When confronted by a completely unidentified glass of
wine, the problem is not so much that some aspect is likely to be
missed as much as it is that the taster doesn't know how much
weight to give to what is apparent, and that's what provides clues
to identification. Besides, not knowing what a wine is may turn
the normal process of assessment and enjoyment into a dogged
search for clues to an unnamed wine's identity.

The moral: Guessing games at the dinner table can be great fun. But they're not very enjoyable—nor very instructive—if it's impossible to guess.

The subject of mystery wines reminds us of an experience that could be described as the ultimate blind tasting. Following a tasting of some of Simi Winery's state-of-the-art Chardonnays and Cabernets in a small restaurant in Santa Rosa, Zelma Long, its well-known winemaker, pulled out some of the winery's older "library" wines (all reds), served them to us blind, and asked what we thought of them. We gamely offered guesses that we were tasting marvelous Cabernet Sauvignons and in one case, possibly a Zinfandel, probably from the 1940s. "You may be right," said Long. "But we'll never know for sure."

She put down her glass and explained that a cache of older bottles had been discovered in Simi's cellar *sans* labels, supporting records, dated corks, cases, or any other significant clue to their identity. The shape and color of the bottles seemed to point to the 1930s or 1940s, and it was unlikely that the wines were anything other than Cabernet Sauvignon, Zinfandel, Carignane— or blends of the same. But that still left a great deal of mystery.

It was a blind tasting, all right, but a particularly frustrating one because in the end there was nothing to reveal. We weren't able to verify that Zinfandel can last as well as Cabernet, or discover how a particular vintage had developed, or confirm or deny any of our tabletop theories. All we knew for certain was that we had several magnificent old reds on the table.

Later we wondered *why* we felt cheated of some aspect of enjoying those wines. Did we really need to know anything more about them than what was gloriously right there in our glasses? Those who like to drink wine but could care less about its production and pedigree often wonder why wine lovers sometimes act as though they'd rather talk about it than drink it.

The answer is, surely, that for many the intellectual component of wine enjoyment—knowing what it is, how it was made, how it's developing, the romance and lore—is just as important and pleasurable as the sniffing and savoring. Let's admit it: in some cases knowing what you're tasting is not just half the fun; it may be essential to your understanding.

WHEN IS A WINE READY TO DRINK?

How many times have you read a carrot-and-stick wine description like this:

The wine has a simply ravishing nose, marvelous mouth-filling flavors, and a finish that just won't quit. Wonderful as it is, it's still a baby. It won't be ready to drink for at least eight years and won't peak until age twelve, maybe fifteen. Considering its great potential, it would be practically criminal to drink a bottle prematurely.

Attracted by that glowing description but cowed by the stern admonition to keep hands off during the long mandatory waiting period, many wine drinkers would be puzzled and frustrated. Is it really foolish to drink a fine wine before it's peaked—or even supposed to be ready? Will it taste good? How much will be missed?

Since most of the world's wines will never be better than when first bottled, the question *When?* doesn't apply to them. It only applies to wines that show definite improvement after time in the bottle—whether it takes six months or sixty years.

We want to cast a cold eye on the whole idea of what it means for a wine to be ready to drink or to be at its peak, and whether that should influence anyone's enjoyment. Obviously a wine is ready to drink when it tastes good. It's at its peak when it tastes best.

Many wine lovers know that certain wines don't show the

character for which they are famous until they've been given a couple of months—or even a couple of decades—in a good cellar. They know that good vintages of Rhône wines, California Cabernets, Barolos and Barbarescos, and red (and even white) Bordeaux are all routinely described as "begging to be cellared."

Perhaps that's why wine journalists receive so many inquiries from consumers about when the wines they've collected will have realized their maximum potential. Quite sensibly, they want their money's worth and are looking for reassurance that they'll uncork their treasures at just the right time.

A generation ago, it was assumed that older almost always meant better. English wine writers of that era made a cult of this, hoarding their best bottles as long as possible, taking pride in uncorking them at an advanced age, when all that might be left was a last, poetic gasp in the glass. They painted vivid word pictures comparing the opening of nineteenth-century clarets to rudely awakening old soldiers from a hundred years' slumber so that they could snap to attention one last time before toppling into the grave. Those dinner-table swan songs with old Moutons and Margaux occasioned much purple prose.

No one writes that sort of stuff anymore (marvelous as it was for armchair reading), but one legacy of that school of thought is the persistent notion that there is a magic moment for each wine, when it will finally "blossom" and display all its long-awaited glories. Today a wine's evolution is described as if it could be plotted on a graph, with a bell curve representing its rising improvement, plateau of drinkability, optimum peak, and inevitable decline.

The trouble with all these descriptions is that there is often disagreement among experts about when a wine is *à point*. The French, by and large, like their wines young, when they still show freshness and vibrancy. With rare exceptions, they like Bordeaux before ten years of age, Burgundy even younger, and Champagne as soon as possible. To them, the "full-fledged maturity" the British still revere is really a taste for the passé—like a perverse interest in overripe cheese or long-hung game. Most Americans (as long as we're risking generalizations) don't really care for the taste of old wines, possibly because most wines consumed here, even fine wines, are clean, fresh, and fruity. Not having developed the habit of laying down wines, we haven't acquired a taste for older vintages. Nonetheless, old wines are held in high esteem, if only because in this country any wine more than ten years old is considered a collectible and priced accordingly.

Frankly, we believe that it's often a mistake to think of a wine having a peak at all. Simply put, a well-made wine has a different sort of balance among its components when young, middle-aged, and old, and it can taste very different in character at all these stages. Whether the wine's midlife is always the ideal point at which to drink it depends a lot on the wine as well as on individual taste—not to mention the dishes it might be paired with. (A young, still tannic red might be an ideal choice for roast duck; an old, faded, but pungent wine might be just the bottle to bring out with the cheese tray.)

Consider fine reds. Normally they're mature once they've reached the point when tannin is shed, fruit hasn't yet faded, the bouquet has developed, but the flavor is still fresh. Unfortunately not all reds have a perfectly regular evolution. Take an overly tannic Barolo, for example. The fruit may fade before the tannin diminishes, and if that's the case, it may be at its best far sooner than any theoretical time frame might suggest. Besides, contemporary winemaking worldwide, which emphasizes balance and soft tannins, almost always ensures that even long-lived reds can be drunk with pleasure in their youth. This is true of topflight California Cabernet Sauvignons, such as Opus One, the Barbarescos of Angelo Gaja, and even many '82 Bordeaux.

As we think about it, we often enjoy our wines best before they've really peaked. Certainly it's more fun to taste a wine and contemplate how much better it might become than to realize how much better it must have been.

On the other hand, wines on the downhill slide have their merits, too. Several years ago we tasted a well-stored example of the 1958 Château Haut-Brion. It was small-scaled and a bit short in the finish but perfectly delicious drinking. If we had purchased that wine twenty years ago, would we have had the courage to set aside a few bottles for extended aging, considering how limited a future was predicted for the '58s?

In our view, part of the fun of drinking wine is to taste it at various stages of development, which is one reason to buy more than a couple of bottles of any wine you believe in. Regular tastings prevent miscalculations by allowing you to monitor wines that seem to be gaining with time.

In general, we've decided we like our Bordeaux older than our California Cabernets. Clarets may lose a good deal of fruit and still retain a sort of attenuated delicate sweet ripeness that is most attractive, while the larger-scaled California Cabernets, once they lose their magnificent fruitiness, have a less graceful decline, becoming rather dry and pungent. (That's true of Rhônes and Piedmontese wines, too, which we also prefer in full vigor.)

The progress of red Burgundies is not easily predictable; often luscious from the start, they may seem at their best at eight years of age and yet go on gaining for decades. Balance is the key, as it is for whites, both dry and sweet. California Chardonnay can seem almost tropically fruity when young and benefit from a year or so in the bottle. Sauternes can be appreciated in extreme youth for its freshness and sweetness or years later when it has evolved into a more complex and dramatic wine.

By now, you'll understand why we're dubious of overly precise predictions on when wines will reach drinkability, attain their apogee, and slide off their pinnacle of perfection. Such prognostications ignore much that a wine lover might consider important when it comes time to pluck a bottle from the wine rack. But can a real expert tell by taste what sort of evolution a wine will have over a span of several decades? That's the impression given by the readiness with which many wine pundits offer detailed predictions, sometimes into the next century, of when this or that bottling will give its all.

It can be done, and done well. But the question of how accurate *most* such predictions are—well, that's another story.

NEW THOUGHTS ON OLD WINES

One night at a dinner party we served a 1966 Château Montrose with the cheese course, thinking it would make an interesting contrast to the 1976 Château Montrose served earlier. Though most of our guests found it superior to the younger vintage, one of them—who knows little about wine but can listen to his taste buds—demurred. "Maybe I'm missing something," he said, "but I think the younger wine is a lot nicer to drink." Put that way, we agreed. In terms of drinking pleasure, the younger wine had it all over the older one.

That incident started us thinking about all the fuss that's made over old wines, whether they're twenty years old or two centuries old, like those mysterious bottles auctioned recently that supposedly belonged to Thomas Jefferson.

What *is* the appeal of these old wines? There's taste, of course. Old wines are supposed to offer the kind of complex pungency and attenuated flavors that only extended time in the bottle can confer. To be truthful, though, very, very few wines over twenty years old offer the ultimate tasting thrills to be found in the world of wine. Drinking a famous old bottle is often a great experience, but not necessarily a great pleasure if you think of it in purely sensual terms.

Actually, for many wine lovers the appeal lies in the intellectual interest that comes from discovering how a vintage has developed. There's also the frisson that comes from uncorking something scarce and very costly. In the days before such bottlings became staggeringly expensive, one château owner we know used to serve legendary vintages such as 1870 in an unmarked decanter. He would nod knowingly when his unsuspect-

ing guests failed to go into transports of ecstasy. After revealing
the vintage, he'd nod knowingly again when they began to discover extraordinary sensations from the dregs in their glasses.
(We once tasted a Rhône wine from 1832 and were so bedazzled by the date that it only slowly dawned on us that we
were actually tasting the world's most venerable vinegar.)

The Bordelais—who produce the stuff, after all—don't make
a cult of old wine. By and large they drink their wines young,
under ten years, while they're still vigorous and fruity. Decades-
old wines, if still drinkable, are regarded as survivors or sou-
venirs, historical curiosities that can be enjoyed only if drunk
with some understanding of their limitations.

Not that we don't enjoy a big-deal bottle from time to time.
Not long ago we sacrificed a magnum of '64 La Mission Haut-
Brion (magnificent) and a '55 Cos d'Estournel (wonderful) at a
dinner party we gave for some appreciative wine-minded friends
and reveled in every sip. But we don't do that sort of thing very
often, and not only because we don't have many bottles of that
caliber gathering dust. One reason is that so few occasions are
suitable for grand old wines. They require a certain amount of fuss
in serving and a substantial amount of attention at the table, or
the whole exercise seems pointless. By now, many older wines have
become so expensive that no one but the wealthy would serve
them casually. For most of us, on most occasions, that's enough
reason to regard serving them as uncomfortably ostentatious.

There are also distinct limits to how long any wine remains
attractive. Even wines intended for long aging—such as California Cabernet Sauvignon, red Bordeaux, and Vintage Port—have
definite life spans. For Cabernet, it's rarely longer than eight to
fifteen years; for Bordeaux, ten to twenty; for Port, fifteen to
thirty. To exceed those limits the wines would have to be top-
quality examples from superior vintages that have been im-
peccably stored. Middling wines from average vintages, particularly those with a checkered past—several ocean voyages, many
owners, a spell on retail shelves—may not even last to the minimum expectation.

Once, we visited a huge wine cellar in Texas that was mind-bogglingly complete, with bin after bin filled with famous old vintages—not just prewar, but even prephylloxera. Later at home our modest basement cache looked woefully inadequate until we realized that the majority of our wine was for future consumption; when wines had reached their best they were regularly and happily liquidated. In that vast Texas cellar, the proportions were reverse: virtually everything was in decline.

Wine lovers attracted to the idea of having a key to a museum of rare old wines need to remember that there's a vital difference between collecting wine to enjoy drinking and collecting wine to . . . enjoy collecting wine.

TO BREATHE OR NOT TO BREATHE

Does a wine *really* taste better if it's opened well in advance of being served so that it can breathe? Alas, there's no quick or definite answer. Tradition, science, and the differing experiences of many wine drinkers often contradict each other.

In fact, there's little consensus on the issue even among winemakers. In Italy, the notion that all serious reds require hours of aeration is almost ingrained; on the other hand, Burgundians avoid early opening and shun decanting when possible. In Bordeaux it's common to serve wines at lunch that have been opened since morning, but no less an authority than Emile Peynaud, consulting enologist for scores of châteaux, regards breathing as a pointless practice often harmful to the wine.

Not surprisingly, wine critics are divided over the issue as well. A number hold to the long-standing wine lore that red wines are definitely improved by exposure to air before consumption. A few—the heavy breathers—go further, asserting that it is criminal to serve fine reds without giving them a chance to breathe and even advocate down-to-the-minute aeration periods for specific bottlings (including whites!)—12.5 minutes for one, 22 hours for another, etc.

As the late Frank Schoonmaker put it, "much pretentious nonsense is written about breathing." But then he, too, went on to confuse the issue by adding that breathing can "help in rounding out sturdy young wines and a few powerful northern Italian wines." What is a wine drinker to think? Does breathing make sense or not?

Obviously, all wine drinkers want the best from the bottles they broach. But those who take all the airy advice about breathing as gospel find themselves fretting over when to uncork and whether they should decant early and if so, how soon before pouring. Are they wasting their time? For the most part, we think so.

And here's why:

Enologists agree there is little solid scientific evidence for advocating advance aeration of wines when the facts about wine and air are considered. True, wine is exposed to air during the winemaking process, but in a highly controlled manner. Its development in bottle occurs in the absence of air (corks don't breathe).

Once opened and exposed to air, any wine eventually becomes flat, oxidized and acetic—spoiled, as anyone knows who's ever sniffed a half-consumed bottle that's been forgotten for a week. And what constitutes exposure to air? Uncorking a wine, obviously, but since this exposes only a dime's worth of wine surface, it can be hard to tell a just-opened bottle from one that has been uncorked for an hour. Decanting the wine into another container, however, does amount to vigorous aeration, and that includes, obviously, the simple act of pouring it into a glass. (Recorking a partially consumed bottle or stoppering a decanter will not retard oxidation so long as there is airspace—it only slows it somewhat.)

Since the oxidation process that leads to eventual deterioration starts when the wine is opened, why would anyone think that there could be an improvement in the *early* stages of air exposure?

Well, for one thing, aeration can dissipate the odd smells some wines show when they're uncorked. These "bottle stinks" may result from gassiness, fermentation, sulfur, or mustiness, and they typically mask the wine's bouquet. As one odor fades, another more attractive odor may be revealed. That could have been the case some years back when we tried a bottle of Château d'Yquem from 1954, a long-forgotten vintage—and with good reason, we thought, when we uncorked it and found it a mean, musty, varnishy drink. We dumped our glasses and left the half-filled opened bottle on the kitchen counter. The next morning, out of curiosity, we cautiously sniffed it. Amazed at its improvement, we sampled it and found it palatable.

However, as enologist Maynard Amerine points out, "the claim that leaving a wine open or decanting it results in an increase in the desirable odors is hard to substantiate. What chemical reactions could take place within a few minutes or a few hours that would produce enough additional desirable odors to be recognizable?"

Yet many wine drinkers, ourselves included, have experienced wines that seemed to blossom in the glass hours after being opened. But we've noticed that this phenomenon is especially marked at meals and typically occurs about the time the cheese is served.

"Say," someone will announce, "taste the Château Trop Cher again. It's really marvelous now." Everyone will taste, and yes, the wine will seem much better than it was before. But has it really transformed itself?

Any such apparent change is likely to be the result of what enologists call palate adaptation: the food and the mood—not to mention the preceding glasses—have all paved the way toward heightened appreciation.

Then, too, the change may simply be due to a rise in the temperature of the wine. It's known that the odorous compounds of wine are more volatile (and thus more apparent) at warmer temperatures. A wine plucked from a stone-cold cellar, for example, will not show much bouquet until it has warmed. Yet few people seem to consider that a wine that appears to have improved after early opening may also have risen significantly in temperature.

Aerationists and their scoffers alike, however, do seem in accord about what happens to a fine red after breathing. At best, the taste softens and the wine appears to be smoother in texture. To many, this is desirable. But this usually happens at the cost of diminished bouquet, and since bouquet is a wine's crowning feature, any loss in this regard is (for us, anyway) sufficient objection to the practice of breathing. A hyperventilated red will lose not only its bouquet, but also its firmness of structure, and will taste flat, dull, tired, even soupy. For a very old and fragile wine, excessive aeration can be fatal. Of course, decanting is necessary for older wines with sediment. But considering the vigorous airing involved, it's wise to wait to decant a very old wine until just before serving, as many venerable bottlings can begin to disintegrate right in the glass.

Sure, we've got wines in our cellar—some, but not all of our Bordeaux, for example—that we know from experience strike a better balance between nose and taste if allowed a turn in the air before dinner. But there isn't one we'd hesitate to serve immediately if time were a problem and no decanter were available. We'd simply give it a vigorous swirling in the best aerator of all, a wineglass. If we're not familiar with a wine, we'd rather play it safe, forgo decanting, and let its nuances develop in the glass as we drink it.

In fact, we haven't found it possible to say, as members of the breathing school do, that young sturdy reds benefit more than mature wines from breathing. It just seems to depend on the bottling, and frankly, few of any type seem to benefit markedly from any more airing than provided by simply decanting and serving. In our experience, the vast majority of the world's wines never taste any better than they do when first opened and poured, unless the wine shows some fleeting off-odors or is served too cold. Frankly, we've also tasted wines for which deep breathing is deemed essential that had their winemaking faults made more obvious by extended aeration—some Brunellos, for example.

Actually, the only wine type that we'd say always seems to be improved by a couple of hours in a decanter is vintage Port—that is, if it's still in its prime. The flavor is so intense that most tasters find aeration, which softens the wine, makes it a shade more appealing.

But let's face it. The world over, wines are routinely opened and consumed during the course of a meal without undue fuss over transformations in the glass. Unless you're drinking something ancient and evanescent, timing just isn't that critical—despite what those critics with stopwatches say.

We're all for the romance of wine, including the search for nuance, but think the beverage can be enjoyed—and assessed—with a minimum of mumbo jumbo, and that includes inflated worries about whether it's a half-hour too early or minutes too late to catch it at its best.

Sound too casual? Still wonder if extended aeration, precisely timed, is crucial to enjoyment? By all means, put the matter to the test at your own table, but do it blind. In the end, you may find you can breathe a little easier about the whole business yourself.

COOL REDS

A frequent refrain in our observations of the wine scene is that too many wine drinkers allow themselves to be browbeaten by tradition instead of paying attention to what their palates tell them. A case in point—the serving temperature of red wines. Permit us a story to illustrate: Two years ago on a late summer evening we were dining in the garden of a small, trendy restaurant in New York City's Chelsea district. Though something light and a bottle of white would have been more in keeping with the season, we ordered the 1978 Château Pichon-Lalande we saw on the list, curious about this fine Bordeaux that we hadn't tasted in several years. Besides, we wanted to try the grilled duck with mushrooms.

As the waiter carefully opened the bottle and poured out an ounce or so for us to taste, we noticed that the stylish couple at the next table seemed to approve of our choice. And when we tasted it, so did we. There was only one flaw: the wine was unpleasantly warm. So we had the waiter plunge the bottle into an ice bucket. He satisfied this request without a murmur, but the couple at the next table now watched with barely disguised shock and dismay. A little later, when we resampled the just-cool claret and nodded in satisfaction, the woman quickly averted her gaze and the man turned away with an involuntary shudder. They were doubtlessly wondering why we hadn't ordered the ice-cold Lambrusco our brutish palates so evidently craved.

From their reaction, you'd have thought we'd asked for a pair of straws to enjoy the bottle. Where does the misleading idea that reds can never be chilled come from?

Perhaps it's an overreaction to the American penchant for serving most beverages *ice*-cold. At one time in this country, even fine red wines were labeled—as we once saw on a bottle of Château Lafite-Rothschild from the 1940s—with a recommendation to "serve at room temperature." As word got around that reds don't normally need refrigeration, these cautions became unnecessary. But recommendations about the *ideal* serving temperature for reds are harder to come by. The vague advice about "room temperature for reds" found in many wine texts (which probably takes its inspiration from the drafty dining rooms of English country homes) misleads many wine lovers. As a result, most Americans consistently serve reds five to fifteen degrees warmer than they should for the wines to show their best. Unless they have a cool cellar, many never discover how much more attractive many reds are below 70 degrees (Fahrenheit).

When European winemakers attend tastings of their wines in the United States, they are often distressed at the warmth at which their wines are typically served. We remember Robert Dousson of Château de Pez and Lalou Bize-Leroy of Domaine de la Romanée-Conti, among others, fussing over proper serving temperatures. On their home ground they are used to having their reds far cooler.

As wine lovers who've had plenty of reds served American style, we have to say that we think these winemakers are right. We've come to prefer our reds—all our reds—on the cool side, European style. It's more than just a matter of preference, however. Though temperature isn't a component of wine, it is certainly part of the overall impression a wine makes. The volatility of the various odoriferous compounds present in wine is affected by temperature. Simply put, the warmer the wine, the stronger the scent and flavor; the colder the wine, the less apparent the scent and flavor. Yet a cooler wine is much more refreshing than a warmer one. Many Americans follow that line of thinking to a fault, overchill their whites, and serve them numbingly cold. Still, only an eccentric would prefer an expansively scented but warm glass of white wine to a slightly less aromatic but refreshingly cool glass of the same wine. Although the wine may lack a certain expansiveness of aroma, it gains far more in overall attractiveness.

Few wine drinkers realize that the same principle holds for red wines—albeit within a slightly warmer range. A cool serving temperature accentuates acidity and tannin; hence reds appear firmer when cool. When a low-tannin red such as Beaujolais is served almost as cool as a white (say, in the low fifties), its fruity, grapy character is definitely accentuated.

Cooling a Bordeaux down to the midsixties focuses the overall impression, tightens the bouquet, and restores a sense of architecture to flavors that at a warmer temperature seem to sprawl over the palate. The term "bouquet" evokes a useful image: cooling a red slightly has the effect of drawing together its elements, like a hand gathering flowers. Served too cold, of course, wine will appear to retreat into a shell. A tannic red, such as a

Bordeaux, is a grim, biting mouthful at too cool a temperature. It needs to be served a little warmer than a Beaujolais—both to release its more complex bouquet and to soften its astringent character. But there's an upper limit: over 70 degrees, the more delicate aromatic compounds appear overwhelmed by the alcohol, and the wine seems more soupy than structured.

The ideal temperature for individual reds requires some experimentation, but here are some useful guidelines we've developed. The better the wine, the warmer it can be and still show its best. But there is a minimum level of coolness even for the finest reds. Served warmer than these norms, they seem to have lost a linchpin. For us it seems to be about 62 degrees for Beaujolais or Gamay, 65 for Burgundy or Pinot Noir, 68 for Bordeaux or Cabernet Sauvignon. (Ports should be served slightly cool, too, or the alcohol will seem obtrusive.) Normally we serve wines cooler than the ideal so that they'll take longer at the table to reach the point of being too warm.

This doesn't mean we're constantly taking a wine's temperature—despite the example of a few prominent winemakers who do so religiously before drinking. As a rough guide, we simply feel the bottle. If a taste proves too cold, we let the wine warm up in the glass. At home, it if appears too warm, it's easy enough to put a red in the refrigerator to cool for twenty or thirty minutes or to keep it next to a cool window in the winter (or the air conditioner in the summer).

In a restaurant it can be difficult to get a cellar-cool red, but we've developed a strategy. If we've ordered a white wine to precede a red, we make sure the ice bucket isn't whisked away after we finish the white. A brief dunking may be just what the red needs. Even if we haven't ordered a white, we don't hesitate to ask for an ice bucket if the red is too warm—even if it does raise a few eyebrows at the next table.

CHANGING FASHIONS:
DRY VERSUS SWEET

Do wine connoisseurs invariably prefer dry wines to sweet? Not necessarily. But they're supposed to, according to most casual wine drinkers, who invariably equate dry with sophisticated.

Where does this idea come from? Perhaps it stems from the widely held notion that neophytes have trouble weaning themselves from sweet wines until their palates become more refined. It's an attractive, if oversimple, way of explaining how people graduate from soda pop to St.-Emilion. Embodied in this explanation, however, is the misleading idea that only the unsophisticated have a taste for sweet wines.

Even experienced wine lovers, who ought to know better, are often victims of this gastronomic groupthink and will deprecate their own taste in this regard. We remember the Chicago couple who seemed unaccountably embarrassed when we asked to look at their wine cellar after dinner. It turned out that they thought the preponderance of classic German bottlings in their modest collection might be taken as evidence of arrested palate development.

So prevalent is the idea that dry is superior to sweet when it comes to wine that those consumers who show a preference for sweeter styles of wine can't be sold on buying sweet if it isn't marketed as dry—presumably so that they can satisfy their taste while preserving their self-esteem. California jug wine producers know very well that most consumers prefer wine with a small amount of residual sugar but don't want to be told they're drinking sweet. Hence the phenomenon of "fruity" or "hearty" or "pink" or "golden" or "round" as euphemisms for sweet. Even slightly sweet bottlings of champagne are labeled "Demi-Sec" (Semidry) or "Sec" (Dry) to disguise this preference.

What few people realize is that this attitude toward sweet wines is simply a matter of fashion and has nothing to do with sophistication or the lack of it. Nowhere is this more obvious than with the great classic sweet wine Sauternes.

Several generations ago, the most sought-after wines were sweet. Russian grand dukes doted on the great Sauternes, and the multicourse dinner of Edwardian times always featured rich, sweet wines—Sauternes, German Auslesen, or Tokay from Hungary, and sweeter Champagnes. Château d'Yquem, the greatest of the Sauternes, regularly sold for more than Château Lafite; and in fact, even up to the 1950s, the top Sauternes estates just below d'Yquem in rank commanded higher prices than the Médoc second-growths. This was reasonable: fine Sauternes is far rarer and far more costly to produce than fine claret. But when Bordeaux prices soared in the late fifties, the Sauternes were left behind. Exquisite wines such as Château Climens, Château Coutet and Château Suduiraut sold for little more than the price of mere *cru bourgeois* Médoc!

Why had they fallen from fashion? Perhaps they seemed too heavy, too rich, and too extravagant to find a place on the simpler, leaner menus of the postwar era. Relegated to the dessert course at banquets, they eventually disappeared from most tables altogether. Worse, those who never actually put the matter to the test took for granted that such sweet wines simply didn't go with most foods.

Curious to find out if the gourmands of the Belle Epoque had a perverse liking for overwrought food and drink combinations, or if, in fact, they knew something about these wines that we moderns don't, we tried several dishes often served with Sauternes in the past. We were pleasantly surprised to find that they *do* work. Chicken with garlic or leeks and fish in cream sauce proved excellent with a number of Sauternes, particularly with the lighter, more acidic Barsacs, such as Nairac and Climens. The principal drawback, we've discovered, is that for many people the very idea of serving a sweet wine with other than a dessert course is simply too novel. Recently we were at a dinner with a number of wine lovers at which a heavily sauced steamed fish wrapped in cabbage was brilliantly paired with a German Kabinett; virtually everyone agreed it worked well, but, not believing their taste buds, ended up claiming they would have been happier with a dry wine!

Then there's the school of thought that maintains that Sauternes should be served as an aperitif. We used to think this was an idea dreamed up by the desperate producers of Sauternes, but actually it has long been a Bordeaux tradition and in recent years has been rediscovered with enthusiasm in Paris as well. It is extraordinary in combination with foie gras and in fact, is just as delightful with a handful of salted almonds. We've managed to put away our initial misgivings about starting a dinner with sweet wines, having convinced ourselves by repeated experiment that whatever fine dry wines follow will not be diminished in flavor.

Little wonder that during this past quarter-century-long slump in Sauternes sales, the great châteaux there have produced fine wines largely as a matter of pride, although some ended up tearing out their vineyards and planting red grapes, while others took shortcuts in the vineyard and cellar, which resulted in a poorer wine and a further decline in reputation.

One survival measure that's been widely adopted has been the production of fine dry white wines at these sweet wine châteaux—ostensibly to ensure that even in years when there would be little classic wine made, there would be something to sell. At first these dry wines were modeled on the rather heavy "Y" (pronounced *ee-grec*) of Yquem, but lately livelier, crisper wines have been produced, such as the *vin sec* of Château Coutet, the "R" of Château Rieussec (recently purchased by the Rothschilds of Château Lafite) and the "G" of Château Guiraud.

But Hamilton Narby, Guiraud's new owner, scoffs at the idea that producing an alternate dry wine is the answer to the Sauternes producer's prayers. "We make about thirty thousand bottles of 'G' a year—that's hardly enough to alleviate the cash flow problems of a Sauternes château. Producing a dry wine is partly a matter of prestige." And partly, we suppose, a matter of wisely keeping the château's name in the public eye, in the hopes that wine lovers will become curious to try the real thing—and discover what they've been missing.

THE EMERGING INTERNATIONAL TASTE

Scene: A dinner party in the year 2000. A curious guest savors his glass of wine and turns to his hostess. "This is really rich and smooth. It must be one of those multinational varietals—Transatlantic Merlot, maybe?"

"Tastes just like it, doesn't it?" she replies. "You'd never guess, but it's Pacific Cabernet—from New Zealand grapes, made in Japan, and bottled right here in L.A."

It hasn't come to this—yet. But there are signs that for better or worse, the world of wine is headed that way. Many of the wines we're all going to be drinking in the future will taste surprisingly alike and seem to have as little relation to a particular country or region as "Pacific Cabernet."

Consider the following comments, all heard in the past several years.

"I'm looking for a Bordeaux-type elegance in my Cabernet—a balanced, drinkable style." (From a California winemaker.)

"With our new methods, we extract only the soft tannins. That way we get a suppleness of character that permits us to enjoy the wine in its youth." (From a Bordeaux château owner.)

"I want to make a California-style Chardonnay—very fruity and flavorful, and of course aged in small oak barrels." (From an Italian producer.)

These comments are illustrative of the enormous changes that have taken place in the world of wine in the past decade as a result of the new technology used in making wine and wine producers' heightened awareness of worldwide winemaking techniques and wine styles. The geographically scattered wine regions of the world—each of which formerly produced wine according to local traditions that appealed to local conceptions of style and quality—now seem to be shrinking into one global wine village with an increasingly homogeneous outlook on how wine should be made. In the process the spectrum of tastes in the wine world has begun shrinking, too: diverse regional wine styles are being modified or dropped as more and more wines, regardless of origin, are being made to conform to the emerging international taste.

What are the hallmarks of this international taste? In whites, it means a refreshing, crisp, fruity, whistle-clean style; in reds, a round, soft, fruity style, enhanced by the spice of noticeable new oak, that trades some potential longevity for early maturation. In both instances, agreeableness is paramount, even if some character and complexity must be sacrificed to attain it. Whether this taste will become so dominant worldwide that regional wine styles will largely disappear remains to be seen. But this emerging international taste seems certain to have an important impact on how both everyday and fine wines in the future will be made—and judged.

A number of factors have come together to bring about this phenomenon. One significant change in the past decade has been that the best wines from almost all the world's wine regions are becoming widely available internationally. Today you can buy the best Napa Valley Cabernet Sauvignons and Chardonnays in Paris. Over a dozen different Brunello di Montalcino wines from Italy are available in New York. Some of the finest Australian wines are starting to appear in U.S. shops. This new availability has meant that the tastes and styles of all these wines and scores more—some with strongly distinctive regional styles—have, inevitably, been compared with one another. Some have won international acclaim and some have not. Largely, they've been accepted internationally depending on how closely they conform to established French standards of winemaking.

This state of affairs has come about because prior to the seventies, the only broad range of fine wines traded on the international scene were French. (German wines, by contrast, constitute a very narrow range of styles.) For many people, these French products were the only examples of fine wines they were exposed to—and people tend to prefer what they've become familiar with. Little wonder that the best French wines became the basis of the developing international taste and constituted the benchmarks for virtually all categories of wine, a position still largely held today.

California wines in fact have become internationally acceptable partly because they have successfully emulated French styles. The taste of these California wines is based on the flavors of the classic French (and now international) grapes—Chardonnay, Cabernet Sauvignon, Pinot Noir, Sauvignon Blanc, and so on— and the freshness associated with relatively short aging in wood, a cornerstone of modern French winemaking. Recently the style of California wines has been coming to resemble French wines even more closely as winemakers seek balance, more moderate alcohol levels, and higher acidity. But California wine styles, even where they haven't followed the French, have influenced today's international preferences. It hasn't been lost on French, Italian, and other winemakers that consumers in many countries find particularly appealing the style of wine in which California excels—wines with emphatic fruit, strong varietal character, soft rather than steely flavors, instant drinkability. French wines themselves have been changing, gravitating in the reds toward greater suppleness and attractiveness when young, in the whites toward lightness and freshness. Partly this has been as a result of improvements in wine technology, but clearly it is also a result of consumer preferences in these directions.

In Italy, Spain, Australia, and other wine-producing countries, the success of this new French/California international taste has had its effect. Winemakers there have not only been going to great lengths to clean up and streamline their traditional products but also are planting the international grapes and creating new wines that ignore traditional local styles altogether. To do so, they've turned to the new wine technology, which has also had a standardizing effect on wines produced with its aid.

The impact of the new wine technology has been particularly

far-reaching. Now winemaking equipment is international, as are the techniques promulgated by wine research centers such as University of California at Davis and Geisenheim in Germany, and well-traveled enologists such as Bordeaux's Emile Peynaud. Today winemakers everywhere, like restaurant chefs, think nothing of taking their expertise from one country to another.

Modern wine technology finds application in every aspect of winemaking, but most dramatically in permitting similar styles of light, elegant white wines to be made in hot climates through the use of temperature-controlled fermentation. Winemakers can now overcome certain regional limitations, and cleaner, fruitier, smoother wines everywhere are the result.

Both the spread of the new wine technology and the availability of the world's wines have contributed to global awareness among the world's wine producers. Winemakers who want to stay in the forefront and increase their share of this new worldwide market carefully note changes in fashion and study the styles and types of wines—from whatever countries—that gain followings in various price categories. Parisian wine merchant Steven Spurrier reports that château proprietors regularly call him asking for obscure California wines. "They don't admit *they're* curious," he said. "They say something like, 'My *maître de chai* should taste them.' "

Pressure to keep up has also led to extensive travel on the part of winemakers. It's something of a standing joke in California wine circles that there's hardly any wine region in the world that you can go to that Robert Mondavi hasn't been the week before. But he's only one of many well-traveled winemakers.

The new international consciousness and the possibilities afforded by modern wine technology have led to multinational investment in wineries and vineyard land. European investment in California has been much discussed, and there is growing investment by U.S. interests in Australia. Even Frenchmen are now making wine there, and Australians have returned the compliment with investments in Bordeaux.

Whether today's wine producers intend to make everyday or fine wine, whether they are located in a region where grapes have not been planted before or in an area rich in wine tradition, their exposure to different wine tastes, styles, and winemaking ideas has led to cross-regional borrowing—even of grape varieties— and this has begun to lead to greater similarity of wine styles worldwide.

Is this an ominous development? It depends on the wine. The new everyday table wines made to appeal to the international taste are a distinct improvement over those of the past, in which some of the individual diversity of regional style was due to characteristic defects, rather than virtues—traditional, overwoody frequently oxidized Spanish and Italian whites are two examples. The advent of modern winemaking techniques and an "international palate" outlook has resulted in a number of refreshing, fragrant, ultraclean, modestly priced wines whose only fault is excessive neutrality. Many, regardless of origin, taste as if they came from the same cellar. But in an everyday wine, character and distinctiveness are not as important as reliability, soundness, and simple attractiveness. Standardization is something of a virtue.

"World-wines," which can be made on a global basis—like automobiles assembled with parts from several countries—are not only a technological possibility, but an economically sensible way of making reasonable wines at a reasonable cost. "Euro-wines"—multinational bottlings with grape sources in several European countries and made, blended, and bottled in others— already exist.

But are we in danger of losing something here? On a trip to Italy, we spoke with Pio Boffa, whose family firm, Pio Cesare, produces classically made Barolos and other Piedmontese wines. Boffa concedes that a traditional wine such as Barolo, which is made from a grape (the Nebbiolo) whose taste is unfamiliar to many non-Italians and which receives long aging in wood, may strike an American or a French wine consumer as downright un-pleasant. But although he approves of recent refinements in Barolo production (such as shortening time in barrel), Boffa sees no virtue in changing the *essential* style of the wine. "You can't make Barolo international," he told us. "It would lose its individual character. Then what kind of a wine would you have?"

Exactly. Expectations are different when it comes to fine wine. On this level, we expect character and distinctiveness of taste— both of which almost invariably require specificity of origin. The problem with top-class wines made to the international taste is that they often lack the idiosyncracies, the specific, quirky tastes and flavors of truly individual wines. They offer instead a mild-mannered, easy-to-like and easy-to-get-to-know style. Like the proverbial well-rounded person, they make friends everywhere but aren't half as interesting as a genuine individual who may, in fact, be difficult to get to know and take some getting used to.

That one overly polished, internationally sophisticated wine is liable to be interchangeable with another can easily be demonstrated on the dinner table. A future full of fine wines that, like designer jeans, are pretty much the same except for the label is a bleak prospect.

Why so? We accept standardization in other products, from automobiles to zoom lenses, and consider it a boon. But the attraction of fine wine is that it offers an almost infinite spectrum of tastes, and these tastes are not there by accident. The harvest from no other plant can be made into a product that so well sums up the fruit, the soil, and the season. Thus, wines that excite the greatest interest are those that are authentic to their origins and hold out the possibility of discerning the ground from which they spring and the marks of the year they were born. This is the well-spring, the motivation for the unceasing interest among wine lovers in vintages, appellations, and vineyards, in character, style, and progress in the bottle.

In the rush to improve fine wines as well as *vin ordinaire,* let's not forget how central sheer diversity of styles is to our delight in wine. Too often we hold wines to a double standard—paying lip service to individuality as a vinous ideal and yet constantly comparing wines and judging them against a single model, as if they should (or could) all taste alike. Surely there is a place in the world of wine and in the appreciation of wine lovers for the traditional as well as the innovative.

A few examples spring to mind: from Italy, the meticulously

made traditional Brunellos of Franco Biondi-Santi; from Spain, the old-world flavor of that country's legendary red, Vega Sicilia; from France, the solid, sinewy, untrendy claret made at Léoville-Barton.

The list, fortunately, could easily be extended. These producers and others like them aren't an endangered species—yet. But we should recognize that such traditionalists are more than just refreshingly out of step with the times. They are a reminder that if every winemaker changes his methods and grapes to conform to the international taste, more will be lost than gained.

2

On Bordeaux

A VISIT TO ST.-JULIEN

Henri Martin, proprietor of Château Gloria and Château St.-Pierre in St.-Julien, is eloquent when he talks of wine, and as one would expect from the mayor of the commune's tiny village, he did not have to grope for words to describe to us the singular virtues and style of his favorite wine. "St.-Julien lies between Margaux and Pauillac, and it's an old but true saying that the style of its wines bridges the styles of those communes as well. Here we find something of the elegance of Margaux and the power of Pauillac; so the wines of St.-Julien have more body than those of Margaux, yet more delicacy than those of Pauillac, and are distinguished by a most individual character and a very particular bouquet."

His words found sympathetic ears. We've tasted richer, fleshier Bordeaux and more delicate, more fragrant ones, but none as consistently seductive as the wines of St.-Julien. A St.-Julien makes its impression by more than sheer impact on the senses. Its appeal lies in the fact that it displays all the hallmarks of a fine Médoc—suppleness and structure, delicacy and strength, ripeness and rigor—in a particularly exquisite equilibrium, which is why the wines of St.-Julien have long been the claret lover's clarets, the favorites of those who understand that great Bordeaux doesn't begin and end with the short list of first-growths.

In no other commune is the winemaking of such a uniformly high standard. Though the 1855 classification of the Médoc that ranked all the wines from first- to fifth-growths is often criticized for being outdated, the classification as a whole missed few outstanding properties. St.-Julien is well represented on the list— with eleven growths—and has the highest proportion of classified land of all Bordeaux's communes. Today the quality of wine made from this valuable soil is higher than it has ever been. Several châteaux that had not been making wine equal to their potential in the past several decades seem now to be back on track. Château Lagrange, long in the doldrums, was purchased in 1983 by Suntory Ltd. of Japan, which plans considerable investment. St.-Pierre is under new ownership, and Léoville-Poyferré intends to recover its former lofty reputation. Given the exceptional record of such classified châteaux as Ducru-Beaucaillou, Léoville-Las-Cases, and a half-dozen others, this now makes St.-Julien a very fast track indeed.

The wine lover is the happy beneficiary of this keen competition and these days can hardly go wrong. Bordeaux expert Steven Schneider puts it this way. "Suppose you were given a case of a classified growth from, say, the '81 vintage, but you couldn't pick the château—just the commune. Which one would give you the best chance to come up with a fine wine?" The answer: St.-Julien.

The chance to taste from the barrel the much-talked-about '82 and '83 vintages was too tempting to pass up. In the spring of 1984 we crisscrossed the district, talking with proprietors, tasting their wines, interviewing people in the trade. We came away convinced that the commune of St.-Julien is making some of the most brilliant wine in Bordeaux.

Although the top wines of St.-Julien are of a very high quality and share overarching characteristics of enticing scent, ravishing fruit, and classic Médoc structure, they are by no means identical in style. Among the world's reds, Bordeaux wines clearly share a distinct scale and personality. But when one tastes only wines from Bordeaux, the wines of the Médoc region appear very different from those of St.-Emilion and Pomerol; and within the Médoc, the wines of various subdistricts, from St.-Estèphe to Moulis, clearly have their own character, too. So it's not surprising that in St.-Julien itself one is impressed with the sometimes marked individuality of the wine from each château, within, of course, that stylistic framework they all share.

For the proprietors themselves, the land and the soil explain it all: the shared resemblance and the idiosyncratic differences. What the casual visitor sees as minor dips and bumps in basically flat land and mere shades of color signifying clay or gravel are the ultimate sources of the quality and character of the wine. Even wine critics dubious of the claimed effects of soil find it difficult to argue away the convincing proof in bottle after bottle, vintage after vintage. So in driving north from Bordeaux on the D-2—the two-lane road that parallels the Gironde River and links the villages of the Médoc—we paid close attention to the passing geographical scene.

Just north of Margaux, the landscape features more pasture and woods than vineyards and fewer châteaux catch the eye. Several villages beyond, a motorist alert to the topography might notice a sudden change—a small creek—and a mild curving rise in the road, and he might realize he was about to climb to higher ground. But one isn't allowed to miss it. Even before an impressive cluster of handsome châteaux—Beychevelle, Branaire, and Ducru-Beaucaillou—and their sweeping vineyards become visible, a large sign erected by the proud inhabitants tips off the ignorant and proclaims in French that nothing less than a low bow would be appropriate upon entering the ancient and celebrated vineyards of St-Julien. Should you inexplicably turn west toward less hallowed ground, other signs warn you of your imminent departure from the gravelly, well-drained soils entitled to carry the proud appellation.

No more seductive introduction to the wines of St.-Julien could be found than a glass of Château Beychevelle from a good year. The wine, like its handsome eighteenth-century château, is a model of elegance. Stylish, silky, and supple, it features an enticing scent and an open, almost translucent structure that reveals a delicious, tender fruit quality at the core of its taste. It is not particularly rich or concentrated, but only a wine drinker fixated on weight and power to the exclusion of all else could be immune to its charms. (Deliciousness, however, does not preclude longevity, as still-glorious bottles of the '55 and '28 from the château's own cellars subsequently proved to us.) With the *maître de chai*, M. Soussotte, we tasted the dark and vigorous-looking '83 from the barrel. Youthfully tannic and well balanced, its attractive fruit was already evident. "It's the typical style of Beychevelle in a good year," M. Soussotte commented, then gave us a taste of the not-so-typical '82, which was soon to be bottled. Very dark color, an astonishingly expansive nose, and an amazing depth of ripe fruit gave an initial impression of precocious deliciousness checked by an aftertaste of considerable tannin. Still, like many of the '82s, it will probably be drunk and enjoyed long before the decade or so it will take to really mature.

At Château Ducru-Beaucaillou, the adjoining property, our timing was not good. The '82 had just been racked and was "not showing well," Francis Xavier Borie, the son of the owner, explained. We didn't press for a taste; winemakers, like proud parents, want their children to look good for company or not make an appearance at all. Instead, we compared a barrel sample of the firm, aromatic '83 with the closed, compactly structured '81 and the scented, silky-textured '79, a progression that neatly demonstrated in two-year intervals the different stages in the typical evolution of good St.-Julien vintages of a similar quality. The wine's constituent elements were raw but in the correct proportions in the '83, had begun to knit together in the '81, and emerged harmoniously in the '79, which had matured enough to show that characteristic polish and refinement, a kind of sensual sheen on the palate, that we associate with Ducru-Beaucaillou.

Even in less concentrated vintages such as '79—or to take an even better example, the exquisite '62—Ducru displays its quintessential St.-Julien virtues of appealing fruit and stylish structure in a weightier, more authoritative, and less obvious form than that of Beychevelle, without sacrificing delicacy and finesse. Beychevelle represents what the French persist in calling the feminine type of St.-Julien (translation: delicate) and Gruaud-Larose, farther west, the masculine (rich, powerful); Ducru-Beaucaillou falls somewhere in between. In short, it is as close to the archetypal St.-Julien as one could find and along with Léo-ville-Las-Cases, currently enjoys the highest reputation in St.-Julien.

Such stature isn't easily achieved. "To make good wine is not so difficult," Xavier Borie explained. "But to achieve the last millimeters of quality—that takes work." The château owners of St.-Julien, Borie reminded us, "play all the time on the same instrument." There are, after all, only minor differences in the characteristic mix of mostly Cabernet Sauvignon, some Merlot, and fractions of Cabernet Franc and Petit Verdot at each estate, and only slight variations in the classic Bordeaux cellar techniques. The potential quality possible from each estate is brought out by minute attention to detail. Ducru-Beaucaillou has been in the Borie family since 1942, and its current reputation is credited to Xavier's father, Jean-Eugène Borie, who literally lives above the shop (the château, unlike most in Bordeaux, is built right over the wine cellar).

Inland from the river, across the road from Beychevelle, is Château Branaire, which produces a flavorful, full-bodied, savory style of St.-Julien with a very individual, fine-grained texture, faintly reminiscent of chocolate. Coproprietor Luc Sartor gave us a taste of his promising, stylish '83 and a sample of his soon-to-be-bottled '82, a marvelously deep, rich, tannic, deliciously complex wine.

Farther west lie the immaculate grounds and cellars of Château Gruaud-Larose, where we tasted the '82 and '83 of that property along with the '82 and '83 of Château Talbot. Both these large estates are owned by the shipping firm of Cordier, and both are unusual in that they are neatly surrounded by their own vines—scattered and intermingled vineyard parcels among various châteaux not being at all uncommon in the Médoc.

Gruaud-Larose is dark-colored, rich, thick-textured, fruity, even plummy wine, round and fat in the mouth. There may be less clarity and point in its tasting impressions than with other St.-Juliens, but it rarely disappoints: meticulous winemaking produces attractive, reliable bottlings even in less-favored years. Talbot is stylistically similar and equally reliable, but less concentrated and rich. Both can be very long-lived. We found the '83 Talbot well balanced, with fine color intensity and fruit; next to it, the '83 Gruaud-Larose appeared deeper, riper, yet more refined. The '82 Talbot was very rich and quite tannic; the '82 Gruaud-Larose was even deeper and more "packed," already displaying an incredibly long, scented finish.

The famous three Léoville vineyards farther north represent among themselves the stylistic polarities of the commune, from delicate to powerful. In the eighteenth century, there was only one vast Léoville estate dominating the prime vineyard land of the district. A revolution and several changes of ownership later and there were three: Léoville-Las-Cases, Léoville-Barton and Léoville-Poyferré. Despite having been separated for a century and a half, they are inevitably compared in each vintage. Each has had its era when it was regarded as superior to the other two. In the nineteenth century and through the 1920s, Léoville-Poyferré was proclaimed the best; in the 1940s and 1950s, Léoville-Barton held pride of place; in the 1960s and 1970s, Léoville-Las-Cases gained the ascendancy and is now widely regarded as having no peer but Ducru-Beaucaillou, a view reflected in the prices it commands.

In fact, changing taste has as much to do with the status of the three Léoville marques as does the skill of their winemaking or the age of their vines—factors often cited—for the three are actually quite different in style.

At Château Léoville-Barton there is no château; when Ronald Barton's great-great-grandfather purchased a portion of the Léoville estate in 1826, he was already the owner of neighboring Château Langoa. Since then, the two wines have always been made in the cellars at Langoa. Ronald's nephew Anthony Barton, who runs his own wine *négociant* business and at that time assisted his uncle in the administration of the Barton properties, had set up a tasting for us of the '83, '82, and '81 Langoa-Barton and Léoville-Barton in their traditional *chai*.

We confess that until we'd had the opportunity to taste some older vintages of Langoa-Barton and Léoville-Barton (notably splendid pairings of '49, '53, and '55) a few years ago, we did not fully appreciate their style. These wines are harder, firmer, and less fleshy than the St.-Julien norm and as a consequence, can appear unyielding, harsh, and acerbic, even charmless in youth. But given the requisite fifteen to twenty years of age, what emerges is claret in the traditional mold: architectural in structure, deep flavored, often magnificent, never lapsing into softness. In spite of the trend toward more supple Bordeaux, the Bartons make wines that argue eloquently for the view that a classic claret cannot be made more appealing in youth without sacrificing something in its maturity. In an era when wines are judged, sold, and drunk on the basis of their youthful appeal, it is a style of winemaking largely disappearing from the Médoc.

In style, Langoa-Barton is to Léoville-Barton what Talbot is to Gruaud-Larose, a shade less refined and deep and often a bit more forward, but clearly cast in the same mold. We found the '83 Langoa-Barton big, hard, and intensely flavored; the '83 Léoville-Barton is equally powerful, deeper, and more aromatic. The '82 Langoa-Barton has great concentration and tannin and that precocious ripe fruit character of the best '82s; the '82 Léoville-Barton is more tightly knit with immense depth and character and a finish inky with tannin. The '81s are smaller scale, more typical; the Langoa-Barton has a lean, tight structure and emergent fruit, and the Léoville-Barton is a bit more closed and acerbic.

"Let's go taste some real wine, shall we?" Anthony Barton suggested, and soon thereafter we were midway through lunch and enjoying a glass of the now mature, scented '62 Léoville with him and Ronald Barton. (After overseeing nearly sixty harvests at Léoville and Langoa, Ronald Barton died in 1986; Anthony Barton now directs the two châteaux.) Ronald Barton was proud of the fact that no classified châteaux of the Médoc have been in the same family hands for as long as his, and even prouder of his insistence on traditional techniques in the vineyard and the cellar.

With the cheese came a decanter whose contents showed the brick-red edge of color in the glass characteristic of older Bordeaux. A magnificent bouquet and a marvelous, mouth-filling flavor, austere, yet with a lingering, sweetly ripe finish suggested a tannic wine that must have taken years to reach its present peak. Something from the fifties perhaps? . . . Well then, the forties? "Actually, it's a 1937," Anthony Barton told us, savoring his glass. "But you know, I sometimes wonder if we should be in the business of making wine that lasts forty-seven years."

Ronald Barton peered over his glasses at us. "Ah, but don't you think it would be a pity if no one made this sort of wine?"

Indeed.

Farther up the D-2, in the small village of St.-Julien-Beychevelle, a cluster of buildings on either side of the busy road houses the cellars of Léoville-Poyferré and Léoville-Las-Cases—separately, of course—so that workers at both châteaux must dodge speeding cars several times a day to carry out their tasks. At Poyferré new construction in the *chai*, new equipment, and the presence of Francis Dourthe, the new (as of 1981) *maître de chai* gave us the idea, correct as it turned out, that Poyferré is making considerable effort to regain the high regard in which it was once held.

In style, Poyferré has traditionally been a St.-Julien that deliberately traded power for harmony and finesse, which places it closer to the Beychevelle end of the St.-Julien spectrum than the weightier styles of the other Léovilles. But from the 1950s through the 1970s, the wine was frequently disappointing, its lightness verging on weakness. Yet the potential for superlatively elegant wine remained. In the small, neat, new tasting room of the refurbished *chai*, M. Dourthe poured out samples of his last two vintages. The '83 was strikingly deep in color, with an expansive, attractive aroma; the taste was young but already showed a certain delicacy of balance between its tannic intensity and luscious fruit. The equally dark '82 was suffused with a lovely, ripe fruit scent and round lingering flavor. Different wines, but equally marvelous, they promise to become bottles to elicit the praise of the past.

Next door at Léoville-Las-Cases, everything has the immaculate look of an enterprise widely regarded as one of the front runners of the Médoc. Under the watchful eye of Michel Delon, an administrator who clearly lets no detail escape him, Léoville-Las-Cases is likely to stay in the forefront. Its current reputation lies in the fact that it has made outstanding wine—within the limitations of the vintage—every year since 1959. Stylistically, the Las-Cases is not as hard as the Barton, but is more austere than the Ducru-Beaucaillou; the tension between suppleness and structure, power and finesse is carefully balanced, so that its tasting impressions are brilliantly focused.

"Power and richness, that is the base of the wine. Finesse is a gift of the *terroir*—the soil. Of course, Las-Cases is blessed with good *terroir*," Delon explained, referring to l'Enclos, the magnificent single vineyard of nearly fifty hectares, surrounded by a stone wall that runs north from St.-Julien-Beychevelle to the Pauillac line and the vineyards of Château Latour. Assisted by M. Rolland, *maître de chai*, Delon offered a series of vintages for us to taste: '83, '82, '81, '78, '75, '71, and '66. The '83 was intensely deep in color and concentration, perhaps comparable in weight to the '78; the '82 was extraordinarily powerful, closed, yet lingering on the palate; the fine '81 already showed balance and finesse; the round, rich '78 was still closed, but hinted at its future potential; the '75 is a sleeping giant, with a just-emerging nose of great complexity; the '71 was a lovely, perfectly balanced wine, a model of St.-Julien wine now approaching maturity; the firm '66, by contrast, still needed a few more years. The exquisite '62, drunk several days before at Restaurant Clavel in Bordeaux, fell into place with our overall impression of superlative winemaking.

But if there was ever a demonstration that there is no immutable order in wine, it is Château Gloria. It is a *cru bourgeois*, not a classified growth, and yet it easily ranks in quality with

the better wines of St.-Julien. Little wonder; its vineyards consist of parcels of land purchased over the past four decades from
the commune's top estates. It was created in 1942 by Henri
Martin in the former cellars of Château St.-Pierre, a classified
growth with a very tangled history. At one time that estate was
divided, then reunited; parts of the vineyard were sold off—to
Gloria, among others. (Recently, fulfilling his vinous destiny,
Martin managed to buy the actual St.-Pierre château, then the
marque and the remainder of the vineyards.)

Among the few *cru bourgeois* of the commune, Gloria has
long held pride of place. It is a particularly delicious, round,
fruity St.-Julien, made with a great concern for balance. "Take
the oak, for example," Jean-Louis Triaud (Henri Martin's son-
in-law) explained to us as we toured the modern cellars. "The
tannin of the wood must be balanced by the tannin of the grapes.
If I use too much oak, the effect is like putting on too big a coat.
It won't make me bigger." Triaud suggested we begin our tasting by sampling the lovely '79, a typically fine vintage, to focus
our palate on the Gloria style. We then moved on to a fruity,
balanced, and promising '83 Gloria. Next to it, the '83 St.-Pierre
was bigger, more closed, more tannic, and very impressive. The
'82 Gloria was ripe and glossy and wonderfully round in the
mouth, deliciously forward. The '82 St.-Pierre was incredibly
deep, tannic, and powerful—judging from those two samples,
we'd say St.-Pierre is somewhat reminiscent of the round, fruity
Gloria style but made of much sterner stuff; both perhaps are
cousins of the ripe, fruity Gruaud-Larose style, but a shade
"brighter."

"We thought that if we were going to restore the fame of St.-
Pierre, we must have the quality," Triaud commented, sniffing
his sample glass. "Fortunately our first vintage was '82, and we
made a very severe selection. What do you think of it?"

We were happy to tell him that there's always room for another superb St.-Julien.

CONTROVERSIAL CLARETS: '82 AND '83

Are you one of those wine lovers confused about the 1982 and 1983 vintages in Bordeaux? Little wonder. Some wine critics have described the 1982 vintage as unquestionably great, monumental, and fantastic, while others have called it ridiculously overpraised and overblown. Proclaimed by some critics as a vintage destined to rank with the '59, '47, and even '29, it has been panned by others as soft, fat, and short lived. Some of the same critics who so heavily knocked those '82s even compared the '83s to the '61s!

What are wine lovers to think? Are those who bought the '82s now sitting on tomorrow's legendary bottling? Or did those who passed them by in favor of the more "classic" '83s make the wiser choice?

To understand why so much journalistic cross fire has been generated—even before the wines were bottled!—one has to realize that controversy over Bordeaux vintages is nothing new. It is partly related to the difficulty of judging vintages before they've shown their true form. Anyone assessing infant Bordeaux is in the position of trying to predict what it will become, based on what it is—an unpleasantly raw, aggressive mouthful. One looks for balance, concentration, the requisite structure and hints of future style; then one determines its quality based on what's in the glass, faith in the property, previous experience of similar wines at a similar stage, and knowledge of the growing and harvest conditions, taking into consideration, of course, the projected effect of a decade or so in bottle on the final outcome. It's obvious that good palates can stare into their sample glasses and come up with very different ideas about the same wines. It's also why, in part, there are dissenting critics who, having tasted the identical '82s that have sent others into ecstasies, can find them too delicious now, too soft, too atypical to make classic, long-lived, glorious Bordeaux.

It's also true that in the past quarter-century, several outstanding vintages have been hailed in succession as the vintage of the century. And talk like that is bound to cause controversy. In fact, the vintages of '59, '61, '70, '75, and now '82 were all lavishly praised even before their respective grapes were completely picked. Their much-vaunted virtues and alleged fatal flaws were debated then in the press, and continue to be. Of the first four, only the '61s seem to have escaped serious second thoughts during their years in bottle.

Revisionist palates now think the '59s are in a disappointing tailspin from which there's no recovery. The excellent '70s have largely been demoted from the nectar-of-the-gods category. Even the still-young '75s are now regarded by some as the vinous equivalent of the emperor who has no clothes because of alleged signs that the wines are drying up prematurely.

We think these negative hindsights are the result of discovering the obvious: that not every château makes a great wine even in a great vintage and that some vintages are best enjoyed while the wines are young and vigorous. In addition, many Bordeaux vintages go through a closed or "dumb" period—a dull phase in the aging cycle when the grapy appeal of youth has gone but the subtleties of maturity haven't yet developed. Yet some years, unusually enough, are relatively attractive throughout their life span.

The controversy is just beginning with the '82s and '83s, whose merits will undoubtedly be debated for a decade or so. Having tasted more than fifty '82s in the fall of 1983 in New York, and visited some fifty châteaux, from *cru bourgeois* to *premier cru,* during a month's stay in Bordeaux the following spring, where we tasted the wines just before bottling, along with the youthful and promising '83s, we're willing to take sides. In fact, four years and many bottles later, we find a distinct profile of these vintages is emerging.

In 1982, an excellent growing season and unusually warm harvest conditions yielded very ripe grapes and unusually big, rich wines with slightly, but not alarmingly, lower than normal acidity levels. From the barrel they were impressively aromatic, with wonderfully round, concentrated, lingering flavors. The large proportion of ripe Merlot in these wines gave even the normally angular Médocs a Pomerol-like lushness. That ripe surface gloss—the vinous equivalent of baby fat—is unusual; rarely is the ripeness of a Bordeaux vintage so apparent in cask. Some critics took its appearance as an ominous sign, as if only Bordeaux that are awful in their youth can amount to anything later. (In fact, after bottling, most '82s shed some of their early glossiness, revealing substantial tannin.) The '82 Bordeaux *are* precocious in appeal but are *not* developing ahead of schedule.

While it is possible to indulge in opening some '82s now—even certain *crus classés*—simply to revel in their richness, such sneak previews of glories to come are certainly premature. We take the degree of ripeness in the '82s not as a sign of quick development; we think it simply means that they will be more drinkable for longer over their life span than many leaner vintages typically are. As David Peppercorn, the British Bordeaux expert, points out in this context, it's worth recalling that the still-viable '47 Cheval Blanc was being served as an "infant prodigy" in 1953.

All this does not mean that we've found our tasting notes on the '82s uniformly enthusiastic. We failed to go into an expected swoon over the '82 Palmer, for example; fine as it was, it lacked the concentration of other wines in its league. But apart from a slight diffuseness in some of the '82s from Margaux, we've found no wines with the loose, structureless quality of some of the oversoft '76s.

Perhaps the most misleading criticism of the '82s is that they are not classic. As Anthony Barton of Château Léoville-Barton and Langoa-Barton told us recently, "The word *classic* is now being used as a synonym for *typical,* which means good vintages are now called classic, while exceptional ones aren't." This sort

of wordplay has left wine consumers with the idea that the '82s
are somehow abnormal in a negative sense.

Yet who doesn't regard such atypical, exceptional years such
as '28 or '49 as classic? It's easily forgotten, too, that there are at
least three different kinds of great Bordeaux vintages. To over-
simplify, let's call them the hard ('45), the beautiful ('53), and
the plush ('59). The '82s definitely fall into the plush category—but are no less classic for that.

That the '82s won't last and won't be long-lived is another
criticism. Perhaps they won't last as long as some vintages, although it's difficult to believe the best-balanced wines won't be
magnificent well into the next century. But will it really matter
if some '82s prove to be at their best at twelve years instead of
twenty? Greatness in wine should be measured by the height it
reaches at its peak—not how long it lasts. The '82s that are less
concentrated will mature early and will be delicious that much
sooner.

Which '82s have impressed us the most? Well, there's little
point in rattling off the names of almost every major property
in Bordeaux, but it is true that many estates made more exciting
wine in 1982 than they had in years. In looking over our notes
we seem to have been particularly taken with the wines of
Pomerol and St.-Julien. Interestingly, the most extraordinary red
wine we've ever tasted from the barrel was the '82 Château
Ausone. It was tannic and unformed, to be sure, but suffused
with amazing complexity and incredible length of flavor. To
taste it in the damp, dimly lit cellars, hewn from solid rock below the vines of this tiny vineyard, was an unforgettable experience. (Alas, we were unable to locate more than a token bottle
for our own cellar. Not being willing to taste it until it is, by
strong consensus, à point, we can't say now how it might be developing.)

And the 1983s? Virtually everyone agrees that it is a very
good, but very mixed vintage. The real controversy is over how
good the best wines are. Unlike the '82s, the '83s taste the way
a fine young Bordeaux usually tastes. From the barrel they were

bitterly tannic, biting, and closed. In 1988 the more successful specimens were still firm and acerbic, although the lighter examples are drinking well already. But the size, concentration, and balance of this vintage is in many instances impressive. The '83s are big and powerful wines showing the flavors of a year that favored the Cabernet Sauvignon; at some châteaux in the Médoc, they are comparable in quality to the '82s from the same property, occasionally better, particularly in the district of Margaux. A direct comparison of the '82s and '83s of Château Pichon-Lalande or Château Margaux, for example, will leave one with the distinct impression that neither vintage is superior to the other, merely different in style.

Claret lovers who didn't lay down enough of '82 or '83 to feel a partisan interest needn't feel left out. They can discuss, compare, and take sides on another contrasting back-to-back pair of top-class vintages, '85 and '86. Those twins will doubtless divide the critics once again, this time between advocates of the precocious, deeply fruity, elegant '85s and the firm, intensely tannic '86s. . . .

Say, haven't we seen this controversy before?

FROM OUR TASTING NOTES:
CHÂTEAUX HAUT-BRION AND
HAUT-BRION BLANC

In the spring of 1986 we attended a remarkable two-day tasting of the wines of Château Haut-Brion held by Marvin and Sue Overton of Fort Worth, Texas, at their longhorn cattle ranch. There are only a handful of wine collectors in America with cel-

lars that can rival the Overtons', but what really sets them apart
are the extraordinary wine tastings they host. The Overtons, like
other serious collectors we know, have a refreshingly informal
attitude about wine and appear—to the novice—to be amazingly
generous with their bottles. Actually, their willingness to share
their wines is part and parcel of a love for wine. There may be
some collections that can be enjoyed in private—stamps, or first
editions, perhaps—but wine isn't one of them. You don't really
enjoy your wines unless you open them, and you don't really
experience a fine wine just by drinking it; you have to discuss
it, and you can't do that alone. (As a natural consequence, wine
lovers who start collecting soon discover that they aren't ac-
cumulating bottles to fill up a cellar—they're collecting them
to share with like-minded friends.)

Along with the other tasters who came to the ranch, we felt
it was a unique opportunity to compare not only forty-nine vintages of Haut-Brion's first-growth red wine dating back to the
last century, but also over two dozen vintages of the château's
ultrascarce white, Haut-Brion Blanc, in company with the château's proprietors, the Duc and Duchesse de Mouchy, and its
articulate winemaker, Jean Delmas.

But we weren't there merely to taste wine; we were there to
enjoy it. Some wine lovers have the mistaken idea that the more
great wines you serve, the more solemn the occasion has to be.
Not the Overtons, whose Texas-sized imaginations are only exceeded by their sense of fun. If we needed proof that it's possible
to be both analytical and convivial at the same event, we got it
there. Vintages of Haut-Brion Blanc were tasted open-air, next
to the cattle pens and accompanied by fried catfish, Texas bull-
frog legs, and home fries (a wild but wonderful wine and food
match). We tasted recent vintages of the red in a creekside
grove of pecan trees—wild turkeys gobbling in protest at our
presence—and later, back at the ranch, resampled them along
with spit-roasted pig. The final black-tie tasting of the older
vintages took place in the barn—by candlelight, to be sure, but
accompanied by a cowboy stew of longhorn beef served up by
the ranch hands.

And the wines? We went to the tasting knowing that despite being famous for three hundred years, the wines of Haut-Brion are curiously underrated in some quarters. We find this puzzling, since both the red and the white are arguably the most complex and individual Bordeaux of either type, a viewpoint confirmed by the variety of vintages we tasted.

Haut-Brion shares with the other fine reds of the Graves district a leathery, tobaccolike bouquet and a meaty, savory flavor with a curious, minerallike, faintly iron tang. In many Graves reds, these characteristics come across as coarseness, but in the case of Haut-Brion, they add up to a refined complexity. Despite its lightness and elegance, Haut-Brion takes years to develop fully, although it reaches drinkability relatively soon—a characteristic of the wine that's not always appreciated. Tasting youngest to oldest, the first wine we thought had a fully developed, mature bouquet was the 1960! Earlier vintages, except those from truly poor years, obviously had a way to go.

Among the most promising recent vintages, we'd include the wonderfully fruity '85 (a barrel sample), the powerful '83, and the extremely rich '82. We found the '84 smaller-scaled but harmonious and thought the '81 would be lovely, given about ten years of aging.

Vintages '79, '78, '76, '75, '71, '70, '66, '64, and '62 were, as expected, classic examples of those years, but we weren't the only ones to prefer the '79 to the '78. We also preferred the elegant '71 to the presently backward '70.

And the older vintages? The '61, a fabulous, faultless wine that will develop further, overshadowed the marvelous '59. Our notes were effusive on the '55, '53, and '52, a remarkable trio in full-blown maturity, with the '53 perhaps the best. With very old wines, how they have been kept and the condition of the particular bottle can be as important as the vintage. But even under perfect storage conditions, only the greatest years can last for decades. We thought the '49, '43, '40, '37, '34, '29, '28, '21, '18, and '07 in the tasting were past their best. Yet other vintages—'47, '45, '26, '24, '20, and yes, even the 1899—were still magnificent.

Even more impressive was how remarkably good the "off years" (light and poor years) were after some bottle age. Considering the vintages, '69, '68, '67, '60, '58, '57, and '50 were surprisingly good. Tasted against food instead of against more spectacular bottles, they would have been more than satisfying. On the basis of this, we expect that the best of the more recent "little" years, 1980, to develop classic Haut-Brion character by 1990, though it won't have the depth of richer vintages.

The opportunity to trace the development of the red's style from youthful to senescent examples was rare enough, but rarer still was the chance to taste the château's scarce and legendary barrel-fermented white. Only some 1,500 cases a year of this blend of Semillon and Sauvignon Blanc are produced, about a tenth of the amount of red. Haut-Brion Blanc is as expensive as the red (when you can find it), but it tastes like a first-growth's white should—if given a decade or more of aging. A great vintage can last and develop even longer.

At its best, Château Haut-Brion Blanc is an extraordinarily complex wine, full of exotic lingering nuances and flavors that hint of caramel, lanolin, lemon, burnt almonds. It is similar in character to a great Sauternes, but bone-dry—not surprising when you consider that it is made from the same mix of grapes.

The high points: Among the younger vintages, '85, '83, and '82 were particularly rich, scented, and lingering (we especially favor the '83); '78 and '71 were deeper in color, unctuous, and savory. The vintages from the sixties—'67, '66, '62, and '61— were amazingly fresh (perhaps in part due to heavy sulfuring, which was common practice then and which retards oxidation). The '61, with its butterscotch flavors, was outstanding. The '53 was superb, mellow and harmonious, but the '49 was simply fabulous, with a nose like *crème brûlée* and a wonderfully round texture. The '47, with its lemon-peel hint of bitterness, was only slightly less spectacular.

Among the older bottlings, it wasn't surprising to find that many vintages, such as the '43, '37, and '28, were past their best, hinting of coffee and varnish, which was why the 1919, which was utterly magnificent, savory, and very long on the palate, had all the tasters shaking their heads in amazement.

If we didn't know it before the event, we knew it after: No one makes a red and a white quite like Haut-Brion, and nobody puts on a tasting quite like the Overtons.

LA MISSION HAUT-BRION AND PÉTRUS:

WONDERFUL, BUT . . .

To the uninitiated, talk of vertical or horizontal tastings sounds vaguely gymnastic, like specialized exercises for the wine palate. In fact, they are. Vertical tastings compare the same wine in different vintages; horizontal tastings compare different wines of the same vintage. A vertical tasting gives one's palate an opportunity to trace the "house style" of a particular wine estate through successive vintages, and can be particularly revealing.

No category of wine offers more scope for such intellectual exercises than Bordeaux, whose vast array of similar but highly individual wines stay on a plane of maturity long enough to permit meaningful comparisons of vintages decades apart. Several years ago we attended a pair of vertical tastings of two well-known Bordeaux châteaux: La Mission Haut-Brion and Pétrus. The tastings, which occurred close in time, were fascinating, but not for the reasons we expected. Since the Second World War, both properties have become widely regarded as producing some of the finest wines of the region. As a consequence, both are much in demand. La Mission commands prices close to the first-growths, while the scarce Pétrus regularly tops the famous Médocs in price.

Of the two events, the La Mission tasting sponsored by Seagram's (this country's principal importer of Bordeaux) was more extensive, with wines going back to 1924. In brief, our notes were as follows: The '78 was a big, rich wine with everything in abundance, and a long future ahead of it—more impressive now for its potential than for what it currently offers. The '75 was still very dark in color right to the rim. Extremely intense, with just-emerging cigar-box scents, it was a massive but perfectly focused wine, surely a classic in the style of the great '61. The '70 was superb, a huge, ripe, but well-knit wine, just beginning to open. The smaller-scale, more austere '66 suffered by comparison but was top-notch claret all the same, probably at its best. We found the '64 an impressively huge fruity wine with the firm structure often missing in many '64 Bordeaux. Even in such company, the '61 struck the equivalent of a pedal-note: incredibly deep in color and flavor, it had a marvelous bouquet that hinted at cassis, tobacco, cedar, earth . . . a fabulous wine, and clearly still developing. The glorious '59 had an almost enveloping richness of bouquet and ripe flavor. While in no danger of decline, we thought it probably had attained its peak. The lovely, lingering, fully developed '55 had much of the luscious appeal of the '59 without the same scale; the '53 had a strong tobaccolike nose, a delicious flavor, but a somewhat open, loose structure that suggested further aging will not improve it. The '49 was extraordinary, so harmonious that it quelled analysis while it encouraged superlatives. (It is, however, clearly at its best now.) From the perspective of that peak, the '47, grand as it was, seemed a shade overblown—all truffles and tobacco—or perhaps simply a few years past its best. The '34 was also in magnificent decline, as was the fast-fading '29 and the still impressive '24, which was now an echo of the wine it must have been.

The Pétrus tasting, which was held at L'Académie du Vin and consisted of ten vintages between '79 and '61, inspired us to equally lengthy tasting notes, which we summarize here. Of the two youngest and least developed wines, we preferred the fruity, stylish '79 to the more powerful '78, although both have the impressive richness and spicy concentration characteristic of this

property. The big but lighter-textured '76 had a somewhat pungent nose and a softer structure, which suggested early and not
especially splendid maturity. The '75, however, was inky and
firm, a concentrated wine, still closed but obviously packed with
all the elements to make a superb bottle, although it seemed to
lack the plump fleshiness of Pétrus at its most individual. The
mouth-filling '71 was firm and fruity, an outstanding wine. The
first bottle to show the full-blown style for which Pétrus is famous, however, was the '70, which was opulently rich and
scented, almost glossy-fat in the mouth, a fabulous wine, and still
developing. By comparison, the '67 was soft, open, and smaller-
scaled; excellent, but not exciting. The highly reputed '66 was,
alas, an off-bottle with a peculiar nose and flavor. However,
the '64 was in prime condition, a lush, fat, lingering wine.
The '61 lived up to its near-legendary reputation by overshadow-
ing everything that came before. More of an essence of wine
than a wine, it had an exotic compote of a nose and a palate-
dazzling concentration.

Yet despite being forced to search for superlatives by the
sheer quality of the wines of La Mission Haut-Brion and Pétrus,
we found ourselves, upon reflection, with certain reservations
about their style.

Admittedly, these are Bordeaux wines of very different origin
and taste, but our stylistic criticisms were curiously similar. Pétrus
is 95 percent Merlot from Pomerol; La Mission Haut-Brion is
primarily Cabernet Sauvignon, with some Merlot and Cabernet
Franc, and comes from the Graves region. The impression each
makes on the palate is sensual, sometimes stunning, but rarely
ethereal, exquisite, sublime, haunting—adjectives that can sometimes be aptly applied to wines of greater delicacy and refinement. There is a certain bluntness to La Mission and a certain
muffled quality to Pétrus that is apparent when they are compared directly with the hard-edge clarity, the almost architectural
structure of a first-class Médoc. (This is particularly true of
Pétrus, which seems to have a kind of characteristic opacity of
flavor.)

Interestingly enough, the dramatic rise in La Mission's reputation and the near apotheosis of Pétrus has neatly coincided with the modern wine drinker's preference for powerful, concentrated, thick-textured wines. It is this preference that has made virtues of what were once considered stylistic shortcomings. Neither wine has anything like the grossly corpulent tasting qualities found in that now almost extinct creation, the hulking California Cabernet—the sort of wine that left you feeling more mugged than seduced. By contrast, La Mission or Pétrus are pinnacles of refinement.

But their stylistic emphasis on strength and richness leads to a curious contradiction. Both châteaux have a deserved reputation for producing fine wine in years when most Médocs produce pallid, barely palatable bottlings; yet to our taste neither château's wine really achieves great individuality except in strong vintages—when La Mission demonstrates its vaunted muscular power and Pétrus attains its much-praised overstuffed style. As a consequence, we suspect that these wines are best enjoyed in their lusty prime; in some vintages their declining years in the bottle run the danger of being more mawkish than graceful.

Of course, these remarks constitute *intellectual* criticisms of these wines; La Mission and Pétrus are so much above the norm of ordinary Bordeaux that one would have to be a teetotaler or a vinous ignoramus to turn down a glass of either, and only in rather enviable circumstances could you be offered a glass of anything better than the weaker vintages of these wines.

1961 BORDEAUX

Scene: A Saturday morning at 10:59 in a windowless private reception room at a hotel in Coral Gables, Florida. Twenty-eight people from various parts of the country and some from as far away as Sweden, England, and Ireland sit on one side of five rows of long, cloth-covered tables facing the front of the room. Although the day is sunny and the temperature a balmy 75 degrees, no one would rather be at the beach. We're all extremely pleased to be right where we are: at an extraordinary tasting of fifty of the greatest red wines of Bordeaux from the 1961 vintage. The first is due to be poured at eleven o'clock sharp.

The event, broken into three tasting sessions over two days, was the brainchild of Dr. Louis C. Skinner, Jr., a physician and wine lover who thought of holding such a tasting a few years ago and had been planning and discussing it with fellow wine enthusiasts ever since. "When the '61s reached twenty years of age, I thought it would be interesting to see how they were coming along," he explained. Dr. Skinner has a reputation among his friends of being a generous host, but he entered a special pantheon after opening up one hundred bottles whose replacement cost then was somewhere around $10,000. Forty-two of the fifty wines came from Dr. Skinner's own air-conditioned cellar, where they had remained since the good doctor purchased them in the mid-1960s. (Those were the days: He remembers paying $86 a *case* for the 1961 Château Pétrus, which now sells for around $800 *per bottle*—if you can find it.)

Although 1961 was one of the most perfect vintages of this century, ranking with but two other previous extraordinary harvests, 1929 and 1945, it was not universally superlative in all European districts, as 1945 was. What makes 1961 a magic year for wine enthusiasts is based primarily on what happened in Bordeaux. The crop was especially small, about a third of the average; and a warm summer and ideal picking conditions resulted in intense, concentrated wines with a superabundance of bouquet, flavor, fruit, alcohol, and tannin.

The '61s have taken a long time to mature in bottle, but their increase in value has been anything but gradual. After they came on the market, they disappeared quickly and are now extremely scarce (usually available only at auction) and expensive: several hundred dollars a bottle in some cases.

To someone immune to the attraction of great wine, it might seem strange that grown men and women would be willing to travel thousands of miles just to sniff and slurp these fabulous wines—and then spit them out ignominiously into styrofoam cups. Well, one either sees the point of certain activities or one doesn't. From the standpoint of sheer gustatory satisfaction, of course, it would have been far more pleasurable to try one or two '61s at a pleasant meal than to huddle behind dozens of glasses for hours on end just to scribble notes on fifty wines. But the attraction of the event wasn't merely the chance to taste these wines. For the serious wine collectors (such as Texans Dr. Marvin Overton and Lenoir Josey), members of the wine trade (such as John Avery of England and Julius Wile of New York), and the sprinkling of wine writers who made up the group, it was the chance to taste them *all together*. For the true wine lover, such comparisons aren't merely sensory experiences; they are eagerly sought intellectual exercises. To have an entire overview of the greatest wines of Bordeaux in one of the greatest vintages ever was an experience to sustain a hundred animated discussions.

Dr. Skinner had enlisted the aid of Michael Broadbent, head of Christie's wine department, to help organize the proceedings. The various possible approaches to, and order of, the tasting, and the logistics of coordinating glasses bottles, and tasters, were thought out in exquisite detail. The wines were conveyed the few short blocks from Dr. Skinner's house to the hotel in suitable style—his 1961 Rolls-Royce. To ensure the wines would have equal footing in terms of aeration at the time we tasted them, each wine was decanted precisely one hour before it was to be poured, and the wines were served two, three, five, or ten minutes apart, according to an exact timetable. One further refinement was contributed by the writer Alexis Bespaloff, who suggested that the two bottles of each wine opened should be poured alternately. This gave everyone a chance to double-check his impressions of a given wine by tasting the wine in his neighbor's glass, which had been poured from a different bottle. This was particularly helpful when defects were noted—one could verify whether it was the wine itself or just an off bottle.

Although at first the rapid, almost military serving sequence struck us as ridiculous, the schedule actually worked very well; in the same way one can linger so long over the paintings in one room of a museum that the succeeding masterpieces become a blur, so too there is a danger in concentrating unduly on the first wines and tiring out before reaching the first-growths.

Since fifty wines would be too much to taste at one sitting, they were organized commune by commune, and since the tasting was intended as a review, the wines were not tasted blind. "In blind tastings one simply spends too much time wondering what château a wine might *be* instead of paying attention to what it actually *is* in the glass," explained Broadbent. "Besides," he added, "with this many wines it would be an awful sweat." Within each commune grouping, the order of the wines was roughly from the lesser growths to the first-growths. The comments that follow record highlights within each group.

The first morning session began with the St.-Emilions. These were followed by the Pomerols, and the morning ended with the Graves. It was apparent from the first group that with the exception of an occasional disappointment—such as the Clos Fourtet, which appeared thin and acetic—almost any of the wines would probably have seemed marvelous tasted on its own. The extraordinarily high quality of the best of these wines forced one's standards upward so that châteaux that might have earned high marks in another context seemed merely satisfying when tasted alongside the likes of the superb Cheval Blanc, with its marvelous flavor, rich texture, and distinguished complex fragrance that hinted of tea roses. By comparison, a lesser château such as Pavie seemed rather pungent and muffled. By and large, the St.-Emilions struck us as fully mature.

This phenomenon would be repeated with every commune—in most cases the first-growths summed up the outstanding qualities of the wines that led up to them. But as expected, there were a good many wines in the second-, third-, fourth-, and fifth-growth categories so striking and individual that, even when tasted alongside the greatest châteaux, they still commanded attention. Within the Pomerols, for example, which were richer and more flavorful than the St.-Emilions, we found the Trotanoy wonderfully ripe and plummy, with an exquisite "sweet" finish. It was overshadowed, but not completely overwhelmed, by the huge, incredibly dark, concentrated Pétrus: so heady, spicy, rich, and fleshy that it seemed almost more of a vinous essence than a wine.

Following these opulent Pomerols, the Graves struck a distinctly firmer note. The La Mission Haut-Brion had all the massive magnificence, depth of flavor, assertive character, and structure that has made this property, in the opinion of many, virtually the equal of the first-growths in most postwar vintages. Typically the Haut-Brion lacked the emphatic qualities of the La Mission but offered clarity of structure, a particularly lovely dried-flower bouquet, a beautiful flavor, and an elegant finish.

A lunch break (to which several tasters, including ourselves, brought their glasses, in our case, the Pétrus) and a welcome swim in the hotel pool put us in an enthusiastic frame of mind for the afternoon session: St.-Julien and Margaux. St.-Juliens at their best are eminently elegant, stylish, and deliciously drinkable; but curiously, the '61 St.-Juliens struck us all as the most backward—the least mature—of all the communes sampled at the tasting. As a group, they were hard, tannic, and rather closed, although we personally found the three Léovilles—Poyferré, Barton, and Las-Cases—and the lovely Ducru-Beaucaillou that followed them, classically proportioned, sweetly fragrant, and full of emerging ripe fruit, charm, and finesse.

The superbly scented Margaux wines were introduced by Cantemerle, an impressive, flavorful, stylish, and completely harmonious wine. The Palmer was near perfection—perfumed, packed with flavor, a sweet-textured, seductive wine impossible to fault, and clearly in the first rank of the '61s despite its official classification as a third-growth. But when the Château Margaux was poured, we were sorry to have depleted our meager stock of superlatives. For sheer elegance, class, and beauty, we placed it ahead among all the wines we tasted, and the wines tasted later failed to change our opinion. It seemed to us about as close to the ideal of claret as any wine can hope to come.

The next day's session found us bright-eyed, eager for the grand finale, and completely unrepentant about the praise-ridden notes we had scribbled the previous day.

We commenced with the St.-Estèphes, which showed the firmness, earthiness, and solid claret style for which these wines are known. The Cos d'Estournel was particularly distinguished and handsomely structured, while the coarser, thick-textured Montrose was positively steely with tannin, and at first struck us as downright nasty. After half an hour in the glass, however, it opened up dramatically, hinting at its possible future development.

The noticeably higher proportion of Cabernet Sauvignon in the Pauillacs was clearly evident in the marvelous cigar-box and cedar bouquets of the wines of this famed commune—from the spicy Lynch-Bages to the magnificent, mouth-filling Mouton-Rothschild with its intense, lingering black-currant flavor. The incomparable Latour was even more powerful, concentrated, and stunning; its underlying fruit was masked by heavy tannin, and it clearly was nowhere near maturity. The Lafite, while obviously a superb wine, was to our palates not in the same league as the sublime Margaux, Pétrus, Latour, Mouton, Palmer, and several others.

Plenty of lively discussion followed this last session, accompanied by glasses of one's favorite Pauillac. Was it worth doing? Here there was unanimous agreement. In two days, we had experienced a measure of the greatness of which claret is capable.

No scores were kept or group ratings given, and if there had been, the results would have been misleading, for there was no general consensus on which wine was the "winner." At the exalted level of quality these wines represented, there isn't one, lone pinnacle of quality; the greatest '61s constitute an entire range of vinous peaks. And whether one peak seems to reach a little higher than its neighboring giants depends largely on one's stylistic preferences. We took no survey, but we got the impression that those who looked for dramatic power as well as finesse put Mouton or Latour at the top of their lists; those who leaned toward sheer lusciousness awarded the palm to Pétrus or Palmer; those who admired elegance above all else elevated Margaux.

To have reviewed these clarets in early maturity allowed us to savor their power before too many began to fade, as arguably some of the St.-Emilions had already begun to do. Decades hence there will still be viable '61s, but no wines are forever; at some point it will only be possible to compare survivors, as is now done with the '29s. Of course, there could never be a time when those fifty wines could be viewed at an equal stage of *individual* development. In its evolution in the bottle, each vintage progresses like a long wave, led by its early developers and followed by its laggards.

All of us felt, however, that most of the better '61s had not yet reached maturity, and the best will last another twenty years. We all enthusiastically agreed that the '61s would definitely be due for another review of their development in ten years' time. Dr. Skinner heartily concurred. But then, it shouldn't be *his* turn to pull out all those bottles.

IN SEARCH OF BARGAIN BORDEAUX

"It's a curious thing," remarked Bruno Prats, proprietor of Château Cos d'Estournel, during a lunch in Bordeaux. "I've noticed many American wine lovers like to show their connoisseurship by serving wines from famous châteaux. Many of the French, however, like to impress their guests by doing just the opposite. They prefer to serve a less well-known wine, even an obscure one, that is their personal discovery."

Sure, it was a clever if simple characterization of national differences in wine snobbery, but the more we thought about it, the more we realized that the French have a point: those who are interested only in famous, glamorous labels miss the opportunity to drink classic wines for much less. The thought came back to us the other day when we saw the latest quotes on the three Léoville wines (Châteaux Léoville-Las-Cases, Léoville-Poyferré, and Léoville-Barton) from the 1982 vintage—and saw the Las-Cases listed at twice the price of the other two wines. Is it twice as good as the wines of the other Léovilles? In the '82 vintage, all three are magnificent. But even if the Las-Cases is marginally better (which it may be), is it worth twice the price? Maybe for a Bordeaux *collector* who simply must have it, it is. But for Bordeaux *drinkers,* these price dislocations provide a real opportunity by making the other, currently less glamorous Léovilles downright bargains. If you'd rather have a case each of '82 Léoville-Barton and '82 Léoville-Poyferré than one case of '82 Léoville-Las-Cases—as we certainly would—then read on; we have some Bordeaux buying strategies to share with you.

To understand how even in the rarefied world of fine Bordeaux, which is widely regarded as synonymous with fine wine, there could be undervalued wines, you have to understand how the wines of some châteaux become glamorous, sought-after bottlings and why others create far less demand.

Obviously, it has a lot to do with fashion. To put a wine in the vanguard, it helps if it ends up on the right restaurant wine lists, is sought by collectors, and drunk by the right people. Naturally, whether the château's proprietor is a recluse or a charming, well-traveled extrovert influences the attention the wine gets. And of course, whether or not a wine becomes glamorous has something to do, ultimately, with its quality.

But there are other factors at work, the most significant of which is the 1855 classification of the Médoc. This classification of the top châteaux into first- through fifth-growths was not the first such attempt by the Bordelaise, but it was the one that stuck and became official. Naturally, it became a powerful marketing tool, giving the first-growths (Lafite, Latour, and company) a permanent advantage in status over the second- through fifth-growths. Anyone seeking the best would naturally look first at those top-ranked estates.

In recent decades, the price spread between the first-growths and the other classified growths has widened. Any wine bearing a Lafite label, for example, even if from a subpar vintage, usually sells for a substantial premium over the best second-growth bottlings. What this means, of course, is that the claret buyer gets far more value for his money by buying top second-growths rather than first-growths.

In fact, in recent years there has been only a small advantage in second-growth status over third-, fourth-, or fifth-growth status. All alike were regarded as *crus classés;* differences in quality accounted for differences in price. Thus, a popular fourth-growth such as Beychevelle could command prices equal to the second-growths, and top-quality third-growth Palmer could exceed them. Now, glamour itself accounts for substantial price differences.

Today, that fashionable pair of châteaux La Mission Haut-Brion and Palmer, which used to share a price niche between the first- and second-growths, have now been joined by Léoville-Las-Cases, Ducru-Beaucaillou, and Pichon-Lalande. These three wines—dubbed the breakaway seconds by the trade and the unholy trinity by their rivals—have joined the small circle of Bordeaux's glamour wines. The superlative. recent vintages these châteaux have been producing account for their increased demand—and increased price over their classed-growth compatriots. But a canny claret drinker can find near-equal quality for far less from neighboring châteaux—such as the other Léovilles—now unfairly put in the shadow by the glare of publicity concentrated on a few properties. (Second-growth Pichon-Baron is hardly as inferior in quality as the difference in price between it and the fashionable Pichon-Lalande across the road suggests.)

Of course, *lack* of classified-growth status is a definite marketing disadvantage, one that a wise buyer exploits. Consider Château d'Angludet, which although given higher ranking in earlier classifications was left out in the 1855 ranking. Despite the fact that d'Angludet is now clearly making wine on a classified-growth level, its price is kept modest by its lack of classified status. Among a host of unexciting minor producers, d'Angludet and a few other outstanding *petits châteaux,* such as de Pez,

Gloria, and Chasse-Spleen, are *petite* only in name and price.

Ah, but surely you exaggerate, thinks the claret lover who believes the 1855 classification was divinely inspired. Drink an unclassified, inexpensive Médoc alongside a true aristocrat of the grape, a *cru classé* from a good year, and the difference would be dramatic—wouldn't it?

Not long ago we compared a 1979 Château d'Angludet, a mere Margaux, against a '79 Château Margaux, a first-growth and a wine considered by many (with no argument from us) the finest wine not only of that commune but of that excellent vintage. True enough, the lovely d'Angludet definitely lacked the first-growth's depth and exquisite refinements when compared directly. But these are the sort of subtleties noticed when such a pair are tasted together analytically.

From the perspective of the diner, however, who is facing glasses of those two wines across a plate of lamb chops, as we did shortly thereafter, their differences, though still apparent, matter less. In the role of beverages—their *raison d'être,* after all—their gustatory value was surprisingly equal. As a subject of discussion, the Château Margaux offered more to talk about; but the d'Angludet, especially when alternated with forkfuls of lamb, was a completely satisfying wine. In our experience, a good measure of the style and appeal that the Bordeaux reds offer can be found in many well-made but modestly priced clarets—the so-called *petits châteaux.* These are estates other than the classified growths, some of whose labels carry other *cru* designations such as *cru bourgeois exceptionnel, cru bourgeois,* or *cru bourgeois supérieur.*

French consumers have always understood this. They typically look for value and drinkability when buying wine. They believe in buying *petits châteaux* such as d'Angludet in good vintages. Behind this approach is the surmise that many châteaux, including the minor ones, will excel in a fine year; but the minor ones won't be overpriced.

Just how much enjoyment there can be in drinking inexpensive Bordeaux was brought home not long ago at dinner at a friend's house. He served only wines from *petits châteaux,* such as Châ-

teau Loudenne, but from vintages such as '64, '66, and '70. They
were superb. Our host had worked out his own version of a Bordeaux layaway plan, buying a few cases of wine from reputable
but minor properties now and then, when a good year and a
good price coincided. Although by now most have been drunk,
he still had quite a few mixed cases of mature, eminently satisfying '62s, '64s, '66s, and '70s for Sunday dinner, enough so that
he wouldn't be tempted to dip into his cache of '75s and '78s prematurely.

Most wine lovers, even those with a modest wine budget,
could follow his example. Too many have the mistaken idea
that only the *crus classés* benefit from years of cellaring. Not so.
Perhaps the greatest strength of the red wines of Bordeaux is that
the modestly priced wines from the better *petits châteaux* also
benefit from some aging. Eventually they will afford wine lovers
the pleasure of enjoying fine wine at its peak, but as inexpen-
sively as possible.

All this doesn't mean wines from just any old *petit château*
are worth buying or laying away. Many properties have little following because their wines aren't very good. But the best of them
match not only the taste but the longevity of *crus classés*. We
once attended a tasting of the wines of Château de Pez, a *cru
bourgeois supérieur* estate in St.-Estèphe, at a New York Wine
Writers Circle luncheon at The Four Seasons. The proprietor,
Robert Dousson, lives at the château and has been managing the
property since the 1955 harvest. For the luncheon he brought fifteen of the better recent vintages, from 1980 back to 1945, all
from the château's own cellars.

Overall, they were remarkable for their intense color, rich,
mouth-filling flavor, and excellent balance. The wines of the '70s
were well-made and full of promise. The '66 was a classically
proportioned claret with a wonderful cedary bouquet and a warm,
intense flavor. The '61 was magnificent—an opulent, rich, fat,
marvelously concentrated wine that has yet to reach its peak. The
fully mature '55 had leathery nuances in the nose and faint hints
of licorice in the finish. The '50—largely a forgotten vintage—
was still very satisfying even if evidently past its prime. Despite

having to follow fourteen wines, the '45 managed to stand out above all the rest. This huge, powerful wine had a glorious bouquet and seemed in no danger of rapid decline. It would have been an impressive showing for any Bordeaux estate. We went away with lots of stars next to our notes on the '45, '61, and '66 as well as a generally mellow outlook on the world; but more, we went away convinced that wines from the top unclassified properties can age as gracefully as any.

Frugal French wine buyers, while savvy enough to seek out top *petits châteaux,* don't ignore *crus classés,* however. They simply buy top châteaux in the lesser-rated years. In a so-so year, their thinking goes, only the top châteaux can afford to be selective and bottle under the château label only the best lots of wine made in that vintage. (The rest is either bottled under a second label or sold off in bulk.) These châteaux do this, of course, because they have a reputation to defend. Because such vintages are poorly rated overall, however, even top châteaux sell at a discount. One advantage to this strategy is that the wines will be ready to drink sooner since those from lesser years are typically ready before the highly rated vintages.

Clearly, anyone looking for bargain Bordeaux should not fail to exploit so-called off vintages, which are so widely misunderstood. Let's consider what an "off vintage" really means.

The wine-drinking public certainly is aware that some vintages are distinctly better than others; to many, in fact, there are only great vintages (those high scorers on a pocket vintage chart), good but perhaps not great vintages, and . . . the rest.

"The rest" are lumped together as "off vintages," which, to many wine lovers, means vintages to avoid. They fail to realize that an "off" vintage, unlike an "off" bottle, doesn't mean the wine is spoiled. It is merely a vintage that is off the usual standard—below average in quality. Such vintages are sometimes called "useful" vintages, meaning that the wines can provide pleasant, if not ecstatic, drinking. Naturally, their ultimate attractiveness is largely dependent on price. Even in vintages marked by the worst weather, it's likely that in any sizable fine wine area (such as Bordeaux) someone, somewhere, made a fine wine.

Early (or late) picking and rigorous barrel selection are among the measures that can be taken to redress the particular faults that nature may have stamped on most of the year's production. In fact, as we think about it, we've had a number of remarkable wines from so-called off vintages in Bordeaux: the 1950 Château Haut-Brion, the 1958 Château Ducru-Beaucaillou, and above all, the magnificent 1960 Château Latour.

But there's something else to this idea, too. So much attention is paid to the outstanding vintages that many wine lovers, warned off lesser years for fear of buying bottled disasters, never discover what enjoyment can be had from lighter vintages of Bordeaux precisely because they *are* light. A case in point: Several years ago we attended a tasting of recent vintages of Château Giscours, a third-growth Margaux, at Le Cirque in New York. An elegant luncheon followed a tasting of the '75, '76, '77, '78, and '79 vintages. We'd scribbled notes on the superior wines—and the best were superlative, confirming our view that Giscours is currently making wine on a par with the better second-growths.

We were particularly impressed with the '79, a brilliant, stylish, fruity, already delicious wine. We also made a charitable note that the thin, acerbic '77 seemed about all one could expect from that miserable vintage. Food followed and we dutifully sampled all the glasses again.

At the end of the meal we were taken aback to see that the '77 was the only empty glass. We, along with the other guests we talked to, found the "better" vintages not just too young, but also too rich, while the underappreciated '77 had proven the perfect light "luncheon claret"—lean, dry, aromatic, and drinkable right then.

Since that time we've been on the alert for additional first-rate luncheon clarets. The '77s are now long past their best, as are most of the wines from the next "off vintage," 1980. Examples from that latter lightweight harvest constituted a veritable bonanza for those seeking fruity, light, delicious wines for near-term drinking. We can't say how any '80s might be holding up in the late 1980s because we've long since polished off the last of our La Conseillante and Pichon-Lalande, both of which, considering their quality, were relative bargains. (Were it not for their steep prices—due to a weak dollar—the lean vintages of 1984 or 1987 would prove a happy hunting ground for wine lovers willing to pick carefully.)

Astute Bordeaux buyers should also realize that the rise and fall of a château's reputation can be a slow process, sometimes taking decades to have an effect on the price. Examples of lackluster châteaux resting comfortably on their *cru classé* status (and undeserved price) are counterbalanced by châteaux whose leap forward in quality hasn't yet been paralleled by a leap upward in price.

Take the example of fourth-growth Château Prieuré-Lichine. The property was in a run-down state when it was purchased in 1951 by the wine author Alexis Lichine. In the decades since, it has had its cellars modernized and even its vineyard enlarged and improved. Despite a string of increasingly successful vintages in recent years, including two wonderful back-to-back vintages, '82 and '83, the wine still sells for modest sums.

These days, new ownership in Bordeaux often signals a renewed commitment to quality. Typically, the wine shows marked improvement before the glamour (and price) recovers. Château Cantemerle, long one of our favorite wines, had slipped in quality in the 1970s but now, under the ownership of the Cordier group, has turned out a series of impressive wines since 1983. Château St.-Pierre, a little-regarded St.-Julien, is now making top-notch wine under its new owner, Henri Martin.

The wine lover in search of bargains should remember that obscurity is an obstacle to glamour. Few wine lovers are familiar with more than the most famous names of Graves (Haut-Brion and La Mission Haut-Brion), and the modest prices of the other top wines reflect this. The superlative reds and whites of Domaine de Chevalier have their admirers (including us), but the price remains accessible. Other worthy Graves include the red of Château de Fieuzal and the white of Château Rahoul.

The district of Pomerol is full of little-known fine wines. But tiny production at these pocket-size properties tends to keep prices elevated. Nevertheless, the claret drinker who enjoys making his own discoveries can do surprisingly well. Apart from the ultra-fashionable, superexpensive ($100 plus) Château Pétrus and its trendy neighbor Château Trotanoy (widely regarded as No. 2 in this unclassified district and a bit pricey), there is a highly competitive group of less familiar châteaux that vie with each other every vintage: Lafleur, La Conseillante, L'Évangile, La Fleur-Pétrus, Vieux Château Certan, Petit-Village, Latour à Pomerol, and Certan de May (among others). All have their advocates who recognize that the quality level can be magnificent, competitive in some vintages with the first two, and well worth the second-growth prices asked. The only trick is to find them!

In fact, if chosen carefully, one could have a collection of classic, superlative Bordeaux—without a single one of the fashionable (and expensive) names.

True, it takes a certain independence of spirit and taste to resist the lure of the glamorous name or vintage. But there's a definite satisfaction in knowing you've bought two or three cases of excellent wine for what someone else has paid for a single case of Château Chic.

3

Considering California

THE NAPA VALLEY TAKES OFF

Every morning of our stay in the Napa Valley we watched the big multicolored hot-air balloons drift above the vineyards in the bright June sky as we drove up St. Helena Highway to the day's first appointment. Finally, near the end of our visit, we decided to give Napa's popular tourist sport a try. "It's tricky trying to land in the middle of the Valley," our jovial pilot said as he gave us a helping hand into a wicker basket that looked no more substantial than a large laundry hamper. Above us towered a huge, flimsy-looking orange and yellow balloon. "Too damn many vineyards in the Valley now—hardly any open space left," he shouted in explanation as the propane jet roared a yard of flame into the open bottom of the giant bag; and then we lifted aloft from a field next to Domaine Chandon's vineyards in the southern end of the Valley for a cloud-high view of what has become one of the most famous wine-producing regions in the world.

As we drifted north, our initial apprehensions vanished as the accuracy of our pilot's remarks sank in: The narrow valley floor now seemed a continuous patchwork of vineyards from the forested Mayacamas mountains on the west to the Howell mountain range on the east and as far as we could see up the Valley to where it curved out of view northwest to Calistoga. From the air, the lush, leafy rows of well-tended vines looked like the ribbing of some bright green fabric—delicate, expensive fabric, we thought, noting the giant fans and sprinkler systems ready to combat frost and drought. Prime unplanted vineyard land in the Napa Valley has recently traded at $42,000 an acre (up from a mere $8,000 an acre in 1970), making it the most expensive wine-growing turf in California, and some of the most valuable anywhere.

The price of land, like the ever-increasing acreage in vines (now 31,000 acres, more than Burgundy's entire Côte d'Or), is just one example of the changes that have taken place in the Napa in the past two decades and one more sign of the Valley's growing importance as a wine district. Although its current fame may have been swelled somewhat by the hot air of publicity that surrounds anything new and fashionable, the popularity of and the publicity for the Valley's wines have been generated by solid achievements during that time: wines that now rank with the world's best in an astonishing number of categories—Cabernets that compare with Bordeaux, Chardonnays that stand up to white Burgundies, late-harvest Rieslings to put against Germany's, and from time to time, Gamays, Chenin Blancs, Pinot Noirs, Sauvignon Blancs, and others that compete on the level of their European counterparts.

These vinous achievements have contributed to another growing trend: foreign investment in Napa's vineyards and wineries. Since 1970 when Nestlé purchased Beringer, a number of other European firms have invested in the Valley, notably Moët & Chandon, which began its Domaine Chandon sparkling wine operation in 1973. Recent investments include the well-publicized joint venture of Robert Mondavi and Baron Philippe de Rothschild, which produced Opus One, a proprietary red made from Valley grapes. Christian Moueix of Château Pétrus fame (and the man behind Dominus, another proprietary red) is only one of a growing list of French winemakers who have come to the Valley. The owner of one small winery told us that he receives unsolicited offers via telegrams from French companies and agents on a regular basis. While some see this European interest as further proof of the international acceptance of California wine, others believe it simply reflects the lack of available (and affordable) top-quality land in Europe, and the desire to try something new and daring on what is, after all, an acknowledged frontier of wine.

Other new developments are more visible. Tourism, for example, is booming. As we recall, when we first visited the Valley in 1971, there was only one motel and one restaurant. Now it takes a directory to list the charming small inns and excellent places to eat—and most require advance reservations during some seasons. The number of new wineries is booming, too. Back then there were only 39. The big boom, some say, started in 1975, when there were 67; the last time we counted, in mid-1988, there were 165. The optimism required to start a winery and enter the competitive ranks of fine wine producers shows no signs of waning. New winery buildings—some clearly intended by their owners to be "architectural statements"—are much in evidence; "opening soon" proclaimed the sign of one winery-in-progress we passed each morning.

The number of new labels has increased faster than the number of new vineyards. Although the majority of wineries make at least some of their wine from purchased grapes, more and more growers have decided to build their own wineries and make their own wine instead of selling their grapes. "There's a growing trend toward 'the estate concept' as in Bordeaux, where those who own the vineyards make the wine," says Robert Pecota, owner of the small Robert Pecota Winery near Calistoga. "But at the same time, there's been another trend—a growing number of small wineries that don't have actual wineries or vineyards at all. They buy grapes and utilize another winery's facilities to make their wine."

What made this winery bonanza possible was "the wine boom"—America's sudden thirst for wine and willingness to pay the price of a bottle of the best—that began in the late

1960s. Feverish planting in response tapered off in the late 1970s, but interest in land hasn't slackened in the least.

The attractions of the Napa Valley have brought less welcome forms of attention, among them land developers who think vineyards make perfect settings for homes and condominiums. While the international attention for Napa's wines attracts developers, "it also gives us more power to beat them back," says one winemaker. "We can say to the county now: 'The most important and prestigious use of Valley land is for vines.' "

If vintners are united on the issue of developers, they are at odds on other issues, even such a seemingly simple one as what "Napa Valley" on a label should mean. Curiously, until 1981, the term had never been precisely defined for labeling purposes. Many vintners had long wanted the historically loose use of the term more clearly defined to ensure that the Valley's growing reputation would not be tarnished by wine from what they considered inferior subregions. At hearings held then by the Bureau of Alcohol, Tobacco, and Firearms, which regulates the wine industry, producers were divided over whether "Napa Valley" should be confined to the Valley proper—the watershed area—or considered synonymous with the entire county of Napa. The latter definition prevailed, to the consternation of such producers as Joseph Phelps, who felt the appellation became too sweeping to be meaningful; others, such as Joe Heitz, felt the decision staved off misguided efforts to constrict producers' viticultural freedom. It was only the first of many such battles; now, concern revolves around subappellations such as "Howell Mountain," "Carneros," and the like and whether their proliferation will water down the broader and much better-known appellation "Napa Valley" itself.

But despite Napa's newfound status as an internationally important wine region, we worry that the Valley may become a victim of its own success. It is already too much of a tourist magnet for its own grape-growing good (it is said to rank second only to Disneyland among the state's attractions). Valley winemakers take pride in the fact that Napa has become a fashionable name, while bemoaning the tourist traffic on Route 29. After our most recent visit, we found the unrelenting trendiness disquieting. Has the Valley become too much of a fast track? The excessive attention given brand-new wineries, for example, has reached the absurd point where the maximum amount of attention is generated not by new wines *per se* but by new wines *before* they ever appear in the market—Opus One and Dominus are the perfect examples.

We wonder if the desire to create the next breakthrough bottling doesn't encourage experimentation for its own sake. California, of course, is the land of triumphant upstarts, wineries that pop up overnight on a back road, make their first bottling with borrowed equipment and brash new ideas, and then rocket to fame after a well-publicized blind tasting puts them at the top of the pack. That scenario, which is a part of modern California wine lore, fuels the ambitions of every new winery that breaks ground.

That mythology, however, also has its unfortunate dark side: some wineries begin to fall out of favor just because they've been around too long and have become too familiar—even if their wines are as good as ever. Not long ago we were at a dinner party at which a Napa Valley Cabernet from a winery once considered on the cutting edge was poured. "Why, I haven't had that wine in years," murmured one guest. "You don't hear much about it lately," he added, eyeing his glass with the nostalgic curiosity of someone about to watch a now-forgotten Hollywood star on the late movie. It was obvious that he would have been far more impressed if served the latest pressing from the newest kid on the block. A winery that produces excellent wine year after year, with nary a change in cellar or vineyard technique, wine style, or even label design, is liable to be regarded as dull stuff. The value of an unchanging tradition, so prized in European wines, doesn't make for hot copy in the Napa Valley.

As a result, the old guard often seems old hat, despite the achievement of a settled style and a library of wines going back enough years to show the glories of maturity. But in the end isn't that what securing the Napa Valley's reputation will be all about?

STAG'S LEAP: WHAT'S IN A NAME?

Not many wine lovers realize it, but a small funnel-shaped corner of the lower Napa Valley has been responsible for some of California's most ravishing Cabernet Sauvignons. Its vineyards lie in the shadow of the prominent rocky outcroppings known since the 1880s by the romantic name Stag's Leap. At that time financier Horace Chase built a residence there and apparently adopted the name from a local legend of a stag's escaping a hunter by leaping the chasm.

That attractive name has been the subject of a tangle of lawsuits between competing wineries, but the principals in those disputes finally joined forces to identify and enhance the regional character of their wines. In 1985 the area's wineries and grape-growers sought official recognition as the "Stag's Leap District," an action which precipitated further squabbles with neighboring wineries (which wanted to be included) over just where the boundaries should be drawn. Finally, in early 1989, the federal government approved the appellation, adding 500 more acres to the 2,200 its original proponents thought appropriate.

There would have been no such effort (nor would there have been such a controversy) if there wasn't something special about the wines. It may have to do with the long, cool growing season and the well-drained bale loam soils, but Cabernet Sauvignons from this area have proved remarkable. They can be drunk with pleasure four years after harvest, are superb after eight, and are still beautiful after twelve years.

The name Stag's Leap first entered public consciousness over a decade ago. In the now famous 1976 Paris tasting, a wine from a new Napa Valley winery was selected by French judges over a field of reds that included Château Mouton-Rothschild and Château Haut-Brion. The winning wine was a 1973 Stag's Leap Wine Cellars Cabernet Sauvignon, and the event—easily the most discussed transatlantic taste-off ever held—propelled Warren Winiarski's then four-year-old winery into the front ranks of California producers.

Cabernet Sauvignon was first planted in the Stag's Leap area in 1961, but no wineries existed there until the early 1970s. By the time Winiarski purchased land and began producing wines in 1972, there were several other wineries in the area, notably Clos du Val with its French-trained winemaker, Bernard Portet. But it was the founding of Stags' Leap Winery (apostrophe after the *s*) by Carl Doumani at about the same time that precipitated a twelve-year legal battle with Winiarski over trademark rights to the name—the first in a series of bitter squabbles over the name Stag's Leap. This wrangle was terminated recently by a decision that allows both wineries to use the Stag's Leap name and similar labels that feature stags.

The list of wineries in the newly defined area now includes: Stag's Leap Wine Cellars, Stag's Leap Winery, Clos du Val, Steltzner, Shafer, Pine Ridge, Chimney Rock, S. Anderson, Sinskey, and Silverado. In addition, wineries located outside the area, such as Robert Mondavi and Joseph Phelps, own part of the 1,300 acres of vineyards situated within the district.

As the Stag's Leap name became identified with the region as a whole and all its Cabernets, the battle over who could use it expanded. But now, individual disagreements are being transformed into a shared view of what's special about the area and what might be done to identify that on wine labels. "We have the opportunity to make this appellation meaningful," Warren Winiarski explained as we drove through his vineyards on a recent visit. "But to do that, the use of the name has to be more than a marketing gimmick. It has to stand for more than just mere geography."

Winiarski was referring to the fact that, at present in the United States, practically any group of wineries—or even a single one—can argue successfully that it should be granted its own viticultural-region designation. The criteria considered for permitting such specific label language don't include wine quality, cohesive style, or any of the considerations that might make knowing the geographic origin of the wine significant to the consumer. As things now stand, there would be nothing to prevent an unscrupulous winery from flooding the market with jugs of cheap Stag's Leap District wine (Bambi Blush?), thereby diluting the image of the region's fine Cabernets.

This geography-only approach is far different from the *appellation contrôlée* laws in France, where regulations go beyond authenticating origin to set forth the grape types, yields, and production methods permitted in a given wine region, measures that are intended to enhance wine quality. That's why some of the Stag's Leap–area winemakers are discussing the idea of additional self-imposed restrictions, such as agreeing not to use the Stag's Leap District appellation on any wines except Cabernet and Merlot, the only two varieties for which anyone claims a regional character.

Skeptics might wonder if the area's wines are distinctive enough to deserve singling out in this fashion. To find out, we spent time at the wineries, did comparative tastings there, and held follow-up tastings to compare examples from the area against Cabernets from elsewhere. The vintages ranged from 1973 to barrel samples of the 1985s. We're now convinced that there is a Stag's Leap character, even though it isn't always possible in blind tastings to identify wines made there from other Napa Valley Cabernets, or even from other California Cabernets. (It isn't always possible to tell St.-Juliens from St.-Estèphes either, but that doesn't mean there aren't differences, and these differences make it just as meaningful to talk in terms of the Stag's Leap District style in comparison with other California Cabernets as it is to talk of a St.-Julien character in comparison with other Médocs.)

In most cases, we found that the Stag's Leap wines share a striking fruitiness, a berry or cassis quality, rather than the olive or herbaceous character sometimes encountered in California Cabernets. The fruit flavors have a specific taste. Dick Steltzner, who has been growing grapes in the area since 1967 and making wine since 1977, calls it black cherry. The tannins, while evident, have a fine-grained texture rather than an aggressive or biting character. The result is a balanced, appealing wine with none of the overly powerful, overripe qualities California Cabernet is often criticized for.

The two Cabernets that stood out as exemplars of the Stags Leap style at its best are the Stag's Leap Wine Cellars and the Clos du Val. The Stag's Leap Wine Cellars is a shade deeper, perhaps a bit more perfumed, but the Clos du Val cedes nothing in finesse—it is one of the most consistently elegant Cabernets in California. Both the Clos du Val and the Stag's Leap Wine Cellars Cabernets go back to 1972. Winiarski and Portet share similar stylistic goals—to create beautiful rather than merely impressive wines—and both did so even when fashion favored power over polish.

The area's other Cabernets, with fewer vintages behind them, are less easy to peg in terms of house style. But we'd venture that the Pine Ridge is the most open-flavored and charming, quite delicious, in fact; the Steltzner, firmer, strikingly fruity; while the Shafer is particularly rich and thick-textured, almost plummy. Silverado and Stags' Leap Winery have been producing Cabernets only since the early eighties, and the few examples we've had don't seem to fit the Stag's Leap taste profile precisely. . . .

But there's no rush yet to sort out their various styles. After all, they just got their appellation.

ARE CALIFORNIA WINES COLLECTIBLE?

Should you collect California wines? Our answer: yes, but . . .
And to explain that *but,* herewith a saga of the pleasures and pit-
falls of collecting California wine. By the time we moved back to
New York from the West Coast in the early 1970s, we were
budding California wine collectors—though hardly on a grand
scale. Squirreled away among our household effects were cases of
vinous treasures we'd discovered—wines from then little-known
producers such as Heitz, Stony Hill, Ridge, Chalone, and Mayacamas.

We enjoyed, and anticipated, all the same pleasures as that of
any collector of French wines, plus we had the added thrill peculiar to collecting California wine—discovering a great wine few
people have ever heard of. The wines we didn't drink immediately, we looked forward to enjoying. We imagined ourselves
swooning over that 1966 Heitz Martha's Vineyard Cabernet (purchased for a mere $7.50!) at some future time when it would be
perfectly mature, knowing full well that its scarcity ensured that
then it would be a rare, coveted bottle. We added to our collection by snapping up from New York wine shops dozens of Cabernets that on the West Coast were sold one to a customer only,
congratulating ourselves on our prescience.

It took nearly a decade before fashion made it acceptable, even
trendy, to serve a fine California wine on the East Coast, much
less to collect it. Yet we'd known it was only a matter of time before many wine lovers would want to collect the best of America.
The labels are in English, for one thing. And California, like
France (and for that matter, Italy), is one of the few wine-
producing areas of the world that produces fine wine in every
category—red, white, sparkling, fortified, and so on. It's possible
to have a comprehensive, first-class wine collection composed
solely of California bottlings broad enough to cover every dining
need (which, of course, is why many top restaurants can feature
all-California wine lists).

Like many, we collected California wines not just to have something on hand to drink, but to learn. How exciting it was to taste the first Merlots, the first late-harvest Rieslings, the new-wave Cabernets—not to mention fascinating experiments such as botrytised Chardonnay. With each new wine came an insight, and we felt vindicated in filling our wine racks with one California label after another.

But ironically enough, as the fashion for collecting California wines has spread, our ardor for cellaring those wines (as opposed to drinking them right away) has cooled somewhat. By now we've discovered that there is a big difference between possessing a wide variety of wines to sample and a substantial collection of wines intended for long aging before enjoyment.

Because our interest in learning about California wines at first easily exceeded our meager wine budget, few of our early purchases lasted long enough for us to discover their aging potential. To be honest, we gave little thought to what those wines would eventually become. Many seemed so exciting to begin with that an even more glorious future seemed assured.

Surely, we thought, there was enough tannin and fruit in those marvelously deep reds for them to last a decade, perhaps two or three. And wouldn't that richness and oak keep those Chardonnays alive for years? But when we began trying the odd bottle or so of wines we thought called for additional time in the bottle, we weren't always impressed with the results.

Wine enthusiasts who haven't had the experience of opening a long-hoarded wine and discovering it to be long past its prime sometimes think that all the talk about age-worthiness is mere snobbishness. True, in terms of drinking pleasure, ageability is often irrelevant, but if the wine will be cellared and drunk over a period of years, the question is of vital importance. Who wants to end up sitting on a stock of fading wines that should have been drunk in their youth?

Since first collecting California wine, we've had the opportunity to taste many more of various ages and at various stages of development. We're convinced that most of the wines of California age faster than wines from Europe of comparable quality.

What this means in practical terms is that the keeping quality of many types of California wines is limited, despite their impressiveness when first released.

Sure, we've tasted forty-year-old Cabernet Sauvignons still in their prime and twelve-year-old Chardonnays in glorious condition, but those have been rare exceptions. And when it comes to California wine, it isn't so easy to pick out the exceptions. Unlike the wines of Bordeaux, where long-standing similarities in grape variety, method, and geography allow a consensus on a given vintage, California's bewildering variety of grapes, vineyard sources, microclimates, and methods undermines easy predictions about the outcome of certain vintages or the progress of given bottlings—even those of one varietal.

All this isn't to say that collecting California wine is a risky business—on the contrary. As long as you collect with certain time frames in mind, it's hard to go wrong. And what are those guidelines? When it comes to California whites, we think most collectors ought to live hand-to-mouth, so to speak, buying only what they'll drink within a year. That period can be stretched to two years for top Chardonnay and most reds, and it can be doubled (say four or five years after purchase) for Cabernet Sauvignon. You'll discover some wines will defy these limits—perhaps a certain year of, say, Inglenook Charbono that just keeps on getting better. That's part of the fun of collecting.

It is important to remember that just because Joe Blow's aggressive Petite Sirah tastes as if it will take twenty years to develop table manners, that doesn't mean you ought not to open a bottle until 2005. The prudent course—if you have enough faith in it to buy a case—is to try a bottle every year or so after, say, the age of five, until you like the way it tastes, then plan to finish off the remaining bottles within a year or two. If you're really curious, set aside that last bottle for additional aging. If a particular wine seems to have a great future ahead of it, you can always wait a few more years to finish it off.

From our point of view, it's better to end up wishing you'd bought more of Winery X rather than less.

AGING CALIFORNIA CHARDONNAY:

DOES IT MAKE SENSE?

We hear a lot of talk these days about how well California Chardonnays age. "They offer so much more if given additional time in the bottle," many California winemakers are wont to say. It's true that there are a few splendid decade-old examples that support the notion, but we don't think this is sound advice for *most* of the state's Chardonnays.

When we uncorked an '83 Chardonnay a few months ago, we found it was alarmingly decrepit: stinky in scent and oxidized in flavor. Since it had been kept in a cool, damp cellar where numerous other wines have matured in textbook fashion, we knew it hadn't suffered in our hands. After trying several more disappointing '83 Chardonnays, we concluded that at just under five years of age these much-vaunted California whites were simply too old. Concerned as well as curious, we then tasted sixty different Chardonnays from the '81, '82, and '83 vintages (including three dozen from our own cellar) over a period of three months. Okay, it wasn't an exhaustive survey, considering that more than three hundred California wineries produce Chardonnay, but it was a fairly representative sampling.

Interestingly, in reviewing our past notes on these wines, we found that we had thought highly of most of them when they were first released about a year and a half to two years after harvest. At that time most had a fresh, ripe fruitiness, pleasantly apparent nuances of oak, and the fleshy, rich character that makes fine California Chardonnay so appealing. Many of them had merited upbeat descriptions such as "citrusy-crisp" and "buttery-rich."

Now, four to six years after the harvest date, many of these same wines made us reach for less complimentary descriptions— "woody," "tealike," "lemon drops," "rubber and varnish." Most were tired and dull, and some were downright unpleasant. Very few had improved, developing complexity or subtlety. Hidden flaws had emerged; those that had seemed somewhat flamboyant early on now seemed very overblown; lean examples now appeared harsh and hollow; and simple, straightforward wines tasted boringly monotone.

In fact, there were only six wines we still liked. Among the '81s the Robert Mondavi and the Rutherford Hill Jaeger Vineyards were superb; both were deep, golden, harmonious bottlings that had the layered flavors age gives while retaining much of the flesh and vigor of younger wines. All the '82s we tried were weak and wizened. (Considering the rain-soaked vintage, perhaps that was only to be expected.) There were four '83s that had gained depth but still showed a great deal of freshness, fruit, and balance, notably the Sonoma-Cutrer Les Pierres, Inglenook Reserve, Clos du Bois Calcaire and Robert Mondavi Reserve. Even these wines struck us as fully mature and now at their best.

To be fair, some California wineries have produced remarkable Chardonnays that seem to defy time. The 1975 Alexander Valley Vineyards, the 1978 Chalone Reserve and the 1979 Freemark Abbey, all tasted in 1987, were marvelous. They had done more than survive—they had developed. And we remember a number of others—1973 Château Montelena and 1976 Trefethen, to mention two—that still dazzled the palate after a decade. But these are exceptions to the rule that governs the great lake of Chardonnays the state produces every year.

If we're right that the vast majority of California Chardonnays not only don't improve but actually get worse with extended bottle age (say, beyond three years from the vintage date), then why do so many producers recommend laying them away for "further development"? Partly, it's because "age-worthiness" confers a certain status on a wine because longevity is associated and often confused with greatness. The real issue, of course, is not how long it takes for a wine to reach its best, but how good it is when it gets there. And what's wrong with getting there sooner rather than later?

As chance would have it, shortly after expressing our doubts about the wisdom of aging Chardonnay, we attended an extensive blind tasting of older Chardonnays held by Joseph DeLissio, the wine director of New York's River Café, an event occasioned by the restaurant's newly expanded California Classic wine list. We'd gone into the tasting claiming that few California Chardonnays are worth keeping three or four years beyond the vintage date. After sampling twenty-two Chardonnays back to '73, all in drinkable condition and some in magnificent form, were we ready to recant?

No. In fact, the tasting showed that our cautionary advice was sound. The examples poured at the River Café tasting had been winnowed from a field of fifty-five possible candidates. Since the group of wines was composed strictly of stellar performers, it could hardly be regarded as a representative cross section of older Chardonnays. Even so, the '83s and '81s were fully mature, and we doubted that there was anything to gain by keeping them longer. Impressive as some of the older wines were, we thought they probably had been more impressive a few years back.

When the labels were revealed, it was interesting to see some recurring names among our favorites: the 1981 and 1980 Trefethen, the '83 and '81 Robert Mondavi Reserve, the '83 Long and the '80 Grgich were all splendid examples. Some once-glorious older wines such as '76 Trefethen and '73 Château Montelena were now fading, but others, such as the '75 Montelena, were still relatively lively. Most amazing of all was the '74 Robert Mondavi Reserve, an astonishingly fresh wine that had not yet developed the toffeelike flavors age inevitably confers on Chardonnay.

Clearly, a handful of Chardonnays can gain in the bottle, but predicting their development is no science. Why had these whites lasted when so many others hadn't? True, they had some highly regarded names on their labels, but they didn't share any special production technique, such as barrel-fermenting or absence of malolactic fermentation. Vintage seemed to be as vital a factor as any in giving the wines the balance and concentration that would make an intriguing complex mouthful at ten years or more.

How do you find the exceptions worth laying away? It's not easy. Even a Chardonnay that tastes terrific when first released may not have a bright future ahead of it. Wines are like spinning tops: they begin to wobble and fall apart when slight imbalances so difficult to discern early on become obvious with time. A winery's past performance in producing long-lived Chardonnays may not be any help either. The patchwork of California's microclimates, the use of varying vineyard sources, and the constant experimentation in the cellar all militate against making easy predictions about any Chardonnay's potential life span.

Only a gambler would buy a case, no matter what the label, and keep it past its fourth birthday without trying several bottles along the way.

CALIFORNIA CABERNET VINTAGES

California's wine districts, unlike those of Europe, are blessed with a reliable climate that ensures ripe grapes and attractive wines in every vintage. Of course there are variations, but with rare exception California vintage years are a matter of good, better, or best.

Which vintages in the past have been the best for that varietal, however, has been a matter of considerable debate. But we wonder if Californians themselves have always been good judges of their own vintages.

Take the highly regarded 1974 harvest, for example, which was perhaps the first California Cabernet Sauvignon vintage to gain widespread attention. It was also, interestingly enough, the last California harvest where the grape grower's point of view—that superior vintages are associated with high sugar content in the grapes at picking—weighed heavily in the overall consensus on the excellence of the vintage. That's because high sugar in the grapes results in big, high-alcohol wines, and the view that the bigger the resulting wines, the better the vintage was much in vogue when the reputation of the '74s was made.

Since then, there have been a number of dissenting voices. No less an authority than André Tchelistcheff told us several years ago that wines from the '74 vintage fell somewhere between over-rated and worthless for Cabernet, although he'd allow that there were certain exceptions.

Well, we think Tchelistcheff was right. Our impressions of this vintage, derived from tastings both horizontal and vertical, blind and with eyes wide open, are that the majority had given their all at ten years of age and that the tannin often over-shadowed the fruit, giving a curiously hollow-tasting impression. Perhaps the biggest disappointment of that year was the Beaulieu Vineyard's Private Reserve, which always struck us, on the occasions we had it, as a fat, overblown wine.

There were, to be sure, certain exceptions: Trefethen, Caymus, Stag's Leap Wine Cellars, Sterling Reserve, and Robert Mondavi Reserve among them, which had all the complexity, harmony, and character expected of outstanding Cabernets. In particular the Heitz Cellars Martha's Vineyard, with its immense depth of flavor and fruit, always made an overwhelming impression.

It's the fate of every red-wine vintage to be represented in the end by a handful of survivors, but in the case of the '74s, we wonder if a half-dozen wines, good as they are, are enough to uphold its exaggerated reputation.

In 1985 we were able to put the question of California Cabernet vintages into perspective and compare the most highly touted vintages of recent decades—'68, '70, '74, '78, '80—with the so-called lesser vintages (or at least less talked-about ones) of the same period. At the River Café we had a chance to taste California's best Cabernets in a tasting covering six of the state's top producers in as many vintages.

The chance to taste Beaulieu Vineyard Private Reserve, Robert Mondavi Reserve, Mayacamas, Heitz Martha's Vineyard, Stag's Leap Wine Cellars, and Ridge Monte Bello, most in such years as '68, '69, '70, '73, '74, and '77, was extraordinary enough; but Joe DeLissio, the restaurant's wine director, decided to make it really interesting by not telling the assembled tasters either the vineyard or the vintage. By process of elimination, we managed to get most of the vintages and some of the vineyards right, and so we weren't too surprised at many of our comments. Predictably, the '68s were lovely (although completely mature, except for the extraordinary Heitz Martha's Vineyard), the '70s—our favorite older Cabernet year—magnificent and still developing (the Mayacamas is stunning), the '74s—not unexpectedly—powerful and coarse. The '69s were very attractive but had certainly peaked.

But what really surprised us was the strong showing of what many regard as lightweight vintages or even "off years"—'73 and '77. The Stag's Leap Wine Cellars, the Robert Mondavi Reserve, and the Mayacamas were the stars of the former vintage; the Heitz Bella Oaks and the Ridge Monte Bello, the most impressive from the latter.

We might have regarded these bottlings as exceptions in otherwise so-so years if we hadn't coincidentally been privileged to attend vertical tastings of the Cabernets of Chappellet, Conn Creek, and Chateau Montelena within a few weeks of the California Classic event. When we realized in each case we'd preferred the beautiful '73 and perfectly balanced '75 out of all the Chappellet vintages from '69 to '82, and the elegant '77s of Conn Creek and Chateau Montelena out of the recent vintages of these two producers, we began to wonder if there wasn't a reason for our decided preference for these off years.

Could it be that the less powerful build of a wine in a year like '75 or '77 achieves a better balance with maturity than the heavier, more alcoholic vintages, such as '74, '78, or '80? Could it be what Californians have regarded in the past as off years are really the great ones? In any event, there's no question that "lighter" vintages such as '73, '75, and '77 are widely underrated—and that what constitutes an outstanding Cabernet year in California ought to be based solely on taste, not harvest reports.

RIDGE MONTE BELLO

CABERNET SAUVIGNON

Are California Cabernet Sauvignons the equal of red Bordeaux? No, say those who maintain that top California Cabernet Sauvignons start fading at the age when better Médocs are reaching maturity. Yes, say California partisans, who point to the numerous comparative tastings held in recent years at which California Cabernets have emerged victorious over the greatest Bordeaux. Letting the wines themselves settle the question in yet another blind tasting is the most popular way of tackling the controversy: The taste in the glass becomes the final arbiter.

We've long thought that wines from various wine districts of the world can be compared meaningfully so long as the wines are made from the same (or similar) grape varieties, are from vintages of comparable quality, and ideally, are the same age. But many of the comparative tastings of California Cabernet Sauvignons and red Bordeaux of recent years haven't been carefully thought out and have ignored even those basic requirements. They have also ignored something else: A truly valid comparison between the two requires that the wines be of sufficient age to show the qualities for which they are famous. Unfortunately, given the scarcity of older California Cabernets, it's rarely been possible to compare examples more than a few years old.

The single most interesting blind comparative tasting we've ever attended did, in fact, pair excellent vintages for both California and Bordeaux that went back some twenty years. It was billed as a vertical tasting of Ridge Vineyards Cabernet Sauvignons going back to 1962 and was conducted in New York by Paul Draper, who has been the winemaker at Ridge since 1969.

Most wine enthusiasts probably associate Ridge with some of California's finest Zinfandel. But it is also one of the few small-scale wineries that has a track record of fine Cabernets going back decades—to 1962, in fact—when it offered its first commercial vintage. At that time there were only a handful of California wineries devoted entirely to fine-wine production. Today there are scores of such wineries, but Ridge remains firmly in the front rank for its two primary wines, Zinfandel and Cabernet Sauvignon—a position it has enjoyed since its earliest days. We tasted Ridge's best-known Cabernet, which comes from its own vineyards on Monte Bello Ridge in the Santa Cruz mountains south of San Francisco.

We were told that there was likely to be a "ringer"—a surprise wine—in the array, a common practice that helps tasters test their powers of perception as well as keep their prejudices in check. When the wines were revealed, however, it turned out that there were four ringers: the '75, '70, '64, and '62 vintages of Château Latour. These were roughly paired with six vintages of Ridge Monte Bello Cabernet: '74, '72, '71, '70, '64, and '62. In short, it was another transatlantic taste-off.

We found the results fascinating, largely because they upset a couple of our then pet notions about California Cabernet Sauvignon versus red Bordeaux and confirmed others. The following notes on the wines are condensed from the tasting descriptions we made before we knew what they were. In our notes, one star

(*) indicates a fine wine, two stars (**) an outstanding wine, and three stars (***) a superlative wine.

WINE A: *Strong young Cabernet nose with notes of oak and herbs. Tannic, no length or complexity.* **[1974 Ridge Monte Bello]

WINE B: *Weedy, earthy, vegetative nose; some "dustiness" like Bordeaux. Hard core of almost bitter tannin. Short finish, seems to have no fruit.* *[1975 Château Latour]

WINE C: *Almost inky color with hint of browning. Powerful, alcoholic nose with strong cassis note. Impressive, lots of flavor, still tannic, underlying dryness.* *[1970 Ridge Monte Bello]

WINE D: *Less opaque than wine C. Deep pungent earthy nose develops in glass. Heavy hard tannin masking wine. Not much complexity or depth. Not ready yet.* *[1970 Château Latour]

WINE E: *Lovely nose—warmth, spice, fruit, subtlety. Superb harmony—ripe flavors, long lovely finish, balanced tannin. Latour?* ***[1971 Ridge Monte Bello]

WINE F: *Distinctive nose—hints of sweetness; tannins smoothing out; balanced, but a bit green in finish.* **[1972 Ridge Monte Bello]

WINE G: *Weedy scent, tealike hints. Odd volatile note in nose. Not well-balanced, but fruity. Moderate tannin.* *[1964 Ridge Monte Bello]

WINE H: *Fabulous nose, still somewhat closed. Distinction, elegance, subtlety. Real class. Long cedary finish, still some tannin.* ***[1964 Château Latour]

WINE I: *Nose marred by odd fleeting off-notes. Olive-ish flavor; plenty of depth, heavy tannin. Needs time.* *[1962 Ridge Monte Bello]

WINE J: *Superlative pungent nose—very complex. Rich, ripe flavors, tannic backbone, long finish—great class.* ***[1962 Château Latour]

Our first pet theory—that California Cabernets are noticeably different from Bordeaux in style—didn't hold true at that particular tasting. In similar blind tastings, we've found that it was possible to distinguish the California wines from the Bordeaux. This is easiest to do if you know how many of each are represented in the tasting, of course, which we did not. In sorting out the California examples from the French, it helps if they are clearly "Californian" in style—high in alcohol, with ripe, fruity flavors and a more open, mouth-filling taste structure. The Ridge wines, obviously, are more stylistically similar to clarets than most California Cabernet Sauvignons. The alcohol levels, for example, are moderate (below 13 percent, except for the 1970), as they are in Bordeaux.

"In my view, it's California practices—in the vineyard and the cellar—that exaggerate the character of Cabernet Sauvignon grown in California," Paul Draper stated. "There's no reason to expect a California Cabernet to taste like a Bordeaux, but if the techniques are the same, the differences between the two should be no greater than they are between Médoc communes like Graves and Pauillac." The techniques that Draper follows at Ridge reflect the traditional Bordeaux verities: that greatness comes from the concentrated fruit of old vines in low-yield, nonirrigated vineyards, made into wine that is kept on the skins after fermentation and given minimum handling during its time in barrel.

Our notes seem to support the notion that California Cabernet Sauvignons frequently top Bordeaux wines in tastings because they are more fruity and "forward"—that is, they offer much more to the nose and palate when young—than Bordeaux of a comparable age. Finesse, subtlety, and complexity are quiet qualities, easy to overlook in lengthy tastings, and in fact may not be much in evidence at all in young Bordeaux.

We gave some of the lowest marks to the '75 and '70 Latours, which reminds us just how unappealing, even unpromising, young wines from this famed Pauillac property can appear. We thought more highly of the '74 Ridge Monte Bello than the '75 Latour, and the '71 and '72 Ridge Monte Bello than the '70 Latour. In fact, to us, the most impressive wine of the tasting was the superlative '71 Ridge Monte Bello. Its completely har monious structure and perfect balance reminded us, ironically, of Château Latour. (We were interested to hear that Draper himself considers the '71 one of his best to date.) By contrast, some of our highest marks went to the '62 and '64 vintages of Latour, which had developed sufficiently to show their true potential.

We had one other notion that the tasting didn't support: In general, California Cabernet Sauvignons don't last as long as red Bordeaux. There are few California Cabernets from the 1960s—and only a handful from earlier decades—that are still *improving,* which suggests that the appealing qualities of young California Cabernet Sauvignon come at the cost of a relatively shorter evolution in the bottle. We found the '62 and '64 Ridge Monte Bello slightly flawed, so they were not the best examples of the ability of the Ridge Monte Bello wines to age and develop. Certainly the '62 showed no more signs of early fading than the Latour, and the other Ridge Monte Bello Cabernets are all more backward than most California Cabernets from the same years. (This is also true of the '77 and '78 Ridge Monte Bello sampled not long after the event. Both appeared dense, young, and tannic; the '78 riper and richer, the '77—our preference—leaner and less open-textured on the palate.)

Why did Draper choose to measure his wine against what many consider the finest Bordeaux of all? "It's not a question of which is better. Latour happens to be my favorite Bordeaux and a benchmark for claret, a standard of excellence. Tasting my wines against it tells me better than anything else how well we're doing and how much farther we have to go."

Some five years after the Ridge/Latour vertical comparison, we attended a tasting that provided a fascinating postscript to that event. Ridge, of course, is one of the few California producers that can pull out a truly old bottle to defend the claim that California Cabernets can improve with age. So when Paul Draper told us he was going to open the 1984, the 1974, and the 1964 Monte Bello over lunch at New York's Aurora restaurant, we decided that this was one tasting we weren't going to miss.

Ridge is a red wine specialist, but the winery does make a tiny amount of Chardonnay, and we started with a stunning 1984 Monte Bello Chardonnay (alas, available only at the winery). But that was mere foreplay. The real tasting started with a barrel sample of the 1984 Monte Bello Cabernet, which Draper thinks is one of the best of recent years. Although way too young, its rich, soft character and fine balance made it surprisingly approachable—even if the $35 price tag makes one pause.

"At that price," Draper said, "people expect us to provide a Cabernet that not only ranks with California's best but can stand with great Bordeaux in great vintages." Draper didn't hesitate to make a direct comparison. To tune our palates for the main course, we went back a decade to the '74 Monte Bello, a rich, deep, firm wine with an almost mineral tang to the finish. At thirteen years of age it had begun to shed its tannic shell and reveal some complexity. It was a perfect companion to the cassoulet of sweetbreads (we have to eat, too). Those at the table agreed that it really wasn't mature yet.

Draper then poured a 1970 Mouton-Rothschild, a marvelous elegant claret in perfect condition and at its peak, and a '64 Monte Bello. "I wanted to make something of a reasonable comparison," he explained. But the '64 Monte Bello Cabernet dwarfed the famous Bordeaux by its concentrated, cedary nose and enormous depth of flavor. We'd given that particular vintage a mixed review some five years earlier, but now thought it a fabulous, twenty-two-year-old wine with a long life still ahead of it. Draper smiled. "Well," he said, "I think it shows that *some* California wines can develop complexity and quality with age, just as fine Bordeaux does."

We concurred and asked for another glass of the Ridge.

DRINKABLE REDS

"Red wine," Piero Antinori of the Tuscan wine firm of the same name is fond of saying, "is wine. White wine," he always adds with a shrug, "is just . . . white wine."

Many wine lovers, like us, believe the old adage that the first duty of a wine is to be red. Sure, there's a place for white wine—whenever the weather is warm or there's shellfish on the table, or whenever there's a need to wet the whistle in preparation for the suaver sensations of the real thing. All right, that's over-stating it. There *are* plenty of occasions when only a white will do, and we'd be the first to say that anyone who drank only one shade of wine to the exclusion of the other would be missing out on half of what wine has to offer. But asked to state a pref-erence for one or the other in terms of the proverbial desert is-land choice, we'd have to say *red.*

The real point about red versus white is that great as some whites can be, there are greater reds. Certainly, reds are more versatile on the table. It's far easier to serve a multicourse meal matched to a series of red wines than it is to repeat the trick us-ing only whites. Whites are refreshing; reds are satisfying, which explains why whites are the obvious preludes to reds. We've never forgotten giving a tasting some years back of fine Ameri-can Chardonnays for wine-minded friends, after which we served dinner accompanied with the group's top choices. Toward the end of the meal, a good friend of ours followed us into the kitchen when we were clearing plates; he confessed that despite the plethora of excellent whites, he was pining for a glass of red. We hastily produced a decent bottle—a hearty Zinfandel, as we recall—and saw our guests grab for it with cries of joy. Their collective palate had been well primed, to be sure, but clearly they yearned for the gratifications of the real grape. Since then, modest, one-bottle meals and hot-weather dinners excepted, we've always produced at least one red for our guests.

Feeling as we do—and feeling sure that most wine enthusiasts share our prejudice—we are amazed that red wine consumption, despite the overall growth in wine consumption in the past decade, has steadily fallen. At first, when the trend toward white wine consumption began to be felt, we weren't too surprised. We assumed consumers new to wine would be weaning themselves from soft drinks or switching from cocktails and would, therefore, want a glass of something cold. Such drinkers were clearly at the fringes of wine enthusiasm, but once they carried the wine habit from the bar to the dining table, they'd turn to red. Far from it! Having watched the statistics on red wine's declining share of the market for a number of years now, we can only conclude that most Americans don't fit the "progressive palate" scenario confidently predicted by many wine professionals. In other words, Americans, by and large, haven't turned from soda pop to St.-Emilion. Instead, the ranks of wine drinkers have obviously been swelled by growing numbers of people who've turned to white wine, and that includes blush wines, and stayed with these pale bottlings. (By the way, this trend isn't just an American phenomenon. There's a white wine trend as well in such traditional red wine strongholds as France, Italy, and Australia.)

The California figures are particularly interesting, since that state accounts for some 70 percent of the wine in this country. Back in 1970, almost half the wine produced was red, while the balance was evenly divided between whites and rosés. By the mid-1980s, red wine production had shrunk to 15 percent, surpassed by rosés at 18 percent. White accounted for a whopping 67 percent of the wine produced. Red has not only lost a dramatic share of the market, it's lost in absolute terms as well. Despite the fact that California production almost tripled over this period, the amount of red produced actually fell. Imported wines, whose importance in the American market has grown significantly, reflect the same startling color mix: 60 percent of them are now whites.

One of the reasons these statistics seem so strange is that no one would guess that red wasn't wildly popular, considering the elevated prices fine reds command in the marketplace and the amount of press given to them. But this is just where the confusion sets in; the devoted wine enthusiast, fixated as he is on Bordeaux and Burgundy, Cabernet and Port, is by no means the typical wine drinker. For every connoisseur fussing over labels and vintages, there are scores of folks just looking for a glass of something pleasant and not too demanding. And what's so odd about that, really?

The problem is that other than Beaujolais, which isn't to everyone's taste, there aren't very many light, stylish, easy-to-drink reds on the market. Now that every Chianti producer feels obliged to send America his very best *riserva,* there are precious few of those youthful, piquant—and inexpensive—Chiantis available. There are occasional Riojas that fit the bill, and if the wine world were just, there would be an endless supply of affordable top-class Pinot Noir, which is, after all, the ideal light red. But for various reasons, there rarely is.

Since California seems to have such success with Cabernet, we've often thought that it was too bad it couldn't produce the sort of light, stylish, soft wines that you sometimes find from lesser-known St.-Emilion properties—wines that offer some sophisticated flavor but mostly uncomplicated pleasure at around five years of age. Louis M. Martini has been doing just that for years, but its efforts haven't always been appreciated. That's because immediate appeal and drinkability haven't, until recently, been considered red wine virtues, at least in some tasting circles.

A few years ago wine drinkers who took their bottles seriously tended to look down their noses at light reds, dismissing them as vinous wimps. So, unfortunately, did most of the wine press. We remember a tasting of Cabernet Sauvignons given in the midseventies at which Robert Mondavi spoke about his evolving approach to winemaking, which now emphasized elegance over power. The taster sitting next to us snorted derisively in his glass and muttered out loud, "When he says 'elegant,' what he really means is *thin."* Mondavi, as he often does, was correctly anticipating the next direction for the majority of California's Cabernet Sauvignons.

Some critics assert that the scaling down of California's Cabernets amounts to giving up the richness and ripeness inherent in the state's reds for a kind of internationally acceptable but soulless sleekness and sophistication. We're in sympathy with that outlook but don't think it can be applied to every Cabernet bottled. By now it should be widely conceded that only a handful of Cabernet vineyards in California will yield a great, strapping classic that will repay cellaring for fifteen years.

Impressed as we've been with many of the deep, dark Cabernets of the past, far too many were not drinkable when young, nor did they develop into anything very drinkable with age. From our current tastings, however, we see that California's ever-creative winemakers have discovered that if the grapes don't look like the source of bottled greatness, they might still make a light, stylish, drinkable wine that can be enjoyed young—and for a modest price, too. It's nice to think that the best-balanced of these lighter-style reds will mature well in the cellar, but if they provide attractive drinking in their youth, does it really matter what they'll be like in ten years? One often hears young wines that are easy to drink (Jordan's, for example) disparaged as "restaurant wines." Presumably, that's because restaurateurs are always looking for good reds that don't have to be matured for years before they can be offered on a wine list and recommended to diners. But what, we'd like to know, is wrong with that approach or those kinds of wine?

ZINFANDEL: A GRAPE GONE WRONG?

Watching the changing wine scene in California is like watching a speeded-up movie. True, the dizzying pace adds to the excitement, but the rapidity with which wines and wine styles go in and out of fashion can be disconcerting to the wine lover and very discouraging to the wine grower, who can't change the grapes in his vineyard overnight.

A recent example of California's ultrarapid boom-and-bust change in wine fashions is Zinfandel, the formerly beloved red varietal that became a conspicuous sales casualty, only to be reborn as a bland white wine.

It's curious that the taste for Zinfandel should now be on the wane because the wine has never been better. It is particularly hard on a district such as Amador County, whose Zinfandel plantings—some three-fourths of the vineyards there—have yielded superlative Zinfandels of intense character.

Sadly, waning sales have forced many of the wineries in the area to deemphasize its classic red and to plant Sauvignon Blanc. ("You might call Sauvignon Blanc our grape white hope," quipped one vintner.) In the meantime they're producing a good deal of white Zinfandel from their grapes—a wine we find soft and fruity and innocuous at best. (White 'Zin' does have one thing to be said for it: Unlike previous fads—cold ducks, pop wines, sangrias, coolers, and the like—it is a genuine wine, not a winelike concoction.)

But if Zinfandel is so good, how did it become a falling star? A little bit of background on the evolution of Zinfandel's style helps explain its changing popularity. Because it makes fruity wine with an attractive, distinctive, berrylike spiciness (especially when planted in cool coastal districts), Zinfandel has long been widely planted and widely used for blending, as well as for making appealing light table wines. Surprisingly, winemakers discovered, the wine also ages well.

It was during the wine-boom years of the 1970s, however, when experimentation with wine styles was at its height, that Zinfandel came into its own; winemakers began taking it seriously, which meant in those days bottling it as a varietal, but not for early consumption. Convinced that a wine had to have size and substance to last, some winemakers (cheered on by wine journalists who shared this misconception) took advantage of a few hot harvests when much Zinfandel overripened anyway to create wines that were once considered "awesome blockbusters" but are now roundly condemned as "monsters."

People began to get the impression that Zinfandel had a split personality. Side by side on retail shelves were Zinfandels in a proliferation of styles: coarse jug wines; light fruity types; serious, spicy examples; heady, powerful high-alcohol wines; and sweet, late-harvest ones as cloying as cough syrup.

Exciting as all the experimentation was, it had a dark side: Lack of a settled style for the versatile varietal meant that wine drinkers had no idea what they would find in a bottle.

Some wine drinkers bought Zinfandels thinking they had California's answer to Beaujolais, then discovered upon uncorking them that they'd opened up something considerably more muscular and potent—and most important, not as pleasurable as they'd expected. Zinfandels with high alcohol (up to 17 percent), mouth-puckering tannin, and an inky concentration that left one with a stunned palate and stained teeth proved to have few fans. All were described by their creators as suitable for leaving to your grandchildren and were priced accordingly. In fact, most (though not all) of these overblown examples have aged gracelessly. The principal problem with late-harvest Zinfandels, some critics now say, was that wines of such high alcohol have no place at the table. Personally, we never thought much of that argument. Are the classic Amarones of Italy—to pick one example of concentrated, high-alcohol wines—easy to match with food?

Like all unusual wines, truly big Zinfandels do require a special context for appreciation—we find consumption is best confined to small sips with the cheese course. But Zinfandels of normal to moderately big dimensions are first-rate food wines, excellent with Italian dishes and wonderful with charcoal-broiled steak.

It may seem overdone to bemoan the fate of a once-vaunted varietal, but then Zinfandel is not just another grape. Because it has no real European counterpart, it's rightfully thought of as California's own. A well-made, full-flavored, sturdy Zinfandel, with its warmth of flavor, its spice and power, is also California's most individual wine—a wine that for all the current wine talk about "finesse" and "elegance" no wine lover should ignore.

AMERICAN WINE GOES EUROPEAN

It's been popular for over a decade now to claim that American wine has "come of age." Ever since the now-famous Paris Tasting back in 1976 staged by wine merchant Steven Spurrier, when the French preferred California wines over the best of France in a blind tasting, it's been widely assumed that Americans, having proven their worth on the international stage, went on to develop their own wine traditions, their own approach to winemaking, their own attitudes toward wine—or did they? Lately we've begun to think that these new American wine traditions resemble nothing so much as the old European ones.

Really?

In the decade preceding the Paris Tasting, scientific, high-tech winemaking and a distinctly American penchant for experimentation had led to one breakthrough after another. This trend was applauded by an enthusiastic and growing audience of wine drinkers who were attracted to the brash new bottlings that challenged the best of Europe. We seemed to be going far beyond Old World traditions. The stage had been set for a vinous High Noon, which is probably why the Paris Tasting caused such an uproar. The French were dismayed at the outcome, and Americans felt excusably triumphant, but the victory did not mark the beginning of American ascendancy over—or even independence from—European wine and its traditions. Instead, it started our conversion to the European point of view. Americans may have won the Paris Tasting, but we think the French really won the argument.

Each of the European criticisms of the tasting has largely been accepted and incorporated into the national wine consciousness. Increasingly, American wines now reflect the European perspective. Consider these points:

The French argued that the whole idea of comparisons was silly. Comparing American wines and French wines was like comparing apples and oranges, they said. This viewpoint was widely derided then as mere sour grapes, but recently Americans have begun talking the same way about American wines. Just as Burgundians appreciate the difference between Volnay and Chambertin—but never ask which is superior—now we're hearing from U.S. winemakers that Oregon Pinot Noirs are difficult to compare with California Pinot Noirs because stylistically they're too different. Each, we're told, must be appreciated on its own merits.

Wine growers who came to accept the European viewpoint that cooler climates are especially suited for certain grapes discovered that some Northwest and East Coast locales might actually give them an advantage over California in growing certain grapes. In the past decade we've seen the list of non-California successes grow with Oregon Pinot Noirs, Cabernets and Merlots from Maryland and Long Island, Texas Chardonnays, etc., etc. The list gets longer, and with each new addition it becomes clearer that there is a remarkable diversity of valid regional wine styles in this country, and that the California style with various types isn't the only worthwhile one. Even within California regional style is much debated.

We're beginning to recognize, as Europeans do, that wines made from the same grape in different regions can have very different but equally valid styles. The fact that a delicate Chardonnay from Long Island doesn't have the butter-and-smoke flamboyance of a full-blown California Chardonnay is, after all, irrelevant to its quality.

Gone too are the days when a California winemaker would proudly point out a vineyard planted to Riesling, Chardonnay, Cabernet, Barbera, Gewürztraminer, Syrah, and who knew how many other varieties, and would tell you with a straight face that he really believed he could produce a world-class example of wine from each of them. In California the trend for some time has been to search out plots of land where certain grape varieties do their best.

This is all part of a marked Euro-trend: We hear less and less of what's going on in the cellar and more and more about what's going on in the vineyard. We hear talk about regional characteristics of American wines, the style imparted by local conditions, microclimates—even, yes, that European touchstone, soil.

As European critics were quick to point out, finesse and subtlety—the hallmarks of a great wine in the European view—are the hardest things to notice in a comparative tasting. In a blind tasting, even people who should know better invariably give the highest marks to the wine that makes the most powerful and obvious impression, as if a wine could be measured on a sort of vinous Richter scale by its impact alone. In the Paris Tasting, *hélas,* the laurels were given to the attention-grabbing upstarts from California, and if later restagings of the event are any guide, perhaps they deserved them. But the criticism that can be leveled against comparative tastings does have validity in many cases, and not just in transatlantic taste-offs.

The European criticism that many U.S. wines were overly obvious, overly powerful, and overly aggressive has also been widely accepted. We're pleased to see that more and more wines with the subtler Euro-style virtues of balance, finesse, and elegance are being produced—even if they risk being the sort of bottlings that are easily ignored in blind tastings. Today terms such as "finesse," "elegance," "proportion," and "balance" have supplanted talk of "concentration," "tannin," and "mouth-filling dimensions." Wine writers have had to revise their vocabularies to keep up: they've had to dust off words such as "suave" and "supple" because there aren't so many wines left they can call "potent" or "swashbuckling."

Then, too, varietal intensity is no longer automatically confused with character, nor is tannicity always mistaken for structure. Consider recent Cabernet Sauvignons, for example. There was a time when "Cabernet Sauvignon" on the bottle—100 percent, of course—was like a designer's name on a pair of jeans—an imprimatur of taste. But now, in an effort to make not just better Cabernet Sauvignons but better wines, Cabernet Franc, Malbec, even Petit Verdot, are being planted to add complexity to the final blend. One hundred percent Cabernet Sauvignons have begun to give way to the sophisticated red blends available under proprietary names (Opus One and all the rest) that even withhold varietal information—another idea imported from Europe.

One of the most telling criticisms that was made of the Paris Tasting was that fine wines aren't made to be drunk with each other, but with food. The implication was that American wines were made for blind tastings, not the dinner table.

Today, however, all wines in America are, according to their winemakers, "styled to go with food," which leads you to wonder what they were supposed to go with before that idea became prevalent. The current emphasis on stylishness and proportion in California wines might be regarded as something of a concession that there was something to be said for the lightness and finesse of classic European wines after all. As Californians now openly acknowledge, balanced wines do go better with food than overwrought bottlings do. And being compatible with food, all now agree, is something that is very useful for a wine to be able to do. In fact, the endless blind tastings of yesteryear have been mercifully replaced by ever-more-frequent food and wine matchings, which are certainly more civilized for the wine press. (Who wouldn't rather taste a new Chardonnay to determine its compatibility with poached baby salmon than sit and scribble notes on a scoresheet and expectorate into a plastic cup? Fortunately we don't foresee any end to the trend of drinking wine with food.)

What we've been describing here—the Europeanization of American wine—was probably inevitable. As our wine industry matured, perhaps we shouldn't be surprised that it has come to resemble the older parent wine culture. And is it a bad thing really?

We're beginning to celebrate geographic and stylistic diversity and the role of wine on the table. Perhaps we'll come to rely more and more on our own taste and less and less on marathon judgings, incessant comparison tastings, rankings and medals. At that point we can stop worrying about what's the best and start thinking about what's most enjoyable.

CALIFORNIA WINES IN REVIEW

We were among two hundred guests who had just finished a fourteen-course meal with twenty-nine wines, ending with an array of splendid Cabernet Sauvignons. We'd just put a series of stars next to the most memorable wines and dishes, and were thinking that next year's dinner would have to be spectacular indeed to top this one, when we heard the announcement that it would be the last act—at least in New York—for this particular gala. We were at the tenth annual California Barrel Tasting Dinner at The Four Seasons, and co-owners Paul Kovi and Tom Margittai had just explained that next year the barrel tasting would move to San Francisco to the Stanford Court Hotel.

Many of the California winemakers who had looked forward each year to the chance of having their new wines open on Broadway, so to speak, felt that they'd lost an important rite of spring. After the dinner we spotted Tom Burgess of Burgess Cellars waiting for a taxi. We talked. "I'm standing at Fifty-second and Park," he said, "and it's the end of an era. How did it happen?"

How? As we thought about it, it hadn't just been a decade's worth of dinners that had come to an end. A significant phase in the development of California wine—its late adolescence, perhaps?—had passed, too.

What made the annual event so exciting over the years was that it coincided with one of the most exciting decades in California wine history, and many of the frequent and remarkable changes in the wine industry were faithfully reflected in the wines presented and the issues discussed at the barrel tastings. In effect, it was a barometer of fashions, issues, and trends. We began to realize just how much we'd taken away from all those dinners besides notes on hundreds of brilliant debut wines matched to scores of dazzling dishes.

In 1976, when Kovi and Margittai and wine merchant and critic Gerald Asher conceived the evening, it was an audacious and daring undertaking to bring barrel samples of California wines, many of which were little known except by reputation on the East Coast, and present them alongside older bottlings of the same wines for comparison at a grand dinner featuring some of The Four Seasons' most remarkable dishes. Understandably, the barrel dinner became de rigueur for the wine world and the hottest ticket in town. Soon thereafter, similar barrel dinners proliferated, and cask samples from California were soon staples at wine tastings. (In fact, the '76 barrel dinner may have been the first time the public was ever exposed to wines before they'd been bottled.) Sure, veterans liked to sound blasé to each other, pretending it was less a wine tasting than a social event. But the lofty arguments on the merits and shortcomings of the various wines the dinner showcased was the raison d'être of the gathering—even if it wasn't always easy to get a fix on the wines presented.

It can be tricky to assess California barrel samples. Surprisingly enough, over the years we've learned that our prognostications on the whites were less accurate than our assessments of the reds. California Chardonnays, for example, despite their reputation for rapid evolution, seem to need six months or so in the bottle to reveal their final balance, which may be rather delicately wrought and not so easy to pinpoint early on. We were unenthusiastic about many of the Chardonnay samples over the years, some of which—the '76 Freemark Abbey, for example—later proved excellent.

By contrast, the essential composition of the California Cabernet Sauvignon samples was usually blocked out on the palate from the start. The '75 Chappellet Cabernet struck us as a powerful, yet elegant, well-knit wine even as a raw sample back at the first barrel tasting in 1976—and that's just how it tastes today, although it has finally begun to fade. And, judging by our before and after bottling notes, many of the reds we thought clumsy in their infancy we still find clumsy in their maturity.

But the Barrel Tasting Dinner was far more than a chance to get a sneak preview of soon-to-be-bottled wines and how they might age. For many on the East Coast, these dinners of the mid-seventies were their first opportunities to taste and compare an entire spectrum of those breakthrough bottlings from the Golden State that had been making such an impact on the wine-world's consciousness, challenging and in some cases triumphing over the best of Europe in well-publicized bottle-to-bottle comparisons.

One dominant trend that was evident in the beginning was the reliance on the wizard winemaker who employed, often with startling success, the high-tech science of modern winemaking in the quest for greatness. There seemed no pinnacle of winemaking achievement that couldn't be scaled by an audacious California winemaker given a free hand in a state-of-the-art winery.

We remember the moment at one of the earliest dinners ('77, perhaps?) when Walter Schug, the brilliant winemaker long associated with the Joseph Phelps Winery, described to a rapt audience the drama of creating a great botrytised dessert Riesling by letting the beneficent mold shrivel the crop of a ripe Riesling vineyard to a tiny fraction and the tension of risking all to create a remarkable honeyed nectar equal to the greatest German Trockenbeerenauslesen (the '76 selected Late Harvest, we seem to recall). Gasps of astonishment punctuated his recital of the extraordinary sugar levels achieved, and an excited babble broke out over the nectarlike samples that were poured.

In those early days the California wine boom was cresting, and each succeeding barrel tasting seemed to offer some startling surprise in yet another wine category. But ten years later, there was less talk of that wizard winemaker who can create great wines in every category. Sheer novelty no longer guaranteed an eager reception for any new wine.

Because each year the barrel dinner gave a dozen or more winemakers a chance to discuss their wines, dramatic shifts in winemaking styles of the late seventies and early eighties were reflected in the rapidly changing winetalk.

Take one example: Traditionally, California Cabernet Sauvignons were judged more by their power and impact than the subtler qualities now so much in vogue. When Warren Winiarski, the iconoclastic winemaker/proprietor of Stag's Leap Wine Cellars, announced at one barrel dinner (1979?) that he'd filtered and fined one of his recent Cabernets ('78, perhaps) in order to restrain its aggressive tannins, audible boos and mutterings about "taking the guts out" greeted this admission of what many then regarded as wine abuse.

At the last couple of barrel dinners the winetalk reflected a new era of balance and restraint: techniques that were once regarded as "stripping" are now called "sculpting," and elegance and mild-mannered behavior at the table are the bywords. (Can talk of "breed" be far behind?)

Over the same period the fortunes of many varietal wines have been changing. At first all the attention was on Chardonnay, Cabernet Sauvignon, and California's own grape, Zinfandel. Now Pinot Noir, Merlot, and Sauvignon Blanc are being taken seriously as well. In fact, we'd been thinking that Sauvignon Blanc in particular was showing signs of having been taken *too* seriously. Current examples appear to have traded the simple, crisp, assertive style we enjoy for a rounder, deeper, Chardonnay-like complexity. A mistake, we thought. After all, it's not a wine that improves in the bottle, right? Yet the pair of Robert Mondavi Fumé Blanc versions of this varietal served at the tenth barrel dinner—'84 and '74—effectively made the point that some bottlings of this wine can age beautifully and gave the attractive sample of younger wine an aura of hidden potential. (Maybe *we* should start taking Sauvignon Blanc more seriously.)

Over that ten years, Zinfandel fell from grace, although the new popularity for its "blush" wine versions proved to be the growers' salvation. Yet at that last barrel tasting, as if to remind everyone that the grape can't be written off as a serious red, Louis P. Martini presented a couple for consideration. A sample of Martini's 1984 was a soft, pleasant wine that seemed destined for early enjoyment. But alongside it was one of the astonishing wines of the dinner—a 1968 Zinfandel that was surprisingly vibrant and delicious. It had probably not been regarded as worth keeping beyond five years either when *it* was first released.

As the evening demonstrated, there are plenty of surprises left in California wine. But the heady excitement of a decade ago has clearly given way to sober reassessment of style and purpose. And that's exactly what occurred at the end of the tenth Barrel Tasting Dinner in a duet on Cabernet: a discussion between two of California's most articulate winemakers, Paul Draper of Ridge Vineyards and Warren Winiarski, accompanied with a quartet of wines—an '84 barrel sample and a '78 from the two wineries.

Draper's advocacy of classic techniques was firmly buttressed by the track record of the Ridge Monte Bello, one of a handful of California Cabernet Sauvignons that lasts and improves magnificently after a decade or more in the bottle. Winiarski took the opposite tack, arguing that longevity and even varietal expression were actually extraneous issues. "What counts," he asserted, "is the creation of beautiful wines."

Their wines seemed to support each point of view. The Ridge Monte Bellos were deep, profound, persistent on the palate; the pair from Stag's Leap Wine Cellars were softer, more scented, more obviously seductive. We were left with the distinct impression that these two schools of thought will still be arguing their merits a decade hence.

Despite having influenced wine everywhere, California is still defining its own vinous stances, refining its own multiregional individuality. It's noteworthy that this past decade began with California winning its laurels against the best wines of Europe and ends with the talk in California taking a decidedly European turn. There seems to be a realization that the next advances for California wine will not come from the cellars, but from the ultimate sources of wine quality, the vineyards—and advances in viticulture can't be accomplished overnight.

It may not be as attention-grabbing for the wineries as producing a new breakthrough bottling each season, but settling down to the hard work of creating consistently classic wines is bound to have solid, even profound, results—and they'll be well worth another string of celebratory dinners, too.

4

New Wines, Old Classics

MARYLAND CABERNET SAUVIGNON

When we joined over a dozen California winemakers for a blind tasting of forty Cabernet Sauvignons from the 1980 vintage, we thought the results might prove interesting. But we had no idea how startling they would be: a Cabernet Sauvignon from Maryland tied for third place, edging out such famous producers as Stag's Leap Wine Cellars and Château Margaux. Even more startling, we'd put it *first*. For a virtually unknown Cabernet from a virtually unknown wine region to leapfrog over world-class competition in a serious tasting is about as likely as having a 100-to-1 horse end up in the money at the Kentucky Derby. But that's just what the 1980 Byrd Cabernet Sauvignon did. ("Maryland?" queried the tasters. "Are you sure you read that label right?")

First, a bit of background. The setting was an oceanside res-taurant in Monterey, California, in 1984. The sponsors of the tasting, Gary and Nancy Andrus, proprietors of one of the Napa Valley's numerous small fine wineries, Pine Ridge, had an-nounced that twenty-one of the forty wines were from eight states other than California. (While the Californians and the

French have been watching each other, wine growers in the rest of the United States have obviously been planting.)

By the time the last note was scribbled, two things were clear. First, 1980 was an excellent Cabernet vintage producing big, fruity, powerful reds for many California wineries. Second, it wasn't possible to separate the California and non-California bottlings by assuming that all the weaker specimens in the tasting were produced outside the Golden State.

When the names were revealed, everyone was astonished to find the 1980 Byrd Maryland Cabernet Sauvignon ranked close to such standouts as the powerful, tannic Monterey Peninsula and the lovely, deliciously balanced Pine Ridge, which placed first and second respectively in the overall voting. The Byrd—a wonderfully rich, firm, elegant Cabernet—was a virtual third-place tie with the fine, fruity Fisher from Sonoma County. (Alas, only two hundred cases of the '80 Byrd were produced, and all of it has disappeared from the market.) The harmonious Stag's Leap Wine Cellars was next, followed by the scented, well-knit 1980 Château Margaux—the only non-U.S. wine in the tasting. In addition to the top six high-scoring bottlings, we also liked the Monticello, Vichon, and the Caymus.

But the Byrd was on everyone's mind. Considering the group's understandable bias toward the richer, concentrated California style, we thought the wine's showing all the more impressive. The only other non-California Cabernet Sauvignon to place in the top third was the eighth-place Chateau Ste. Michelle Cold Creek Reserve from Washington State.

"The Byrd was really the inspiration for the tasting," Andrus told the group. He explained that after tasting the wine in Washington, D.C., he had been impressed enough to begin gathering other American Cabernet Sauvignons to try against their California peers. "Our feeling is that just because we make wine in the Napa Valley doesn't mean we can afford to be provincial in our outlook—especially these days."

Neither can wine writers, which is why, several months later, we were standing in the Myersville, Maryland, winery's well-equipped hillside cellar while Sharon and William "Bret" Byrd poured tastes of their latest wines into our waiting glasses. We savored the samples and made our notes as Bret Byrd told us about the origins of their enterprise. It's not quite the typical story. A former pharmacist who had long been interested in wine, Byrd first planted vines on the hill sloping down from his house because he "didn't want to see houses cluttering the view." That was back in 1972, and before long the Byrds had planted eleven different vinifera and hybrid grape varieties. Now the views of the Catoctin Mountains from their hilltop home about an hour and a half from Washington, D.C., are well protected by thirty acres of vines. Having weathered such problems as high humidity in the vineyard, crop-damaging winters (1982), restrictive state regulations, and a moribund eastern wine market, the Byrds are now committed full-time to their winery. The cellar boasts the latest equipment (temperature-controlled tanks, centrifuge, etc.), and a California-trained winemaker helps run the operation.

Cabernet Sauvignon is only one of a variety of Byrd bottlings. We tasted a series of his vinifera offerings, including Johannisberg Riesling and Gewürztraminer, which we found light, delicate, and attractive, similar to some of the better examples of these varietals from New York State. To judge by the samples we had, the Byrd Sauvignon Blanc, aggressive and herbaceous, and the full-flavored Chardonnay are on a par with middle-rung California bottlings.

But we were impatient to try barrel samples of the Cabernet Sauvignon, which the Byrds first planted in 1973–74. Was the high-flying '80 just a fluke? Whatever doubts we still had that Cabernet can flourish in Maryland were erased by a taste of the dark, tannic '83, a big, plummy wine that will be blended with an equally ripe and fruity portion of Merlot. The very promising '82 Cabernet sample was amazingly reminiscent of fine young Bordeaux from the barrel and should reach the heights of the classically proportioned '80, which we also resampled. The softer, less focused '81 was a shade off the standard of the other vintages, but still a fine Cabernet. Cabernet production so far is minuscule—only a few hundred cases annually—and distribution is by necessity limited to Maryland and Washington, D.C. But Bret Byrd finds his hardest task is trying to get incredulous wine lovers to take a Cabernet from Maryland seriously. "Maybe in five or six years," he muses, "I'll be able to fold my arms and let them tell *me* how good my wine is."

Had Byrd discovered a magical piece of wine-growing terrain in his backyard? Could other eastern wine growers do as well with this variety? We thought of Dr. G. Hamilton Mowbray, one of Maryland's pioneering wine growers, who has been growing a small amount of Cabernet Sauvignon since 1972 in Silver Run Valley near the Pennsylvania border. To find out how successful Mowbray has been with that varietal, we paid him a visit as well. In the barrel-lined barn of his Montbray Wine Cellars, we started with a glass of a varietal that Mowbray was the first to bottle as such, back in 1966: Seyval Blanc. Here, too, we were pleasantly sidetracked before getting to the Cabernet. A special lot of '81 Seyve-Villard 5276 (Mowbray prefers the original nomenclature) identified with a discreet brown dot on the bottle, turned out to be the finest example of that variety we'd ever come across, making us feel we'd been unduly pessimistic about the possibility of making fine wine from hybrid grapes—well, from Seyval anyway.

Not to be deterred, we soon had another astonishing barrel sample in our glasses: the tightly knit, well-balanced and very promising '82 Montbray Cabernet Sauvignon. In contrast the '83 barrel sample was, as Mowbray pointed out, "a bit too Californian" (you can see where his prejudices lie). Softer, more open in structure than the '82 and marvelously fruity, we thought it would make a delightful bottle in its prime. The lighter, attractive '81 had been in the bottle some months but lacked the concentration of the others. To show us what his earlier Cabernets had been like, Mowbray opened a '77, his second commercial vintage of Cabernet. A small-scaled wine, it had developed some scent and savor in the bottle but had nowhere near the intensity of the '82. "Partly it's a matter of age," Mowbray of fered. "The '82 came from ten-year-old vines." He has only four acres of Cabernet Sauvignon; the tiny production is sold only at the winery. Understandably, he plans to plant more.

We went away with the strong impression that California no longer had an exclusive on top-class American Cabernet Sauvignon.

But four years later, in mid-1988, when we happened to come across a forgotten bottle of the '80 Byrd Cabernet Sauvignon in our cellar, the old incredulousness came back. *Maryland* Cabernet? Had we gotten, well, just a little bit carried away? The Byrd had seemed impressive in its youth, but how would it stack up against a California Cabernet at eight years of age? Lacking any of the original competitors, we decided to compare it blind against the '80 Robert Mondavi Cabernet stored under identical conditions. The Byrd proved far more drinkable than the acerbic Mondavi, which exhibited the characteristic drawbacks of the vintage—excessive warmth and power. Still, it served to point up the virtues of the Byrd, which was still youthful and very well balanced, although it now seems to show a trace too much oak. Clearly our palates hadn't been completely askew back then in Monterey.

And California had better stay on its toes.

GERMAN WINES:

CLASSIC AND PROBLEMATIC

On the coldest winter days we agree with the old dictum, "the first duty of a wine is to be red." By April, however, we are no longer interested in the comforts of a glass of Port by the fireside and have moved on to another vinous prejudice: that German wines are the perfect wines for spring and summer drinking. Their fragrant, fruity-tart style is what refreshing white wine is all about, and their modest alcohol levels—9 to 10 percent— mean that a couple of glasses at lunch on a warm day won't make you feel like spending the afternoon in a hammock. And German wines, besides being the lightest of wines, seem to suggest the delights of walking in the woods on the first warm days of spring. Even Liebfraumilch has its virtues when drunk outdoors with sandwiches and sausages and sunshine filtering through the foliage. But move up a few notches in quality to the top estate-bottled German wines and you can find the sunlight and the smell of spring woods right in your glass.

That is, if you're lucky. Few bottlings show the ideal balance between lively acidity and lush fruitiness and fragrance that is the hallmark of a first-rate German wine. A tasting survey of any given vintage will reveal that many bottlings have all the nobility of lemon-lime soda pop. The presence of one or two really outstanding specimens, however, redeems the breed and justifies the search, for the Germans can still coax more out of the Riesling grape than can anyone else.

The finest of German white-wine grapes, the Riesling, is responsible for all the great German wines, from the sprightly Mosels to the aristocratic Rhines. Of course, the Riesling is grown elsewhere—Alsace, California, Australia, New York State, Washington—but it rarely attains the delicacy and distinction it does in its homeland. Rhine wines, in particular, are unmatched outside Germany: Fine ones are grand, stylish, and dramatic; great ones are arresting, almost operatic, in their opulence. Fine Mosels, on the other hand, are light, lovely, poetic, and very, very seductive. Some people feel about them the way some people feel about Champagnes: They have to be pretty poor before they're unlikable. A first-rate Mosel has a pale platinum color with a tint of green, an expansive flowery scent, and a soft, juicy-ripe flavor balanced by a refreshing acidity and a delicate spritz, or prickle. Such a lyrical mouthful will banish anyone's doubts that a wine can legitimately be called charming.

Years ago we sampled a series of '75 Mosels outdoors on Fire Island and gave our highest marks to the flowery-tart Ockfener Bockstein Kabinett (Dr. Fischer). We weren't the only ones who were impressed with it; a bee, evidently intoxicated by the wine's perfumed bouquet, made its preference clear by diving kamikaze-like right into the glass, which shows that even experts can get carried away by their enthusiasm.

Alas, not every Mosel or Rhine can be expected to make music in your mouth; a lot depends on the vintage as well as the vintner. Germany's grape-growing regions are the most northerly in Europe, and when the weather is poor, the grapes barely ripen. In such years, the Mosels taste thin, tinny, and tart; the Rhines, lean and wiry. Ironically, the high acidity of those "off vintages" can make them ideal candidates for cellaring. Wine lovers hear enough about what wretches they are for uncorking their wines ahead of their prime—but it is true that fine German bottlings can develop marvelously in the bottle, gaining burnished, round depths that balance out the acidity.

Why then are these classic wines so neglected? For a variety of reasons they have become specialists' wines, giving great satisfaction to those with the will to master their complexities while frustrating the majority of wine lovers.

Why? Because the production of the great German estates is broken up into a variety of different wines—not only from different vineyards but of different levels of sweetness as well. Because this fragmentation results in modest-to-minuscule quantities being available of any one wine, finding a specific bottling of fine German wine can be maddening.

Then, too, what puts off many wine drinkers are those long names in gothic script on otherwise attractively slim bottles. The key to understanding German labels is to realize that most producers offer several different wines with different levels of sweetness from the same vineyard. Without getting too technical about it, these Prädikat wines are qualified on the label as Kabinett (just off-dry), Spätlese (late harvest, hence richer and deeper), Auslese (selected harvest, hence even sweeter), Beerenauslese (made from individually selected grapes, hence extremely sweet), and Trockenbeerenauslese (a nectar made from dried or shrunken grapes). Auslese wines of the Beeren and Trockenbeeren class are supersweet and superrare, as one might expect of wines produced from individually selected berries. A taste of a rarity such as the staggeringly rich yet perfectly harmonious 1976 Eltviller Sonnenberg Trockenbeerenauslese (Schloss Eltz) explains the German zeal for such selectivity in the vineyard even if it complicates matters for the consumer.

Another reason fine German wines aren't more popular than they are is that virtually all are noticeably sweet, even those outside the dessert wine category—as they have to be to balance their naturally high acidity. But because many people won't make the effort to find dishes suited to such wines, the standard advice is to drink them on their own. What German wine producers have come to realize is that wines that are "too perfect" to serve with food run the danger of not being drunk at all. In an effort to produce wines that are thought to be more compatible with food, many producers (notably Schloss Vollrads) have been in the forefront of the current trend toward half-dry and totally dry bottlings (*halbtrocken* and *trocken* respectively).

But a totally dry German wine with its naturally low alcohol of 9 to 10 percent has nothing to mask its equally natural and razorlike acidity. Apart from a few impressive Rhine bottlings, the majority of *trocken* and *halbtrocken* wines are very steely, and some are about as charming as raw lemon juice.

But at least one group of Rheingau estates may have found a viable approach to dry German wines. The association of Charta Wine estates was formed several years ago to revive the prestige of "hock"—the English term for the dry, dramatic Rhine wines the Victorians laid away in their cellars alongside claret and Port. Those wines were higher in alcohol and extract than the more sugary examples of recent decades, but they were held in high esteem at the table and aged marvelously. We were not impressed by the Charta group's first efforts, although the association has a number of famous names among its members. Apart from a remarkable '83 Rauenthaler Baiken Spätlese from the state domaine, we found them rather steely. Lately, however, the Charta selections—which are identified not on the label but by a special embossed bottle—appear better balanced: we found the dryness of the '85 Schloss Vollrads Kabinett Blausilber, for example, offset by considerable depth of flavor.

One final paradox bedevils the would-be German wine lover. For the world at large, a great German vintage is one in which it's possible to produce large quantities of sweet wines. Yet, as many recognize, it is the drier German wines that are now increasingly finding favor with Germans themselves and are widely perceived as the answer to the long-standing difficulties of matching the traditionally sweeter-style German wines with food. And in fact, don't many of us think of the drier German wines (QbAs or Kabinetts) when we're looking for a delicate, refreshing white to serve with fish or fowl? Yet the "off vintages" that produce such wines in abundance are routinely passed up in favor of years rated higher on the vintage chart when drier wines are actually in shorter supply.

IN PRAISE OF PINK FIZZ

Call it fizz, bubble, or pop, the way Evelyn Waugh used to do. Or be precise and say Champagne and *méthode champenoise* sparkling wine when you're referring to effervescent wines at

their most elegant. Either way, you're talking about the unquestioned symbol of the high life. Champagne has never gone out of
fashion since the day it was invented some three centuries ago,
but styles of sparkling wines go in and out of vogue.

Take rosé Champagne, which is currently *the* fashionable fizz.
It's nothing new, having been around since the late eighteenth
century, but its charms seem to be rediscovered by every other
generation. Pink fizz reached its previous height of popularity
during Edwardian times, when it was the preferred tipple of the
fashionably dissolute, who used it freely to toast chorus girls and
to greet the dawn. Imaginative types were even said to have
drunk it from their mistresses' slippers. In its latest revival, there's
not much of the ooh-la-la aura left, and nobody we know drinks
it out of shoes. But when we want to underscore the bubbles, we
pour flutes of rosy-hued froth.

No raised eyebrows, please. We're not talking about pink plonk,
we're talking about the really good stuff, the kind of fine-bubbled
fizz whose enticing color—shading from pale coral to pale crimson—makes it the prettiest wine in the world. Understand: we're
talking Krug, Taittinger, Bollinger, Pol Roger. Only the hopelessly jaded could fail to feel a lift of the spirit after being
handed a glass of such enlivening sparkle.

Partly it's the color, and perhaps it also has to do with the connotation of taking something special just one step further, as if
Champagne alone weren't extravagant enough. Pink fizz is the
extra string of pearls, a picnic with china, or black tie at a
disco—you get the picture. All right, it's a bit Hollywood, but
it's all the more fun for that. Whatever the reason for the magic,
it's a never-fail hit. Years ago, when we were attending a dinner
at the Château de Saran, Moët & Chandon's guesthouse in Épernay, a fresh young rosé Champagne was served with a dessert of
fraises des bois after a succession of grand and dramatic older
Champagnes, which we had been savoring and dutifully analyzing.
The purely direct pleasure of the young rosé was a sensual shock
to all the guests and brought some fun to what had been, up to
that point, a rather intellectual approach to the evening.

It was a reminder that Champagne, complex as it can be as a

wine, might as well be served flat as drunk without a sense of delight. And what, we ask you, is more obviously delightful than a glass of pink Champagne? Little wonder that pink fizz is drunk with enthusiasm even by snobs who wouldn't be caught dead drinking a rosé in any other circumstance.

In recent years, the fashion for fine sparkling wines has resulted in strong sales of all Champagnes and other sparkling wines. Although only 2 percent of the millions of bottles imported annually fall in the rosé category, the demand is brisk enough that virtually every Champagne house now produces and exports a rosé style. The boom in bubbles has had a dramatic effect in California, where joint ventures between European Champagne and sparkling wine firms and top California producers have added new labels to a growing list of superb sparkling wines, a number of which are blushingly pink.

Maybe it has something to do with the fun-and-froth associations, but some wine enthusiasts have the mistaken idea that rosé fizz can't be as subtle as the paler cuvées. From our tastings, we'd say that most producers make their rosé blends with as much care as their *blanc* siblings, and some houses even specialize in such bottlings. Admittedly not every rosé is particularly distinctive or distinguished. Among the rosé bottlings now on the market, there are many that are indistinguishable in flavor from the nonpink styles. (To test this, it's necessary to taste blindfolded—an eye-opening exercise.)

All the good rosé Champagnes and sparkling wines are more or less Brut (which is to say bone-dry to slightly off dry), and range in flavor from light, simple, and fruity to deep and lingering. Color is equally varied: some are quite pink, as if a drop of cassis were added to a pale base wine; others shade toward a salmon hue. The variations depend upon how it's made.

In Champagne, rosé bottlings are usually made by adding some still Pinot Noir wine (often the excellent red of Bouzy) to a traditional Champagne cuvée of Pinot Noir and some Chardonnay. The alternative method of imparting just the right amount of color to the wine by letting the clear juice of Pinot grapes stay in contact with the skins for precisely the right amount of time is far trickier, which is why it's not often used.

In any case, the production of rosé cuvées is difficult, which is why Champagne makers, after telling you that rosé Champagne makes women smile (or some such Gallicism) will add that it also drives enologists wild.

Interestingly, we've found that some of the most attractive rosé cuvées on the market today (such as Domaine Chandon Blanc de Noirs and Iron Horse Brut Rosé) come from California. There the warm climate at harvest makes it easy to add an attractive rosy hue to sparkling wine by permitting a little of what's unblushingly called skin contact (allowing the juice to remain in contact with the skins of red grapes before pressing).

In either case, what's imparted along with the color is a fuller flavor and a hint of tannin, which makes them go so well with foods. In fact, many rosé Champagnes and sparkling wines, particularly the very dry ones, can have a lightly bitter grip to the finish. From our dinner table trials, we'd say that rosé Champagne pairs marvelously with rich entrées of veal or duck and is the obvious choice for the main course if you'd like to serve sparkling wine throughout a meal. The rosé could be preceded by a pale, crisp Blanc de Blancs style for openers and followed by a sweeter Demi-Sec or Extra-Sec bottling with dessert. Rosé fizz is perfectly suitable for an aperitif when accompanied by rich and luxurious appetizers such as foie gras, pâté, or smoked salmon, and it's wonderful with not-too-sweet berry desserts such as strawberries and cream.

Because it's the sort of bubbly to have when you want just a touch more than the usual flair, it's equally at home with midnight suppers on penthouse terraces, extravagant picnics, and lazy breakfasts in bed. In fact, the very act of pulling out a bottle of rosé bubbly defines you as an expansive type. We have a neighbor in the country who likes to start his dinner parties with a literal bang, indicating to his arriving guests what they can expect by standing in his doorway and letting the Champagne cork fly across the lawn from a hip-held bottle. He feels the wasteful gush is outweighed by the gleeful response of his friends, who realize they're not just going to dine—they're going to celebrate.

He could get an equally enthusiastic response by just pouring pink.

CHENIN BLANC

By harvest time, the grapes are pale-green, tough-skinned ovals that hang from the vine in compact, conical clusters. To wine-makers in the Loire district of France, in California, and in a few other wine-producing regions, they are immediately recognizable as Chenin Blanc. In their minds, these ripe grapes have already been translated into wine, but the various wines they envision depend on growing conditions, tradition, and their own view of the grape's ultimate expression as a wine: bone-dry or unctuously sweet, still or sparkling, simple or serious, fresh and appealing, or deep and complex. In fact, the differences are so marked among the various possible styles of Chenin Blanc that they tend to obscure the similarities all of them share. Those who are only familiar with the ubiquitous bland bottlings made from the grape scoff (as we used to) at the idea that it can be the source of bottled greatness.

But consider the grape. According to ampelographers, who make a study of these things, there are more than 10,000 grape varieties, and each can be made into something resembling the dictionary definition of wine—"fermented grape juice." Only a fraction of these vinous legions—a few dozen varieties—can be made into attractive, enticing, even beautiful wines of individual character. These "great grapes," selected over centuries for their distinctive aromas and flavors when made into wine, are unique, refined plants, far removed from grapes in the wild state. Centuries of culling and coddling and coaxing have given each its individual characteristics. Indeed, winemakers talk about wine grapes almost as if they had personalities. When describing their behavior in the vineyard, during fermentation, or in the bottle, they say one grape is "difficult and quirky," another is "lovely to work with," a third is "easy to control."

Chenin Blanc is widely considered a docile grape; one winemaker says it "has the personality of a well-behaved child." It ripens in the middle of the harvest season, sparing vineyardists protracted late-fall agonizing. Its compact, tight clusters make it easy to pick. Its tough skin allows it to be transported from vineyard to crusher with minimum damage. And Chenin Blanc is generous to growers in another way: It is prolific, almost too prolific, in fact, for the purpose of fine winemaking. The only worry with Chenin Blanc is that bunches may rot on the vine—a problem in certain areas because its tight clusters prevent the grapes from drying properly after heavy rains.

The vinous character of this "well-behaved child" is not so simple, however: witness its multiple personality as a wine. The profusion of possibilities has been a characteristic of Chenin Blanc for centuries in the Loire Valley of France, where it originated, and where it has been cultivated, some say, since the eighth century. It remains one of the region's principal varieties. Local variant names include Pineau de la Loire (although the grape is not actually related to the Pinot family). Chenin Blanc is the only grape that can be used to make wines labeled with such Loire appellations as Vouvray, Savennières, and Coteaux du Layon.

Although the variety is cultivated in Russia, New Zealand, Australia, Argentina, and California, nowhere is the grape made in such a diversity of wine styles with such distinction as in the Loire Valley. Only a handful of the scores of producers of Chenin Blanc in California (where it is the single-most-planted white variety) make wines that approach the appeal of the better Chenin Blancs from the Loire, though when tasted side by side they are not likely to show the class of their French cousins. The California version with which most people are familiar is the intensely fruity, fragrant, not-quite-dry style of the wine that cold fermentation techniques have made possible. With this method, fermentation is arrested by chilling to leave about 2 percent residual sugar in the wine, and the wine never touches wood before bottling. The result is that drinking the wine is just as delicious as biting into a piece of fresh fruit—and just as simple. But maximizing Chenin Blanc's simple fruitiness masks its potential as a complex, dry wine. After tasting a dozen examples, one yearns for something beyond picnic fare, something less cloying.

A few Californians strive for character with the grape by treating it as a kind of shadow Chardonnay. Donn Chappellet, of Napa Valley's Chappellet Vineyard, has been making big, full, bone-dry Chenin Blancs for nearly two decades at his mountain winery. "Distinction in Chenin Blanc depends on where it's grown," he says. "To have real character the grapes have to come from low-yield vineyards." Chappellet ages his Chenin Blanc in French oak barrels "just like our Chardonnay. It spends about a month in oak to give it a little more complexity."

By contrast, the remarkable diversity of styles in which Chenin Blanc is made in Loire districts not only varies from area to area, but also—making a commercial virtue of climatic necessity—from year to year. In wet, cold years when the grape fails to ripen and the resulting wine is thin and unpleasantly tart, it is made into sparkling wine; an average year yields a pale, attractive, dry to off-dry wine (sometimes helpfully labeled *sec* or *demi-sec*); in years when conditions allow the growth of the beneficent mold *Botrytis cinerea* to shrivel the moisture content of the grapes and concentrate its natural sugar, fragrant dessert wines are made. Because each of these variants has its following, some of each style is produced each year, weather permitting, although many districts make a specialty of one style. As with any region, those styles will vary in quality according to the producers and vintages.

A middling example of a Chenin Blanc from the Loire is a fragrant, fruity-tart wine. The aromas in better examples are more subtle—vaguely fruity-floral, or grassy or melonlike. Sometimes the scents are laced with hints of wood or chalky soil, and the sweeter versions can suggest wild honey. Dry or sweet, these better examples have a lively, refreshing, vivacious acidity that balances the fruit and gives a piquant, lingering sappiness to the flavor.

One of Chenin Blanc's more remarkable—and surprising—qualities is its ability to age. "We say in Vouvray that our wine has two lives; the first when it is young, fresh, acidic—up to two years of age. After that, there can be a difficult period," explained Armand Monmousseau, head of the Loire firm of J. M. Monmousseau, producers and shippers of Vouvray and other wines of the region. "Then, perhaps five years later, the wine gets a second wind—another life. It becomes a different wine. In a great year, it may live a very, very long time. We still have bottles of 1893 in our cellars, and they are still drinkable."

We met with M. Monmousseau on one of his visits to New York to learn about some of his latest vintages and some older ones that demonstrated his thesis convincingly. We sampled his delicious '82 Vouvrays, including a light, vibrant Vouvray Blanc de Blancs and two very distinguished special bottlings from his own vineyards, a Vouvray Château Gaudrelle and a Vouvray Clos le Vigneau. The latter two bottlings had an enticing balance of very crisp acidity and lingering fruity intensity; even so, it was hard to believe that these pale, stylish delicate whites—perfect luncheon or summertime choices—could evolve into deeper, more complex wines. "The '82s are not for long keeping," Monmousseau cautioned. "Only about ten years. But let me show you some others at dinner that have the balance for long life. It takes a great vintage."

With a slice of foie gras we drank the round, slightly sweet '75 Clos le Vigneau and began to understand what age can confer on Vouvray: a deepening of flavor that accentuates the balance of fruity acidity. With the poached salmon there was a 1969 Château Gaudrelle. Still pale gold in color, it was magnificent, mouth-filling, dry, rich, and lingering. In a different way, it had all the weight and authority of Puligny-Montrachet.

Before the dessert, by itself, we drank one of Armand Monmousseau's cellar treasures: a 1959 Château Gaudrelle. Made from botrytis-infected grapes, this concentrated, but not overly sweet, deep-gold wine was perfectly balanced by its refreshingly high acidity, giving it an exquisitely tart, ripe character. (In truth, we don't remember the dessert.)

There are several of the world's dry white wines that will age and improve in the bottle. But few wines other than Vouvray can boast of changing personality completely as it matures, evolving from a delicious, delicate, light wine to a deep, weighty, memorable one.

The Loire has other vinous surprises made from Chenin Blanc—as we were reminded on a recent visit. The region is a patchwork of subregions and appellations and is full of producers who make a variety of wines from different areas; Vouvray is only one of several well-known dry whites in the region that are made in sweet versions when harvest conditions permit. The most highly regarded of these little-known (and inexpensive) sweet wines are from the Coteaux du Layon area, which also includes Quarts de Chaume and Bonnezeaux.

Coteaux du Layon itself is surrounded by the larger region of Anjou, which produces a number of wines, including 3 million cases of its popular Rosé d'Anjou. But the pride of this region is its great sweet whites, which are a lighter and brighter alternative to Sauternes. Their high degree of acidity not only balances the sweetness perfectly, giving the wines a lively fruity character, but also allows them to age for decades. When the energetic Jacques Beaujeau at Château Beaujeau learned of our interest in these late-harvest Chenin Blancs, he gave us a barrel sample of his lovely '85 Coteaux du Layon, followed by his lemony-floral '83, a deeper, apricot and honey '76, and an expansive '70, all hazelnuts and butterscotch.

By the time we arrived at the cellars of Joseph Touchais at Doué-la-Fontaine, we were unabashed converts to these delicious bottlings; but even so we found ourselves unprepared for the sight of cave after cave filled with bottles—over 2 million, according to the proprietor—with vintages of great sweet wines going back to 1870. His top wine, Moulin Touchais, is offered only when the vintage allows a fine sweet wine to be made. For various complicated reasons, Moulin Touchais is usually labeled with an Anjou appellation.

As things turned out, we had no extensive tasting there, but in New York we made up for lost opportunities at a Moulin Touchais tasting featuring a dozen vintages from 1979 back to 1875. Our tasting notes read like a repetitive list of superlatives, but even so there were standouts: a brilliant, round-textured, lingering, peachlike '76; a soft, unctuous '59; a superlative, astonishingly deep and still fresh '49; a still-delicious '28; and a trio of amazingly alive veterans, 1885, 1879, and 1875. The 1879 was not the least oxidized.

Not a bad showing, we thought, for a bunch of old Chenin Blancs.

C'EST BEAUJOLAIS

Whenever we think of Beaujolais, we inevitably think of wine at its most casual. . . . We recall a spring in Paris when we discovered an excellent Beaujolais at a tiny wineshop on the Rue St.-Antoine around the corner from the apartment we'd rented. On our frequent forays for the essential *fromage, pâté, et pain,* we always picked up a bottle or two. One day the proprietor informed us that if we returned the empty bottle, we could save a franc on our next purchase. We must have looked a little puzzled, and to clarify things he pushed the curtain behind him aside to reveal a barrel-shaped, somewhat wine-stained worker, Gauloise dangling from his lips, filling empty bottles with Beaujolais from a hose-equipped tank.

Parisians love the unfussiness of Beaujolais. For them, it's a wine for drinking, not contemplation—a café wine, what you order standing at a wine bar, a wine for couples who still want to talk about each other rather than the wine. And the younger the Beaujolais the better, to judge by the growing fashion for Beaujolais *nouveau* (more precisely, *primeur*)—the weeks-old wine that every year is rushed to Paris for consumption starting the third Thursday in November. Amazingly, something like one-third of the crop is now made into *nouveau,* so that instead of serving as a sample of the coming vintage, this cotton-candy version of the wine has practically become the image of Beaujolais. Perhaps it was inevitable—the charm of youth is widely regarded as the principal appeal of Beaujolais.

Actually, that simple formula isn't quite right. The charm of Beaujolais is not just a matter of age—or lack of it. Part of it is surely due to the Gamay grape, which in the right circumstances and the right location makes a wine whose appeal to the senses is instantaneous: The aroma is intensely grapy, almost to the point of floweriness; it is an appetizing scent, one that urges you not to pause and ponder, but to drink. The taste gives its all with equal immediacy—a sort of expiration of fruitiness balanced by a lively, tart, almost sappy quality that verges on the gulpably delicious. Little wonder Beaujolais' popularity continues unabated, despite the fact that some of the best bottlings can no longer be regarded as an inexpensive quaffing wine.

But it's quaffing wine all the same—isn't it? We used to think that until Georges Duboeuf put on a remarkable tasting for us during a visit he made to New York in the early 1980s.

M. Duboeuf is known in some quarters as "Monsieur Beaujolais," and for good reason. He is one of the biggest shippers in the region, with an inventory of millions of bottles, specializing in wines from around eighty individual properties and five cooperatives, virtually all of which are kept separate. He is also one of the busiest, tasting up to three hundred wines a day during the peak season. Duboeuf supplies Beaujolais in various styles, from delicate to muscular, to suit his customers—which include several three-star restaurants.

When we arrived at his hotel suite, Duboeuf was busy uncorking and cooling an impressive array of bottles from his own cellar. The Beaujolais he brought with him were chosen out of his extensive wine library to make the point that with careful selection (of growers who have old vines, favored plots, and are careful with vinification), it is possible to find *primeurs* that can age for years, *crus* that can rival Burgundies for sheer impressiveness, and individual estates that manage to make superior wine in vintages that in the public's mind have largely been written off.

Duboeuf is a thin, energetic Frenchman who speaks little English but conveys his enthusiasm for his wines in rapid-fire French, punctuated with animated gestures. He first marshaled a range of Beaujolais-Villages *primeurs* from several small growers to illustrate the ability of some specimens to last despite the widely held belief that they deteriorate within six months of bottling. He explained that after two months *primeurs* go into a decline because unlike traditional Beaujolais they are vinified quickly and lack the requisite stuffing for aging. If well-balanced, however, they start to recover within a year. A three-year-old example was tart, stemmy, and small-scale but still holding up; a five-year-old bottling was darker and heavier and older, but still very much alive. Most impressive was an eight-year-old *primeur,* a Beaujolais-Villages La Varenne from the forgettable vintage of 1974. It had, amazingly enough, a fine bouquet and considerable richness.

After that warm-up exercise, we were ready for the next step: the continuity of style that can be found in the wines of a single top proprietor (Manin), even in poor years. These wines came from Fleurie, one of the nine *crus* of Beaujolais. We asked Duboeuf how he would describe the character of Fleurie. He replied that each of the nine *crus* has its own *goût de terroir,* except for Fleurie, which to him "is like a super Beaujolais-Villages." With the exception of a rather ponderous '76, the wines were outstanding—lively and flavorful.

After a pause, during which Duboeuf checked the temperature of the wines to be tasted by popping a thermometer into the wineglass (Beaujolais shows best from 58 degrees to 64 degrees Fahrenheit), we tried the top *cru* of Beaujolais, Moulin-à-Vent, from a variety of producers. With these wines, the deliciousness of Beaujolais took on added complexity: The highlights were a 1978 Moulin-à-Vent (Le Balme) that was simply stunning—lovely in scent, luscious in flavor, and long on the palate. We were wondering whether it might not have been the best Beaujolais we'd ever tasted, but only until it was eclipsed by a taste of a truly remarkable 1976 Moulin-à-Vent (Bloud Réserve), which had the intensity of a first-rate Volnay and enough tannin to suggest it would age well. Our eyes had been opened. Some Beaujolais, we decided, are not only worthy of cellaring but also worthy of contemplation. (Ever since, we've laid away some of Duboeuf's Moulin-à-Vents to see what develops. In our latest experiment we find that at three years of age his 1985 Moulin-à-Vent is just beginning to unfurl its flavors.)

As we were leaving, we asked Duboeuf what he looked for when selecting Beaujolais. "What counts for me," he said, "is the fruit—the agreeableness." He smiled and shrugged. *"C'est Beaujolais."*

THE QUEST FOR GREAT BURGUNDY

The historic Hospices de Beaune wine auction that takes place in Burgundy each fall is widely regarded as a barometer of the region's wine prices. When prices fell an average of 40 percent at the 1986 auction, breaking a six-year upward spiral, many wine lovers naïvely thought marvelous Burgundies might soon be available for a modest sum. But that's a fantasy. And not just because of the weak dollar. For a variety of reasons, great red Burgundy will always be scarce and can never be cheap.

The sad corollary of this is that Burgundy—remember, we're talking red here—frequently falls considerably short of what Bordeaux, California Cabernet, some Italian reds, among others, deliver consistently, and for much less. Too often all that lingers is the sting of an expensive disappointment. As a result, you don't shop for great Burgundy—you go on a quest. No wonder Americans drink only 15 percent of the region's reds, although they drink half the world's supply of its far more reliable whites.

At this point a cynic might wonder whether the wine is worth the bother.

But what wine enthusiast who has been exposed to Burgundy at its seductive best hasn't become a passionate convert? Years ago we admitted to ourselves that Burgundy at its best gave us more of a thrill than great Bordeaux or any other red, sublime as they all can be. Maybe it's because we find drinking Burgundy a more purely sensual experience. A great Bordeaux can make you feel like saluting; a great Burgundy can put you into a swoon. Maybe it's because among the red wines of the world, only Burgundy offers such dramatic impressions: a heady, savory-pungent bouquet of mingled earth and fruit, a delicacy of body that belies a depth of lingering spice, and a texture that makes one think of silk, satin, taffeta, velvet. . . . Burgundy is probably the only wine for which such highly romantic associations don't seem ridiculous. André Tchelistcheff, the dean of California winemakers, once told us the bouquet of a great Burgundy reminded him of a "lady's fine leather glove, still warm from the hand."

Having once tasted a truly great Burgundy, the seduced are always hoping to repeat the experience of a taste that can't be found (except fleetingly) elsewhere. In truth, there's nowhere outside the borders of the thirty-mile-long Côte d'Or in France to turn for wines that taste quite like Burgundy. Although California Cabernet Sauvignon is not identical to red Bordeaux, it does stand on its own terms as an example of an equally impressive, somewhat similar wine made from the same grape varieties. The great Rieslings of Germany and the Chardonnay-based whites of France, among others, have their stylistically similar counterparts in other wine-producing countries. But the character and quality of red Burgundy has yet to be consistently equaled (or echoed) outside the district itself. There are a few exceptions, including some we've tasted from Oregon. But so far, one can practically rattle the names off in a single breath (Eyrie, Adelsheim, Sokol Blosser, Knudsen-Erath, and a handful of others in that charmed circle). Their wines have enlarged our experience of great Pinot Noir and will continue to do so. Joseph Drouhin, the highly respected Burgundy *négociant,* has even purchased vineyard land in Oregon—the ultimate acknowledgment of that region's potential. But grateful as we are that such wines now supplement the original source, they are not a substitute for it.

But why is the truly sublime stuff so hard to find?

First of all, good red Burgundy is rare because of the region's cold climate, and the frequency of hail, rot, and other natural disasters. Bordeaux averages four weak vintages in a decade; Burgundy is lucky to have four good ones. Furthermore, even in a good vintage there are many disappointments. So despite the importance of knowing harvest conditions, it isn't enough just to know the "good years."

Second, not much red Burgundy is made. The region produces only a tenth of the amount of red wine that Bordeaux does. Demand regularly outstrips supply, elevating prices. It's rare to find an exciting Burgundy for less than $25 a bottle. What's more, spending $50 won't guarantee ecstasy. Burgundy prices are a guide to rarity, not to quality.

Third, this small amount of wine is broken up into a bewildering variety of bottlings. Because 10,000 growers, 150 *négociants,* and 44 *cave* cooperatives are producing wine, there are thousands of different wines, but none available in large quantities. Because good, bad, and indifferent growers may each own a tiny chunk of a famous vineyard, a great Burgundy and a poor one may come from the same vineyard in the same year.

We once sampled over 120 examples from '78 and '79, as well as some from the spotty 1980 vintage, in a half-dozen blind tastings. We found again and again that one proprietor's or shipper's success with some of his wines had no bearing on how good his other wines might be—even if they were made from grapes grown on adjoining parcels of land. We also had a clear demonstration that differences in winemaking can cancel out regional differences dramatically. We found big beefy bottlings from communes whose wines are traditionally noted for their delicacy, and vice versa.

Furthermore, Pinot Noir is a notoriously difficult grape from which to make wine, and the wines it makes are exceptionally fragile and heat sensitive, suffering more from poor storage than any other fine red. This makes it extremely difficult to buy older vintages of red Burgundy in good condition.

None of this is any news to longtime Burgundy lovers, who often like to complain about their favorite tipple. What neophytes need to know, in addition, is that they may find it difficult to judge young Burgundy, particularly if their palates have been formed on Bordeaux and California Cabernet Sauvignon.

Robert Haas, a well-known importer who has been visiting Burgundy and tasting in its cellars for the past thirty-five years, points out that "when you taste young Bordeaux, you always find it a mouthful. In contrast, young Burgundy can taste pretty insubstantial—but that impression can be deceptive."

Consider the typical flavor development a fine Bordeaux or Cabernet undergoes as it ages: the rough, raw textures become smooth, the bouquet evolves from grapy aromas to a complex scent, and the flavor becomes more refined.

But fine Burgundy develops differently. A young one, while direct in flavor, can seem small, tight, and unyielding, offering little depth, richness, or concentration to the nose and palate. It doesn't have the raw astringency and bite of Cabernet-based wines, so even a very good one may seem less than stunning, a lightweight that you are apt to think couldn't possibly improve with age.

The color of a Burgundy may show a tawny tinge at the edge of the glass at an early stage, making a taster think the wine is alarmingly advanced. In fact, Pinot Noir wines characteristically lose pigment quickly, unlike Cabernets.

But with five, ten, even twenty years in the bottle, fine Burgundies do seem to put on weight. Pungency and depth develop in the nose, and richness and spice emerge in the flavor so that one has the impression of layers of complex, lingering flavors. (Not that development follows a rigid pattern. Burgundies may reach several attractive points of balance in their evolution. The better '83s, once deep and fruity, are now dull and sullen in the glass and will, it is hoped, pull themselves together again in the 1990s. The 1985s, by contrast, have been delicious from the start and may never go through an out-of-sorts phase.)

Now consider the last step: you've done the legwork, tasted around, and found a good one. All that's left is to remember that Burgundy will not show its best unless it is served noticeably cool—around 60 to 65 degrees. It shouldn't be decanted, and it needs a generous-size glass to develop its scent and to give you room to revel in it.

Hey, after all you've gone through, you deserve it.

THE DOMAINE DE LA ROMANÉE-CONTI:

STILL GREAT?

Not counting the crew or the waiters pouring Champagne, there were twenty of us on board the fifty-six-foot yacht. But most were crowded on the flying bridge, watching the sunset and luxuriating in the soft offshore breezes of a South Florida evening in late spring. We were motoring up the Ft. Lauderdale stretch of the Intracoastal Waterway, and to the people in small pleasure boats zipping by us, we must have looked as though we were enjoying ourselves. Indeed we were. Champagne in hand, we were off for the first event of a gastronomic extravaganza—three days of wine tastings and grand dinners, from which we would take away notes on three dozen wines from Burgundy's greatest wine estate: the Domaine de la Romanée-Conti. (Whoever said wine writing had to be a chore?)

Our host was Leonce Picot, coproprietor of three of South Florida's finest restaurants. We were headed for one now, The Down Under, at which we would dock to dine this first evening. Picot pointed out his other Ft. Lauderdale waterfront restaurant as we glided by—the Casa Vecchia, which would be the scene of our forthcoming wine tastings and the grand banquet the following night. We would end with a final dinner at his third establishment, La Vieille Maison in Boca Raton.

When the "Fête du Domaine de la Romanée-Conti," as it was called, was widened in scope from a single black-tie benefit dinner to a three-day event that would include a complete review of recent vintages of the Domaine de la Romanée-Conti (D.R.C. for short), it gained a dozen-member tasting panel equal to the task of forming an opinion on the current efforts of one of the world's most legendary—and controversial—wine estates. Joining the two of us were fellow journalists William Rice, Alexis Bespaloff, Robert Finigan, and Robert Hosmon; screenwriter James Goldman and his wife, Bobby; and Texas wine collectors and connoisseurs Marvin and Sue Overton and Lenoir and Susan Josey. Also in attendance at the events were the co-owners of the Domaine, who had flown from France to take part: the petite, outspoken Madame Lalou Bize-Leroy and the urbane Aubert de Villaine.

To help put our assessments in perspective, the group would also be tasting a number of "oldie goldies"—classic D.R.C. bottlings from such vintages as '71, '69, '59, and '45. In typical, expansive Picot style, all would be punctuated with deluxe Champagne—Mumm's Crémant de Cramant, Perrier-Jouët Fleur de Champagne, Roederer Cristal, Krug Grande Cuvée—just to keep our palates refreshed.

The level of enthusiasm aboard the yacht was high, and to understand why, you have to understand what Burgundy means to
a wine lover. "Great Bordeaux can be really superb," said Dr.
Marvin Overton after Aubert de Villaine asked him which he
preferred, Bordeaux or Burgundy. "In fact, when you're drinking
them, you can't imagine wine could be better. But great Burgundy can send you right out of your mind."

Few would disagree that the greatest collection of vineyards in
Burgundy belongs to the Domaine de la Romanée-Conti. It is the
sole owner of Romanée-Conti and La Tâche. It also owns two-
thirds of Richebourg, large portions of Grands-Échézeaux and
Échézeaux, and cultivates (but doesn't actually own) the largest
holding of Romanée-St.-Vivant, whose wine is sold under the
prestigious D.R.C. label. Besides these superlative *grand cru* red
wine vineyards clustered near the villages of Vosne-Romanée
and Flagey-Échézeaux, it also owns a tiny parcel of Burgundy's
most famous white wine vineyard, Le Montrachet. Total production of the entire Domaine is under ten thousand cases a year.

The demand for the D.R.C.'s wines, particularly Romanée-
Conti, is so disproportionate to the amounts available that the
Domaine can now ask astounding prices—in the case of the
Romanée-Conti, several hundred dollars a bottle. What has given
an edge to the long-standing criticism of the D.R.C.'s pricing pol-
icies is the charge that the wines in recent decades have not lived
up to their almost legendary reputation. Well, we thought, as we
docked at The Down Under, the next few days should provide
some answers.

That first evening's dinner was a chance for those who didn't
know one another to become better acquainted, and for the
tasters to tune their palates on the likes of 1976 Montrachet,
'66 Romanée-St.-Vivant, '71 Grands-Échézeaux, '64 La Tâche,
'64 Romanée-Conti, and one non-D.R.C. bottling, an earthy '55
Mazis-Chambertin from Leroy, Madame Bize's *négociant* firm.
With two days of wine tastings to come on which to base our
judgments, we, like the others, took our notes but held our raves
in reserve. (For convenience, we've grouped all our notes on the
D.R.C. reds below.) The Montrachet, however, provoked im-

mediate comment. Because the Domaine produces only two hundred cases a year of this wine, it is a more than $200-a-bottle rarity. The '76 we drank was so rich and concentrated that its flavors reminded us of butterscotch. In the end we decided that exciting as it was, it was too exaggerated and overblown in style. But there was significant bottle-to-bottle variation. When it was good, many of the tasters, such as Robert Hosmon, thought it extraordinary.

The next day's first event was an eleven A.M. review at the Casa Vecchia of the ten wines to be served that evening at the restaurant's Fête du Domaine de la Romanée-Conti black-tie dinner: '66 and '76 Romanée-St.-Vivant, '76 Montrachet, '71 and '78 Grands-Échézeaux, '71 and '79 Richebourg, '71 and '77 La Tâche, and '72 Romanée-Conti.

There was plenty of discussion on the ultimate merits of the wines. In fact, the '72 Romanée-Conti provoked considerable controversy. Some tasters dismissed it outright, others found it "not harmonious," and some, like ourselves, found it rich and concentrated, full of lingering, earthy, mushroomlike nuances.

The future development of the '71s was also vigorously discussed. One of the '71 Richebourgs we had, for example, was fabulous, all violets and velvet, and seemed to promise even greater things to come. The other bottle lacked equal excitement and finesse. (Until 1985 the Domaine bottled its wines directly from the barrel, a practice that surely accounts for some of the bottle-to-bottle variations encountered in the earlier vintages.)

There was little consensus on the older wines, but the tasters were sufficiently impressed by the younger wines—especially the stunning '79 Richebourg—to regard the next day's tasting—a review of all six vineyards of the D.R.C. from the '79, '78, '77, and '76 vintages—with considerable anticipation. From a wine lover's point of view, it would be the central event of the three-day fete.

But there would be a certain amount of tension in that exercise. In the opinion of many—ourselves included—most Burgundies produced in the last two decades don't compare favorably with the great Burgundies of the past. The Domaine in particular has been heavily criticized for its recent wines. After tasting a

1933 Richebourg from the Domaine—which he described as "pure nectar at forty-four years of age"—Harry Waugh, England's senior wine critic, made a comment that voiced the thoughts of many wine lovers: "It makes one wonder why the Domaine de la Romanée-Conti no longer produces masterpieces of this caliber. The soil is the same as ever, the climate is no different, so it can only be the human element that is to blame."

Burgundian shippers and producers offer different answers to the critics of modern Burgundy. Louis Latour, of the *négociant* firm of the same name, points out that the latest criticism is nothing new; nineteenth-century writers claimed Burgundy had irreparably declined a century ago. Pierre Maufoux of Prosper Maufoux blames the lighter style of contemporary Burgundy on overproduction now possible because modern vineyard practices permit higher yields. Some authorities blame the replanting to different clones of Pinot Noir after the Second World War; others claim that many of the "big" Burgundies of the past were actually doctored wines that owed their weight to the addition of Rhône wines or even brandy. Modern vinification has something to do with it, too. André Gagey of Louis Jadot blames modern wine drinkers who "will not appreciate a Burgundy that is hard in its youth."

Even if contemporary Burgundies aren't the giants of yore, they may not be as weak and pallid as many tasters assume. Pinot Noir can start browning a few years after bottling, but that doesn't necessarily mean that the wine is in premature decline. Then, too, tasters often mistakenly assume that a Burgundy without palate-gripping tannin in its youth can't last. In fact, as with every wine, balance is the key to long maturation. Yet Robert Drouhin of Joseph Drouhin concedes that there was a somewhat excessive trend toward lightness in the sixties and early seventies. But now, he adds, Burgundian vintners are returning to a more substantial style of Burgundy. Tomorrow would tell, we thought.

The panel regrouped at the Casa Vecchia at eleven A.M. sharp. Tasters had their own ways of preparing for this *grand dégustation:* some reviewed their notes; others played tennis; still others warmed up on steak tartare for breakfast.

Each participant faced a grid of two dozen crystal glasses—a row of the '79s in the order the Domaine recommends: Échézeaux, Grands-Échézeaux, Romanée-St.-Vivant, Richebourg, La Tâche, Romanée-Conti. Then a row of the '78s in the same order, then the '77s, and last the '76s. The wines were served as the Domaine prefers, at about 65 degrees, all uncorked and immediately poured directly from the bottle.

"It's an incredible array of riches," murmured Burgundy aficionado James Goldman, as he surveyed the wines in front of him. "I don't know whether I should taste horizontally, vertically, or just hop around." Careful pouring began, then silence ensued, punctuated by sniffs, slurps, spitting, and the rustling of tasting sheets.

As we laid down our pens, we wondered if these two dozen D.R.C. wines provided an answer to the frequent criticisms we had made of modern Burgundy. Our notes were full of superlatives, at least for the '78s and '79s. The lively discussion that followed showed some divergence of opinion, but also considerable agreement that there were some extraordinarily impressive and promising wines on the table. These were wines far removed from simple grapiness; instead, a whole mélange of exotic subtle aromas and pungent, haunting, penetrating flavors had made a dramatic impression on the senses. Odd as it sounds, the Domaine de la Romanée-Conti wines, even when young, showed the kind of complex character usually associated only with mature wines. Their color, too, was deceptive: most of the wines already had a tawny edge.

What struck us all was the way in which each of the wines of the six vineyards retained its own personality, despite the definite overlay of the Domaine style and the earmarks of the particular vintage year. In French terms, they were true to their *terroir*—they reflected their soil. Hence we've grouped our impressions of the wines by vineyard, and we've included opinions offered by other tasters, particularly in cases of strong dissent or consensus.

ÉCHÉZEAUX: When compared glass to glass, Échézeaux is invariably overshadowed by the more intense, elegant Grands-Échézeaux, with which it shares a familial resemblance. Nonetheless, along with several others, we gave high marks to the lovely '79. The '78 was weightier, but not as enticing. The '77 was short and sharp, and the '76 attractive but somewhat overripe and unfocused.

GRANDS-ÉCHÉZEAUX: We've always been impressed with the style of this wine: its full, rich, meaty nose with intriguing hints of roasted nuts, wonderful balance, fleshy texture, and penetrating finish. The '79 was a marvelously stylish, exquisitely balanced example. The richer and deeper '78 was a shade less exciting now, though potentially superior. The '77 was a recognizable but dull echo of what the wine can be in a good vintage. The '76 was round and flavorful but marred by a loose, almost flabby structure.

The '71 Grands-Échézeaux sampled previously was ripe and full with spreading flavors and a long finish; stylistically similar to the '78, it lacked the depth of the younger vintage.

ROMANÉE-ST.-VIVANT: To our palates, the Romanée-St.-Vivant seemed the earthiest of the wines tasted—the pungency of the bouquet reminded us of mushrooms, autumn forests, whiffs of tobacco. Along with others, we preferred the rich, full, almost gamey '78 to the lighter '79. The '77 was characteristically earthy, but too thin and acrid to be appealing. The '76 had overripe, almost licoricelike nuances, attractive flavors, but a rather short finish. The fine '66, sampled on both the first and second evenings, seemed past its best.

RICHEBOURG: The one word we used over and over again in our notes to describe this wine was "spice." The '79 was regarded by many at the tasting—including ourselves—as the best of the '79s. Its floral perfume (violets?) was so intense that by turns it suggested gardenias, holly, even ponderosa pines. . . . We stopped searching for an exact equivalent and reveled in the concentrated flavors and already expansive spicy finish. A brilliant wine, it was nearly matched in our notes by the deliciously rich, deep, harmonious '78, which was also marked by lingering spice. The considerably subdued '77 lacked the glossy texture of the '79 and '78, and flavor and finish fell short as well. The '76 was fragrant, fat, and wonderfully flavorful, but as with the other '76s, its overripe, soft structure put its future development into question.

LA TÂCHE: La Tâche is a stunning wine, mingling enticing delicacy with a curious minerallike earthiness. This iron-fist-in-a-velvet-glove personality came through clearly in all the examples tasted. The earthy, fruity '79 was less dramatic and more closed than the '79 Richebourg, but was potentially superb. We found the emphatic '78 more powerful and pungent, thicker textured, more lingering. We weren't alone in finding the '77 remarkable, considering the lackluster vintage. It was small-scale, but well-built, and full of character. The '76 was tannic and deep, a big, bold wine, but like the other '76s, showed softness and lack of definition. The '71 served from magnums the previous day was magnificent: lusty and mouth-filling, almost peppery in its concentration, but not yet entirely focused. The '64, however, with its penetrating but definitely fading flavor, was doubtless past its best.

ROMANÉE-CONTI: The origins of this tiny four-and-a-half-acre vineyard, the crown jewel of the Domaine, date from the twelfth century. Its reputation as the greatest vineyard in Burgundy is long-standing; its wine was even spoon-fed to the ailing Louis XIV as a restorative. Average production is a mere 625 cases annually. Tasting this legendary wine after the La Tâche, we were not conscious of a giant step up in quality. But its placement in the tasting sequence was justified by its extraordinary balance and harmony. It had everything in abundance—perfume, flavor, texture—yet no aspect was overobvious, except the finish, which lingered in the mouth for an incredible length of time.

Many found the '79 stunning. "The spices are fascinating," commented William Rice, "and the roundness and richness are overwhelming." The '78 was far more closed in but already showed its remarkably persistent finish. Some thought the '77 a finish without a wine; we thought it impressive—for a '77. The opulent, tannic '76 seemed one of the better-balanced '76s, but it lacked the tight-knit quality and potential of the '78 and '79. In retrospect, the truffle-scented '64, while superior in elegance and subtlety to the '64 La Tâche tasted against it at the first dinner, seemed clearly to have peaked.

To our palates, the majestic Romanée-Conti seemed to sum up the best of what the Domaine's remarkable vineyards can produce.

What was the panel's overall impression? Robert Finigan probably spoke for most of the tasters when he described the '79s as "lovely across the board." It was his opinion that they would be ready to drink sooner than the more firmly constituted '78s, and added that the '77s should probably have been consumed already. The '76s he found the "least appealing." We thought the brilliant showing of the '79s was in part due to their freshness; we, like most of the tasters, gave the edge to the powerful '78s, which were in a quiet phase, having neither youthful appeal nor the added complexity bottle age can give. The '77s, while anemic in comparison, were impressive for what they were, considering that—as Alexis Bespaloff pointed out—this was a vintage in which many well-known Burgundian firms declined to bottle their top wines.

On the other hand, the '76s, which came from a much-heralded vintage, did not live up to everyone's expectations. "I've never been a fan of the '76s," admitted Lenoir Josey, and he saw little reason to change his opinion. Aubert de Villaine conceded that, in the context of the tasting, they had been "disappointing." But Madame Bize-Leroy warmly took up their defense. "They are going through a difficult phase," she argued. "They are like an adolescent girl with complexion problems. Give them time." The panel, however, remained dubious.

But what about the '78s and '79s? Were any of these the equal—potentially—of "the great wines of the past"? Marvin Overton, who asserted that the wines produced by the Domaine in the late sixties and early seventies "didn't make you feel like clawing your way to the front of the line to get 'em," now felt the Domaine was "on the way back." All concurred with his colorful summation of the tasting: "The '78s and '79s show that the cream still rises to the top."

Perhaps because the "hard work" of assessing the current vintages was over, perhaps because the intimate setting, superlative food, fabulous wines, and congenial company worked so well together, we found the farewell dinner at La Vieille Maison in Boca Raton the most memorable evening of the fete.

Admittedly it's not every dinner where the first two wines are Montrachet and Romanée-Conti. And what a Montrachet! The Domaine's faultless '78 could only be described as the Platonic ideal of Chardonnay. The '72 Romanée-Conti that followed seemed like a generous old friend—rich and inviting. A brace of Richebourgs—'69 and '59—came next. The '69 was heady, pungent, and fruity, and although it lacked the definition of the '71 served the previous night, was marvelous drinking, as was the fading '59, a sweet, soft, and loosely structured wine. As a special vinous entr'acte we reveled in a beautiful, delicate '43 Bonnes-Mares (Leroy). The climax of the dinner—not to mention the entire fete—came close to eclipsing everything before it: '45 La Tâche, hand-carried from the Domaine's cellars. Having written so much about the remarkable Burgundies we'd had over the three days, we actually found ourselves at a loss for words now that we were face to glass with as close as wine ever gets to the sublime.

A NOTE ON THE D.R.C. IN 1985

There are some wines whose names wine lovers utter in hushed tones and consider almost mythical—if only because they are far more discussed than tasted. The wines of the Domaine de la

Romanée-Conti, Burgundy's most famous estate, are the prime example. Their fame and scarcity, reflected in staggering prices of $100 to $300 or more a bottle only add to their allure. But what wine lovers always wonder is, Can the wines really be worth it? Can they be that good?

We recently had a chance to review the 1985 D.R.C. wines at a prerelease tasting sponsored by the Domaine's importer. Not having done a complete comparative tasting of these wines since the fine '78 and '79 vintages, we wondered if our enthusiasm for these fabled Burgundies would hold in the much-talked-about '85 vintage as well. All six reds were tasted in the traditional order from lightest to grandest, a lineup that showcases them perfectly—each wine in turn serves as a perfect foil for its deeper and grander successor. Our conclusions? In the 1985 vintage, easily the best Burgundy harvest since 1978, we think the D.R.C. wines continue to live up to the legend. Though the price is mind-boggling, rest assured that there's a fabulous experience to be uncorked.

To be precise:

The *Échézeaux* has clear, vibrant Pinot character—a nose with an almost hard-candy intensity and a lingering fruity flavor. The *Grands-Échézeaux,* a personal favorite among the D.R.C. wines, has cinnamonlike scents, mouth-filling fruitiness, and a long and lasting spicy flavor. The *Romanée-St.-Vivant,* always the earthiest of the group, has a characteristically smoky-herby-stemmy aroma and a quite penetrating flavor.

The *Richebourg,* massively scented with spice and cherries, was a sumptuous wine. No layers of flavor were evident—that will come with time—but it already has a velvety texture. Those who wonder what wine lovers mean when they talk about "a fabulous finish" will find a perfect demonstration with this wine, whose bitey, youthful fruitiness persisted for nearly half a minute on the tongue.

La Tâche struck an even deeper note, both aroma and flavor showing fruit and spice mingled with earthy, iron-mineral nuances. A powerful and complex wine, its finish can only be described as dazzling.

The Romanée-Conti itself, the most fabled of all Burgundies, is monumental in 1985: deep, incredibly intense, and with a mesmerizing scent. The flavor echoes on the palate for a full minute. Of course the thought of paying $300 or more a bottle to embrace such an experience would dash most wine lovers' fantasies. The price isn't mere Gallic gouging—though that fact may not make it any easier to swallow. There are a mere 453 cases of '85 Romanée-Conti for the world to squabble over. (By comparison, Château Margaux—not exactly a bargain wine—produced some 25,000 cases of its splendid 1985.)

In retrospect it seemed amazing that wines a mere two years old would merit descriptions normally reserved for much older great Burgundies, but such precociousness seems generally true of all the top '85 Burgundies, which promise, at this early stage, to be gorgeous throughout their life spans.

JUST A LITTLE LOCAL WINE

According to one local legend, in the nineteenth century sailboats brought each season's wines from the Hudson Valley down the river in barrels stacked on deck to city dwellers in New York. This served as New York City's own harvest wine festival, but the tradition eventually faded away along with the Hudson Valley wine region. Recently, however, the region—if not the same tradition—has been revived, and it's about time.

The revival of the Hudson Valley wine region in the past two decades, spearheaded by such small estate wineries as Benmarl, Cascade Mountain, Clinton Vineyards, and High Tor, has resulted in some excellent wines. A version of the tradition was revived by William Wetmore, proprietor of Cascade Mountain

Vineyard in Amenia, New York, who began to wonder why New Yorkers celebrate the fall harvest season with French wines instead of local wines. Why the hoopla for the arrival of the first wines from France's Beaujolais region in late November, just weeks after the harvest, instead of the fine *nouveau*-style reds from the wine region north of the city? So Wetmore and two other Hudson Valley vintners initiated a celebration of their own: a sampling of their *nouveau* reds brought down the river by boat to The River Café in Brooklyn.

We sailed the last leg of the journey with them, glasses in hand, across the East River to Manhattan's South Street Seaport aboard the sloop *Pioneer*. As the New York skyline began to loom over us as we sailed nearer (it's especially daunting viewed from river level), we felt like a boatful of vinous missionaries, wondering if the natives would pay attention to the simple message of how nice it is to enjoy a glass of the local wine.

Later that night, at a dinner featuring wines from Europe and California, we wondered why so many Americans eagerly seek out little-known local wines in Europe simply for the pleasure of drinking them on their home ground, but rarely do so in this country. Of course, Californians have been appreciating their state's products since viticulture began there, but how many other wine lovers in this country make an effort to support their local wineries? We recall dining in a Maryland restaurant and spotting a lone Maryland wine—then unknown to us—on the wine list. We tried a bottle and thought it was well made and attractive. We asked the waitress whether it was a popular item. "Well, not exactly," she explained. "You're the only people who've ever ordered it."

Admittedly, there was a time in this country—not very long ago—when very little U.S. wine produced outside California would have appealed to wine lovers. But improvements have been so marked in viticulture in the Pacific Northwest and the East Coast that the best wine from the rest of the United States is challenging the Golden State, at least in some categories. Light, elegant Rieslings in the German style, for example, aren't California's strong suit, but they may be New York's. We've had several examples, notably Dr. Konstantin Frank's from the Finger Lakes district, that compare favorably with fine German ones. Oregon Pinot Noir has already gained such widespread attention it probably doesn't qualify as a local wine—but the state's startlingly good Pinot Gris would.

One lingering problem seems to be that many Americans still think California is the only state that produces good wines in this country. These are the same people who fifteen years ago thought only Europeans produced good wines. Now that wine is made in some forty of the fifty states, recognition that the frontiers of fine wine in the United States are broader than previously imagined is overdue. (Do you like Chardonnay, but as a resident of Connecticut find the idea of a decent local Chardonnay dubious? Try the Crosswoods. You live in Texas? Go for the Llano Estacado. Idaho? Try Ste. Chappelle's.) The list of fine non-California American wines is long and getting longer. Maybe it won't be too long before wine lovers who now fondly remember the marvelous local wines they had on their European vacation will discover that America has great local wines, too.

RABELAIS'S WINE

If pressed to describe our ideal red wine, we'd tick off the following qualities: It should have character and elegance, like Bordeaux. On the other hand, it should have the charm and drink-me appeal of Beaujolais and also something of the light, tender texture of Pinot Noir. It should be at its best slightly cool to make it a year-round red. Then, it ought to be delicious when just a year or two old but should last for decades. While we're at it, we'd like it to complement a wide variety of dishes, from grilled salmon to roast beef. Oh, yes, we almost forgot—let's keep the price modest, too, say $10–12 a bottle.

Would you believe that such a red exists? That in fact it is a classic wine, known since the eleventh century, and praised by Rabelais, who knew a good wine when he guzzled it? Give up? We've just extolled the virtues of Chinon, Bourgueil, Saumur-Champigny, Anjou Rouge, and the other fine reds of the Loire Valley based on the Cabernet Franc grape. When Bordeaux and Burgundy prices recently soared, Loire reds started to show up more frequently on Parisian wine lists. We've even spotted them in New York.

Sure, we'd tasted examples of these wines before and liked them, but their special appeal didn't come home to us until we tasted them on their home ground. One of the great joys of wine is coming across an underappreciated, largely ignored (and therefore underpriced) category of wines that offers something remarkable and different. It was a 1976 Bourgueil from Lamé-Delille-Boucard, with its heavenly bouquet and taste of *fraises des bois,* that reawakened our interest in Loire reds. Wherever we visited we made a point of tasting the reds; we managed to sample several examples with every meal.

We learned that winemaking in the Loire is very old, apparently dating back to Roman times. By Rabelais's time—he was born around 1490 in Chinon—his local red was highly regarded; and as recently as a century ago, it was compared with fine Bordeaux. Today red wine production in the Loire is less important than it was in times past, but still significant.

The key to the style of Loire Valley reds is the cool climate and the use of the Cabernet Franc grape, locally called the Breton. (There are also Loire reds based on Gamay and Pinot Noir and oceans of rosés made from the same grapes, but they aren't in the same league.) Bordeaux drinkers probably associate Cabernet Franc with St.-Emilion, where it is one of the major grape varieties. In the Loire climate, its delicacy and ravishing scent are accentuated. Chinon, Bourgueil, St.-Nicholas-de-Bourgueil, and Saumur-Champigny are the principal appellations and all are quite similar in style.

Local connoisseurs, of course, find that Chinon has an aroma of violets and strawberries, while Bourgueil's is reminiscent of raspberries. They say that Saumur-Champigny is a shade bigger and heavier, perhaps owing to the practice of blending in Cabernet Sauvignon, a variety used rarely in Bourgueil and Chinon. Further distinctions are made between wines that come from sandy (*graviers*) soil, which mature early, and those from chalky (*tuffeau*) soil, which age better.

But when it comes to wines that are so obviously meant for sheer enjoyment, we prefer to leave such classifications and distinctions behind and merely go on taste. Not every bottle you'll come across is seductive, especially in poor years. Some examples can be overly herbaceous, tart, and thin. But the better ones have an enticing fruitiness, buttressed by a certain firmness in the flavor that, in Hugh Johnson's perfect phrase, "achieves a sort of pastel sketch of a great Médoc."

Concerned that our enthusiasm might have been unduly influenced by the charms of the Loire Valley, we attended a New York tasting of the wines of Couly-Dutheil, a top Chinon grower and Loire *négociant,* to see how these reds would taste outside their picture-postcard setting. We weren't disappointed. Three 1985s were particularly fine. The Saumur-Champigny was fruity and delicious, the Bourgueil "Les Closiers" was deeper and richer, and the scarce Chinon "Clos de l'Echo" was spicy and concentrated: wonderful now, but it will be even more splendid in six years.

Partisans claim that with age the biggest of these reds deepen and come to resemble beefier Bordeaux. Dubious of this, we compared a 1964 Chinon "Clos de l'Olive" from Couly-Dutheil that we'd brought from the Loire with a Château Cheval-Blanc of the same year. (Because the Château Cheval-Blanc has a very high proportion of Cabernet Franc, we thought it would be a meaningful, if tough, comparison.) Admittedly, the Chinon was not quite as glossy and glorious in flavor as the first-growth, but it had a fine bouquet, depth, complexity, and lingering fruit that stood out even in such company. It was marvelous in its own right and every bit as vital and alive.

These little-discussed French reds may not have the prestige and importance of Bordeaux and Burgundy, but they are long on charm and sheer drink-me appeal. That's reason enough to deserve a spot in the cellar, wouldn't you say?

DOWN UNDER WINES

Grape growers, like farmers, love to complain about how difficult it is to grow their crop, and we thought we'd heard all the complaints possible—the cold, the heat, the sun or lack of it, too much or too little rain, and of course, various blights and pests. But we were still taken aback when Dominique Portet, winemaker at Taltarni Vineyards in Australia, described his problems. "Kangaroos," he told us. "You haven't seen anything until you've seen a full-grown kangaroo attack a vine." We learned that fencing out rabbits, deer, or even wild boar (a common problem in some wine regions) is a relatively simple matter compared to the enormous lengths—mostly of wire—that one has to go to in order to keep out kangaroos.

Portet explained that a series of high-voltage fences is the answer, though it turns out even that won't deter a truly determined 'roo. But grape-gobbling kangaroos are just part of the challenge Australian winemakers have met successfully. The real test was to make truly fine wines.

After our recent tastings, we think they've passed with flying colors. We aren't too surprised that some wine critics now speak of the wine potential of Australia as second only to that of France. While we think it's a bit premature to relegate the wines of America—specifically the wines of California—to middle rank, it's clear that Australia's best wines rival California's.

None of this is startling news to the wine-keen inhabitants of
that country, but the rapidity of the developments in Down Under wines may surprise Americans who have been used to thinking of Australia's status in the wine world as something less than
first class. Americans, on the other hand, are keenly aware of the
reasons for California's rapid success story. The lack of tradition
after Prohibition and the emphasis on a scientific approach to
winemaking encouraged widespread experimentation. In the last
twenty years the use of cold fermentation, aging in small oak
barrels, earlier picking, and other up-to-date techniques have become commonplace in California. But the truth is that during the
same period, winemakers Down Under have similarly transformed
their industries, and there are now some five hundred Australian
wineries.

When we first came across wines from Australia ten years ago,
however, we were not exactly bowled over. Though we found
the tongue-in-cheek nomenclature ("Kangarouge," for one) refreshing, the wines seemed considerably less so. A decade ago,
the large commercial wineries of Australia were making tenta-
tive efforts at exporting their products but alas, not their best
ones, which sold briskly at home. The bottlings we tasted then
were neither better nor worse (and no more individual) than
comparable California wines in the same modest price range.

What impressed us most were the pungent, lingering old li-
queur Muscats—a superb and unusual category of dessert wine.
We were astonished rather than charmed by reds of such tremendous concentration that they were more reminiscent of extract than table wine. When we suggested to the Australian who
shared them with us that they were perhaps too much of a good
thing, he explained that many of his countrymen had a taste for
substantial reds. What's more, they knew how to judge a good
one. "You put a spoon in the middle of the glass," he said, "and if
it falls *slowly* to the side, then it's got what it takes."

These bushwhacking bottlings represented Australia's mon-
ster-wine phase, which, though even then on the wane, hasn't
altogether disappeared. Like California (which has also largely
abandoned overly big wines), Australia only gradually discov-

ered refinement as a wine virtue and began finding ways to make wines to international (that is, French) standards. Now we've had the opportunity to taste some of these new-wave bottlings, many of which first trickled into the United States in teasingly small quantities. After tasting remarkable wines—claretlike Cabernets and marvelously rich Chardonnays from Lake's Folly, Taltarni, Leeuwin Vineyard, Brokenwood, Rosemount, and a dozen other first-rank producers, our opinion of Australian wines was revised radically upward.

As one might expect from their similarly warm wine climate and open-minded approach to winemaking, Australian wines most nearly resemble California's, but in many cases they are quite different in character. Perhaps that's because there are as many differences as parallels with the California wine industry, and these will clearly shape the future of Australian wine.

Both wine regions started in the 1700s and were noted for warm-climate wines, particularly fortified wines, until modern winemaking took hold. High-tech winemaking made it possible to produce well-balanced, even elegant wines in warm climates whose products were previously associated with coarseness-in-quantity. Australia's climate—like California's—ensures good quality almost every year. There is the same annoying use of European place-names such as Burgundy and Chablis, and the same importance is given to varietal wines, although Australians don't place as much emphasis on varietal character as Californians do. In Australia there appears to be more emphasis on blending—of grape varieties and of grapes from different regions. As in California, the winemaker is all-important, and the best are regarded as cellar wizards. Australia, of course, is much larger than California, and its wine districts are scattered from coast to coast. Naturally, there are differences among these districts, whose names sound exotic to us now—Hunter Valley, Coonawarra, Margaret River, and the rest—but so far Australians don't seem to emphasize the distinctiveness of these appellations (even though some have a marked *goût de terroir*) so much as they make use of them to create balanced blends.

While we're used to seeing simple California appellation wines that may be blended from one or several California counties, Australians think nothing of creating their finest wines from districts many hundreds of miles apart. (No California producer would offer as one of his best efforts a blend of the wines from Napa Valley and, say, the Willamette Valley in Oregon.) Of course, this sort of multiregion blending makes an Australian vintage chart almost meaningless.

So far, there's little interest in single-estate wines, now a California concern and an idée fixe in the French view of quality wines. Australian labels can be very confusing, too. A producer may make a Shiraz/Cabernet as well as a Cabernet/Shiraz, and many wineries offer an array of bin-number wines, which are blended to maintain a particular style from vintage to vintage (or so it seems). California, on the other hand, has largely dropped the practice of labeling different lots of wine by number in favor of "regular" and presumably better "reserve" bottlings.

Both Australia and California are seeking out cooler regions, partly in response to the cooler-climate grapes now emphasized and the desire for more refined wine styles. Australia is a relative newcomer to the Chardonnay and Cabernet sweepstakes (most of its acreage of these grapes was planted in the past ten years), which makes its performance with these grapes even more impressive.

In fact, we decided we'd gain some insight into just how good Australian winemaking is by looking in detail at their efforts with the grape that comes as close as any to having international standards—Cabernet Sauvignon. We were able to taste two dozen of Australia's most highly regarded examples along with a few top California Cabernets. Overall we were impressed with the richness and color of Australian Cabernets, the technical polish of the best of them, and despite the intensity of flavors, the modest alcohol levels. A half-dozen examples from Tyrrell's, Penfolds, Vasse Felix, and Rosemount more than held their own against some top-class Napa Valley Cabernets.

But once the aura of the exotic wears off, will American wine lovers show as much enthusiasm for, say, Cabernet bottlings from the Hunter Valley as they now do for the Napa Valley? Or will Down Under wines be regarded as a world of parallel tastes to California's? It seems reasonable to ask what, in broad terms, Australia can offer wine lovers that California can't. In our Cabernet tasting there didn't seem to be significant differences.

Fortunately, Australia's fame as a wine region rests on grapes other than Chardonnay and Cabernet, and any wine lover who hasn't tried them shouldn't pass up the opportunity to do so.

Australia's most unusual white, and one of its most widely planted grapes, is the Sémillon, which makes a remarkably rich, mouth-filling, and very individual white, notably in the Hunter Valley (where, maddeningly enough, it is often labeled Riesling, a holdover from the loose label language of earlier days). We've tasted some striking young green-gold examples (especially the 1983 Tyrrell's HVD) that offer an almost oily texture offset by a refreshing lemony acidity. With a decade or more of age, as we noted in several older vintages of Lindemans Semillon (notably the 1970), the wine gains amazing depth and character. Len Evans, the Australian wine authority, explained the transformation to us. "When young, Semillon has a freshness, but not much varietal character. Between three and five years of age, it's quite dull. Later it develops a burnt-toast, almost vanillin quality as if aged in oak—which, classically, it isn't." Nonetheless, the variety has considerable affinity for oak and "wood-matured" specimens that can mimic some of the complexities conferred by bottle age. California makes Semillon, too, but they're nothing like the Hunter bottlings.

Australia's most common red is the Shiraz (or Hermitage), which is actually the Syrah grape of the Rhône, cuttings of which are thought to have been taken to Australia in the 1830s. Shiraz produces a round, satisfying red and is widely used for blending, even with Cabernet Sauvignon. Shiraz is also capable of greatness: Penfolds Grange Hermitage, the most famous red of the country, is a brawny and muscular wine, balanced and well proportioned but full of hints of berries, truffles, mushrooms, and chocolate, and often laced with earthy, leathery overtones. Although elegance isn't the first word that comes to mind when tasting Grange, it cedes nothing in complexity and magnificence. Its highly individual style is consistent, to judge from a series of vintages we tasted in New York with Penfolds winemaker Max Schubert. The '80 ("typical but a baby," according to Schubert) already showed a licorice and currant nose, a lovely lingering texture, and a tannic finish. The lighter-bodied '67 had smoky, leathery nuances, the sweet pungency of old claret, and a suggestion of tannin still in the finish. We gave it a slight edge over the '66, which had smoky adhesivelike hints in the nose and a long, lovely, but dry finish. Best of all was the tremendous '71, with its expansive, rich smoke-and-berries bouquet and deep, mouth-filling flavor that seemed to echo on the palate.

California has nothing quite like that, either.

A TASTE OF PORT

Before visiting Portugal's River Douro, we thought we had some appreciation of Porto, one of the world's classic wines. The type of wine most of the world knows as Port—a rich, sweet, fortified wine of about 20 percent alcohol—is widely imitated, but we've long agreed with the almost universal opinion that the original has yet to be matched. And we thought we understood its remarkable range of styles: golden-colored Tawny Ports long aged in cask; inky-dark Ruby Ports, all fruit and flavor; majestic bottle-aged Vintage Ports, with their extraordinary depth, complexity, and lingering warmth. But nothing made us realize what a fine bottle of Port represents as much as going up the Douro to see the harvest. Only then did we appreciate Port's provenance, its pedigree, its achievement.

From the cool white stone veranda of the house it was easy to watch the progress of the pickers: the terraced vineyards ascended in a steep natural amphitheater that swept around the spectacular gorge formed by a bend of the River Douro. Here, not many miles from the Spanish border, was one of the farthest reaches and finest estates of the dry, wild, gray-and-brown landscape of the region that gives birth to Port. From such rocky vineyards the young wine would be shipped the following spring to Oporto, the ancient city fifty miles downriver that gave the wine its name, to be selected, matured, bottled, and shipped all over the world. Each of the major Oporto shippers has a top-quality estate (quinta), which is used as its base of operation in the Douro and whose vineyard may supply much of the superior wine that ends up in its finest Ports. We were at Quinta de Vargellas, the finest estate of the redoubtable firm of shippers Taylor, Fladgate and Yeatman—"Taylor's" to the trade.

The pickers, mostly women and children, seemed oblivious to the vertiginous angle of the slopes, slopes so steep that vines could cling to the hillside only because of the bulwarks of stone terraces connected to each other by crumbly steps or the miniature rock slides that passed for paths. The old men waved sticks and shouted directions; the young men seemed to be standing idle, but when each tall wicker basket that stood at the end of the vine rows was finally filled with fat purple clusters of grapes, it was clear why they deserved their moments of rest. With understandable difficulty they shouldered the 150-pound baskets, which rest on a roll of cloth high across the back and are balanced by a stick held hooked to the front edge of the basket. Without a moment's hesitation, the young men plunged down the slopes at a fast downhill trot, puffs of dust rising behind them all the way, to small trucks waiting at one of the dusty tracks now used for service roads. From there the grapes would be taken down the hill past the house to the cellars.

We were witnessing the vintage as it has been for centuries. It made quite a contrast to the demonstrations of mechanical picking we'd seen in some of California's textbook-perfect vineyards. But not as much of a contrast as what we had seen the night before when, after dinner, we watched wine being made in the cellars the way all wine used to be made: by the human foot. "Actually, the foot is perfectly adapted to the task," explained our host, Alastair Robertson, head of the family-owned firm founded in 1692. "We don't do this for show, you know. We do it because we think it makes better wine. Our Vintage Port has always been produced by treading." Indeed, every drop of Taylor's highly regarded Vintage Port is produced by treading and always has been. "Our vintages have been considered classic," Robertson added, "so we're in no rush to change."

In the stone cellar one large, square granite trough, or *lagar*, was filled with an incredibly purple-black, redolent, pulpy mass of crushed grapes. In the middle of it some dozen men and boys in shorts strode slowly around the tank—when you're up to midthigh in crushed grapes you can't move fast—encouraged in their efforts by an equally large number of women and children dancing to tunes wheezed out on an old accordion. In the next room stood the tall, modern fermenting tanks, empty and ready to receive the grapes Taylor's buys for its less prestigious Ports. The tanks were only one hundred feet from where the grapes were being treaded—but centuries apart.

Treading is still the method of choice for many houses in the Douro for the making of their finest wines. But change is in the air here, as everywhere. Each year it becomes more difficult to recruit the necessary labor to make wine this way, and so it may eventually become a thing of the past.

"Let me give you an overview of Port production," Michael Symington said, interspersing his rapid review of the changes the shippers face with observations on the passing viticultural scene as we drove around the hills surrounding the village of Pinhão, in the heart of the Douro's finest vineyards. "You mentioned treading. Treading fascinates visitors. But we convinced ourselves that modern methods are just as good, if not better. For five years in the late 1960s, we made Ports both ways, and believe me, there was no discernible difference." When a Symington speaks about Port, he speaks with considerable authority. The Symingtons have been involved in the "Port trade" since the late nineteenth century, and today the family businesses account for some 15 percent of all Port sales worldwide and virtually half the total sales of Vintage Port. There are six Symingtons active in various aspects of their enterprises, which include five firms, notably Warre's, Dow's, and Graham's.

Such consolidated ownership of Port firms is not unusual today. "There are fifty-five Port houses altogether, now controlled by twenty-two firms," Symington explained. "In some cases, like ours, the brands are kept separate. Our Port houses have their own tradition—Warre's is over three hundred years old—their own sources of supply, and their own style, which we go to great lengths to maintain. Thank God no one has ever suggested there's such a thing as the Symington taste."

On a mountainside curve high above Pinhão, Symington stopped the car to let us survey the extensive plantings and famous quintas along the Douro. Port, we learned, can be produced only in this area, demarcated in the eighteenth century, of roughly one thousand square miles of the Douro and its tributaries; plantings and production are strictly controlled by the Casa do Douro, a government body that decides how much of the wine produced here may be made into Port (typically only about half; the rest—the poorer half—remains table wine). Vineyards themselves are officially graded for quality according to elevation, exposure, and soil—or rather, what appears to be the lack of it.

Symington ticked off a list of further facts as we drove on. The high quality of the vineyards around Pinhão is due in part to scanty rainfall, poor soil, and harsh conditions—freezing winters, baking-hot summers. In such vineyards, each vine produces only enough grapes to make a mere one-half liter of wine. The major shippers actually hold only 6 or 7 percent of these vineyards, and consequently they buy grapes from thousands of small growers. (There are some 29,000 small growers in the Douro, and a single shipper may buy from 3,000 different ones.) But there are still no contracts in the Douro; a handshake suffices because sources of supply are largely traditional, in some cases generations old.

"But—another change—more and more shippers are doing what we do, buying grapes instead of wine and making the wine themselves to ensure quality," Symington explained. "We now process two-thirds of our requirements from purchased grapes."

Curiously enough, only in recent years has much attention been given to grape varieties; traditionally, dozens of varieties were grown together with little regard for the quality of the wine they produced. New plantings, however, concentrate on a handful of the better varieties.

At the Symingtons' own Quinta do Bomfim, we saw contemporary Port-making on a large scale, from a weigh station for farmers bringing truckloads of grapes, to an impressive battery of autovinifiers, closed fermenting tanks adapted from systems first used in Algeria for rapid fermentation in hot-climate wine production. "And," Symington pointed out, "the best thing about them is they don't quit and go home to bed at midnight, the way treaders do." We clanged across high metal catwalks as Symington explained the process. "We want extraction of color and flavor rapidly—within thirty-six hours—because we want to run it off into a vat and add the grape brandy, which is seventy-seven percent alcohol by volume, about halfway through the fermentation to stop it." The result is a fortified wine with about 7 percent of its natural grape sugar retained and an alcohol level of about 20 percent. It's young and raw, to be sure, but recognizably Port. It looks like ink and stains a porcelain tasting dish a striking magenta; it's also arrestingly inky to the taste but wonderfully fruity underneath.

The train from Pinhão back to Oporto follows the winding course of the river, and its modest pace allows plenty of time for reflection. Since the damming of the Douro in 1961, it is no longer the wild rapid-ridden river it used to be, nor is it the romantic route the wine used to take to the shippers' Podges in Oporto. For hundreds of years the traditional Douro boats, the square-rigged *barcos rabelos,* took the new wine downriver the following spring in large casks, or "pipes," holding about 534 liters; now transportation is by tanker truck, but presumably the drivers don't fortify themselves against the rigors of the trip by frequently sampling, as the boatmen always did.

The history of viticulture in the Douro probably dates back a millennium or more, but the modern history of Port dates from the development of a wine trade with England in the thirteenth and fourteenth centuries. The first officially recorded shipment of *vinho do Porto* from Oporto was in 1678, which was coincidentally the year two young English gentlemen—whose names are lost to history but whose story is repeated in every text—arrived from England to find wines suitable for export to Britain. In the course of their travels in Douro, they stayed at a monastery in Lamego, where the abbot served them his best wine from Pinhão. The travelers were impressed with the smooth, powerful, sweet wine, which the abbot explained was the result of adding a quantity of the local brandy to the wine while it was still fermenting. The Englishman bought some and shipped it home, but this new style of fortified wine did not come into general vogue until much later; around 1850.

The Methuen treaty of 1703 allowed Portuguese wines to be imported into England at one-third less duty than was imposed on French wine, which naturally gave an enormous boost to the early trade. The British firms were the first to make Port as we know it today, the first to export it, and they continue to dominate the trade. A number of firms still in business today, among them Croft, Taylor, and Warre, were founded in the late seventeenth century. But from the beginning the British were joined by the Germans and Dutch—Kopke, Burmester and Van Zeller are well-known names in the trade—and of course, the Portuguese themselves.

"Port is a British creation," said Manuel Poças Pintao of Poças, Jr., one of the most modern and progressive of the Portuguese houses, "but it is unquestionably a Portuguese wine." Today the Portuguese shippers account for half the production of all Port and vary in size, from Royal Oporto, a specialist in bulk Port with 18 percent of the world market, to smaller houses such as the prestigious Quinta do Noval. Most have exported primarily to European countries other than Britain, notably France (now the world's largest Port customer), Belgium, and the Netherlands, and sell a great deal within Portugal itself. Until recently most have concentrated on Tawny Ports, but more and more are determined to gain a reputation for the longtime specialty of the British houses: Vintage Port.

In the tasting room of the historic, highly regarded Portuguese firm of A. A. Ferreira, Vito Olazabal, a descendant of the founder, had set out a long row of Ports to illustrate the spectrum of tastes and styles of the major types. In the bright north light from the broad windows, their colors ranged from pale straw to deep gold to purple-red. Beyond, through the window, was a panoramic view of Oporto across the River Douro; we paused to take it in.

The Douro divides the city into Oporto proper on the north bank and its main suburb, Vila Nova de Gaia, on the south bank, where we were. By law, Port shippers must have their offices and their lodges (cellars) here in this crowded, ancient quarter with narrow, twisting streets built on a hill. The famous lodges are all clustered together under red tile-roofed sheds blackened with age and the fungus that is attracted by evaporating Port. Unfortunately, the close proximity to one another and the Douro exposes every shipper to occasional catastrophic fires and to periodic damaging floods. The centuries-old lodges themselves are warrens of rooms, some tiny, some barn-sized, filled with barrels and huge vats of aging Port resting on dirt floors. But it is in modern tasting rooms such as the one we were in where the young Ports of each firm are carefully graded on their arrival at the lodge the spring after harvest. Lots of similar quality are combined, and initial decisions are made about their potential use in the various categories and styles offered by each house.

White Port, which we tasted first, is a small but significant category at every major shipper, although something of a rarity in the United States. It may be dry or slightly sweet but is always fruity.

Next we tried Ruby and Tawny Ports, the two basic styles offered by every shipper. These two categories make up the vast majority of all Port. The Ruby sample was aggressive and fruity.

For a basic Ruby brand, Ferreira would blend similar lots of young, raw Port together and age them for about three years in large wooden vats to create a dark, rich, soft, fruity wine. "The Tawny, as you can see, is a very different style of Port," Olazabal remarked. The sample was paler and more pungent than the Ruby. Already blended, it had been kept in smaller cooperage to increase oxidation and encourage the lighter, tawny-brown color and special tang associated with this style. An inexpensive Tawny can be produced by simply blending Ruby and White Port, but better Tawnies achieve their color and character through aging in cask. For certain Tawnies, aging may go on for decades.

Later in our visit we had a chance to compare Ports at their most divergent: Ferreira's "Duque de Bragança," a Tawny whose component wines have an average age of twenty years, and Ferreira's 1963 Vintage Port. The golden-brown Tawny was warmly scented, with the deep, lingering, mellow taste and savory character that only years in the cask can confer. The 1963, like all Vintage Ports, had come from the best wines of an especially fine—in this case, a great—year, and had been bottled after two years, so that unlike other Ports its maturation had taken place in the bottle. It was strikingly different in color, still ruby-red and just turning a warm brick color at the edge of the glass. Its rich bouquet was impossible to fix with a single term, but it suggested fruit, flowers, spice; to the taste it offered a sweetly round mouthful of flavor full of texture and warmth. Twenty years had done much for both wines. "I like to say," Olazabal commented, "that Port is a business that takes patience."

Vintage Port is by no means the most familiar Port; but of all Ports it is undeniably the most alluring. Across the Douro from the shippers' lodges, not far from the bridge to Vila Nova de Gaia, stands an imposing gray granite Georgian building whose very atmosphere seems to many to sum up all the romance and tradition of Vintage Port. Known as The Factory House, it was originally the headquarters of the British merchants, or "factors," who formed a guild in the late eighteenth century. Since 1814 The Factory House has been the headquarters of the British Association, which consists of British Port shippers, their partners, and directors. It is so full of history that it seems as much a museum as a club, which in a sense it also is. Its members, twelve British houses—now consolidated by takeovers into five administrative groupings (the Symington group, Sandeman, Taylor, Croft, and Cockburn)—account for over half the world Port market.

At the traditional Wednesday lunch for directors of the members' firms and their guests, the ceremony of "passing the Port" begins once the lunch plates are cleared. A decanter of fine old Tawny (irreverently referred to as "mouthwash" in deference to the Vintage Port that is to follow) begins its clockwise procession around the table. (The origin of the custom of passing Port to the left may have something to do with the fact that it's easier for most people, being right-handed, to pass the Port that way.) And shortly after this, a decanter of Vintage Port begins its circuit in the same clockwise fashion.

The equally traditional game of guessing whose Port it is proceeds openly. At this lunch, it was a good, but not great, Vintage Port, and hence not so markedly individual. But the shippers' experienced palates quickly cornered it: "Bit light—'67, don't you think?" "On the soft side." "Yes, lacks a bit of grip." Criticism is generally muted; the crystal decanter may contain your own firm's Port. A few more guesses and word is passed down: it turns out to be Delaforce '66.

Although Vintage Port accounts for only a tiny fraction of Port production, it gets virtually all the attention of the connoisseur, the collector, the press. It is wine solely from an outstandingly good year, composed of the very best wines available to each shipper, from his own quintas and others. As James Symington, puts it, "A shipper will watch the best wines of a promising vintage very closely, and if satisfied with the results of various trial blends, he will 'declare' a vintage some eighteen months after it's made." Some years only a few shippers will declare; in others, twenty or more may.

Although Vintage Ports are only produced in the best years, it doesn't mean each vintage is like every other. Some—such as '75 or '60—are lighter and faster maturing; others—such as '63 or

'45—are massive, concentrated wines taking decades to attain their peak. A Vintage Port is also the epitome of each shipper's "house style." These range from dark, firm, and elegant (Taylor) to rich, fruity, and luscious (Graham and Fonseca) to lighter and stylish (Quinta do Noval and Sandeman).

Of course not every shipper has the same reputation for Vintage Port; as might be expected, considering they invented the style, the British houses have the edge in this category both for quality and quantity. (Although Great Britain imports only 10 percent of the world's Port, it takes 85 percent of the Vintage Port produced.) Yet even in that staunchly traditional market one Portuguese house in particular has an enviable reputation for its Vintages: Quinta do Noval.

The problem with Vintage Port is that there is so little of it. Generally declared vintages occur on the average about three times in a decade. During a fine vintage—say '77—some 5 to 10 percent of a firm's production might go into Vintage Port, which averages out to 1 to 3 percent of its total production over a ten-year period. Figures are closely guarded, but a shipper would probably produce only around 12,000 cases of Vintage in a fine year, and the total amount of Vintage Port produced by all shippers in a generally declared year is somewhere around 250,000 cases. That's not much more than the Bordeaux first-growths *alone* produce in a good year.

Is there enough to go around? Shipper David Sandeman says, "There is a definite shortage. Vintage Port consumption is steady in England and increasing rather rapidly in the United States." Despite the outward appearance of entrenched tradition that The Factory House epitomizes, the Port trade is not complacent and has for some time been looking for alternatives to meet the growing demand. The shippers' answer lies in what Alastair Robertson of Taylor's calls "the in-between"—Ports that offer some measure of the style and flavor of Vintage Port, but without the initial expense or the necessity of aging it or of decanting it before serving. One approach is to offer, in essence, a super-ruby—an especially fine Ruby Port. Another alternative, one closer to true Vintage style, is late-bottled Vintage Port, a Port that carries a date but is kept four to six years in cask before bottling to hasten maturity.

Yet neither is a substitute for true Vintage Port. Vintage Port is the ultimate Port. In fact, without its existence the everyday Ruby or Tawny on the sideboard would lose part of its image. In some ways Vintage Port is an anachronism in the modern world—in the way it's harvested, made, and bottled, in the way it has to be cellared, and in the ceremony with which it is served. Yet its appeal and romance are surely based in part on those trappings and traditions. The other part is what it offers at its best. "It may sound odd," Michael Symington told us on parting, "but what we Port shippers are saying is: 'Trust us. Get a hold of this wine, which is coarse enough to fill your pen with and write a letter, lay it down for years and years, handle it properly, and it will be magnificent."

COCKBURN'S PORT: 1904–1985

Textbooks, wine lists, and wine lovers alike divide the world of wine into broad taste categories by color and production method, grape, and region. A closer look at Champagne or Pinot Noir or Bordeaux reveals differences imposed by house style, cellar technique, and microclimate. The same is true of Vintage Port. Someone new to this classic fortified wine is more struck by how different *any* Vintage Port is from all other wines than by the subtle but distinct differences found among the characteristic styles of the dozen top shippers' Ports. Dow, for example, tends toward firmness and dryness; Graham is characteristically rich, sweet, and soft; Fonseca is typically fruity and fleshy.

With Vintage Port (as with many other wines) it's easier to

be impressed by (and appreciate) power and intensity of flavor than elegance and balance. Perhaps that's why, when top Vintage Ports are discussed, Cockburn's is often neglected. But should it be? Peter Cobb, one of Cockburn's directors, gave a tasting not long ago in New York that perfectly demonstrated the virtues of the firm's understated style.

The firm (pronounced "co-burns," by the way) is one of the classic British houses, founded in 1815, and it is the most popular brand of Port in England. Like all such houses, it offers a wide range of Ports—Ruby, Tawny, late-bottled vintage, special reserve (a "superruby"), and a top-of-the-line Vintage Port.

It's the Vintage Ports that really reflect shippers' styles, but we tuned our palates on Cockburn's special reserve (a pleasant blend of four-year-old rubies); and the mellow ten-year-old Tawny. Then we got to work on the Vintage Ports, tasting from the oldest and most delicate to the newest and most aggressive so as not to tire the taste buds. We thought the 1904 (which unlike the others was not decanted hours ahead but simply opened and poured) was tart and sharp, still drinkable but way past its best; nonetheless, a fair showing for a so-so year. Next came the two big-deal vintages of the pre–World War I years, the 1908 and the 1912. The '08 was pale and rather spirity, fragrant but fragile; we thought the '12 showed more stuffing and more of the character that once made it famous. Fading classics both, but not hard to drink.

Cockburn did not consider singling out as a Vintage Port any wine made between 1912 and 1927 (although other Port houses did) because none really suited the firm's style, which emphasizes refinement and finesse over power and fruit. We began to see that in the 1927. It was splendid—full, spicy-rich bouquet, layers of delicate flavor that echoed on the palate, elements all in beautiful harmony. It had lost its tannic grip and was clearly at or somewhat past its peak. (Followers of the firm's vintages must have been grateful for that one after fifteen dry years.)

The '47 was soft and lacked fruit but was a long, lovely, fragrant mouthful. Better still was the '55, full of deep, round, complex flavors. The '63 was magnificent, perhaps a shade better, but perhaps still a bit young. The '70 was less intense, but almost flowery, round, soft, and lingering.

Cockburn often finds that "lesser" vintage years—years when only a few firms find wines exciting enough to declare a Vintage Port—are often more complimentary to their house style. They did not declare '66, as many did, but declared '67, which most shippers passed over. Cockburn bottled some '66 for its own use, and according to Cobb, their '67 is preferable to their '66. The '67 was a truly exquisite Vintage Port, not especially deep, fleshy, or thick-textured, but light, smooth, more silk than velvet, perfectly harmonious and at its peak.

Unfortunately it is the "great," widely declared years that get all the attention from the trade, press, and auction houses. When Cockburn, for reasons of its own, did not declare a '77—a highly acclaimed year shipped by most firms—it found itself taken less seriously as a Vintage Port producer. The decision was soon regretted, and the firm, knowing that its reputation was on the line, made sure that the next Vintage Port it shipped would lead the pack. The '83 is clearly the standard-bearer of the vintage, young, dark, all crushed nuts and black cherries and full of flavor. It is a fabulous Vintage Port, and behind the youthful tannins we thought we could recognize the Cockburn hallmarks of balance and refinement. The latest shipped is the deliciously fruity, deep, and lush '85; it may not be in the same league as the '83, but it is not far behind. At current price levels of $40 and $30 respectively, we'd bank on either.

5

Cellar Notes

WINE CELLAR REALITIES

We know the fantasy well, and we know what triggers it: you go to pick out a nice bottle from your modest closet wine rack for Sunday dinner. As you rummage through the immature Cabernets and the bargain Pinot Grigio, you discover a forgotten bottle of last year's Beaujolais *nouveau* behind the skis, but nothing really old or special. You wonder with a sigh what it would be like to have a truly great cellar. In a flash of imagination you're treading down the cool stone steps of a true European *cave,* with its dim, damp brick bins, or alternatively, you're stepping into the high-tech temperature-controlled hum of a Texas-size wine collection. In either case you wander past serried ranks of contemporary vintages—all proscribed for drinking, of course, until they've undergone their allotted maturation—to browse among the rows and stacks of dusty bottles, bin tags revealing the roll call of great vintages stretching back decades. You pause before one of many racks of acknowledged classics. Your hand hovers over a number of grand old rarities before settling on the '53 Lafite, now at its exquisite peak. . . .

Like most people whose passion for wine usually outstrips

their everyday means, we've indulged in that sort of woolgather-
ing almost from the moment we became fascinated by wine.
And like many, we wanted to turn fantasy into reality. There
finally came a point when we found the cruel pinch of want
more than we could stand. We suppose it was obvious—when
wine lovers start thinking about starting a serious wine cellar,
their symptoms are apparent to everyone. They start talking
about the advantages that a cellar of any size offers—even if it's
only a few cases competing for room with the vacuum and boots
in the hall closet. There's no point, they'll say, in drinking hand-
to-mouth, making last-minute dashes to the liquor store just
before guests arrive. If they had a cellar, a bottle of wine would
always be there. Because *they* would have been taking care of it,
the wine would be in excellent condition. They'd actually *save*
money because they could buy wine when it was first available
and relatively modest in cost. Having convinced themselves, they
then take the irrevocable step of "laying down wine"; that is,
these formerly carefree drinkers purchase wine in extravagant
quantities, not to drink now, but to drink at some unspecified
date years hence. Watch out: a harmless hobby has become a
full-blown passion. We speak from experience.

The advantages budding collectors cite are all valid reasons
for collecting wine, and they're why even those who are only
mildly bitten by the collecting bug should consider becoming
microcollectors. After all, even a "cellar" consisting of several
cases affords the same keen pleasures and convenience an enormous collection does.

A planned approach to stocking your cellar is the key to successful wine collecting. The strategy that makes the most sense
for most people is twofold. Purchase everyday wines—your house
red and white, so to speak—as you need them, and lay away in
quantity only those wines that benefit by long-term aging. If
you're methodical, you might enjoy calculating your everyday
wine needs by analyzing your consumption patterns. How often
do you drink at home? How often do you entertain and how
much and what kinds of wine do you serve? Do you drink more
whites than reds? How often do you (or would you) drink or

serve an old, special wine? Remember: it's a fallacy to assume that if you have a cellarful of wines, your consumption will change dramatically. By determining the sort of wines you'd serve if you had them on hand, you know your ideal requirements—which, alas, have to be reconciled with your wine budget.

For convenience, you'll want to have some everyday wines on hand in your kitchen wine rack, of course, or even a couple dozen on the floor of the hall closet—but not more than you plan to consume in the coming months (in which case perfect storage conditions are of less concern). You'll want to have some sparkling wine, some light whites for warm-weather meals, and some light fruity reds. Whether you fulfill these needs with California Brut or Champagne, Mâcon or Chenin Blanc, ready-to-enjoy Rioja or Zinfandel, can depend on seasonal needs and by what bargains show up at retail outlets.

Now for the serious stuff, the real cellar bottlings. Because most collectors find that their tastes and interests change, the most realistic approach steers a course somewhere between haphazard impulse buying and never deviating from a predictable five-year plan. Since in any case your cellar should consist mostly of fine reds and a smaller proportion of whites that age well— mostly dessert wines—you won't have gone too far wrong if you've confined your choices to age-worthy examples among these categories.

(One aside: we think a wine cellar ought to reflect one's personal taste, not received opinion. If you don't like Port, for example, then there's no reason to collect it just to have a "balanced" cellar. In our view, it's much more impressive, and more personally gratifying, to have a selection of idiosyncratic choices than an obvious me-too collection of first-growths.)

If you're a collector who wants to develop a cellar of both ready-to-drink wine and wine for future drinking, initially you'll have to buy more than you plan to consume within the year and keep your hands off the excess cases until they're ready to drink.

As a first step, figure out how many extra cases of wine for long-term aging you can purchase each year over and above your immediate needs. That will be the start of your long-term cellar. After a few years of stocking it, you'll reach that satisfying point where you'll be drinking from that well-aged stock as well as adding younger wines to it.

Let's say you find that you consume ten cases of wine a year at home. If you buy twelve, and drink ten, you'll start your base with two cases. If you did that for ten years (presuming you bought wines that would stay the course), you'd then be ready to start rewarding your patience by dipping into your twenty-case base because half your purchases would probably be nearing maturity. If you'd followed this plan during the 1970s and 1980s, buying an extra case or two of, say, fine Bordeaux or top California Cabernet Sauvignon in good years, you could have accumulated some '70 and '71 Bordeaux and '74 Cabernet, which you could savor now and during the next five years (two cases' worth a year) while waiting for your purchases of '75, '78, and '79 Bordeaux, and '78 and '80 California Cabernet to come around. Once you've established such a base, your task is simply to offset your annual inroads into the cellar by an equal number of purchases every year of the same sort of wine.

If, however, you stock your cellar exclusively with wines that need fifteen years of aging, you'll have only your everyday wines to drink in the meantime. We'd strive for purchasing some older (but not especially scarce or extravagantly expensive vintages) that promise development but can be enjoyed now.

When you're buying for the future, there are several further considerations you should bear in mind when developing your plan. Taste widely, but when laying down wine, don't confuse what's interesting to taste with what makes sense to collect: wines that will age and improve. Who wants to be stuck with cases of over-the-hill Muscadet or an alarming amount of rapidly maturing Zinfandel?

A cellarful of Beaujolais *nouveau*, for example, couldn't possibly be consumed before it faded in the bottle. On the other hand, you can have a cellarful of bottles of mature wine, none of which you need to rush to drink up—if it's the right sort of wine. Top Bordeaux in good years and Vintage Port may take a decade or two to mature, and may stay at their peak for another decade before slowly declining in quality, which is why these two wines traditionally form the backbone of large cellars.

In addition, we strongly advocate buying wines for the long-term cellar in case lots so that you'll be able to try a bottle now and then as it approaches maturity and still have the better part of a dozen to try when it's come into its own. For example, you might have sampled a bottle from a case of '78 California Cabernet Sauvignon purchased in 1981 and enjoyed it, then decided not to try it for three years. At that time you decided it was ready and drank six bottles. You tried one more the following year and decided you were premature, so you're hoarding the last four. But none of this is possible if you haven't purchased enough bottles.

One enthusiast we know disdains this approach, claiming that having to drink the same wine twice amounts to a deprivation of experience. We understand the rationale behind such a promiscuous attitude, but when it comes time to match a wine to a particular dish, or pull out something for a special occasion, it's awfully annoying not to have a single bottle of wine on hand that you've tasted before. Besides, drinking wines only once is like meeting people only once: unless they're very superficial, you can't say you really know them. There is a particular pleasure to be had in following fine wines as they change and develop over the years, and a parallel satisfaction in having a cellar stocked with familiar favorites. (Of course, no one wants the forced intimacy of drinking the same old thing every night— there has to be enough variety to prevent boredom.)

Another advantage of buying in case lots, apart from the discounts offered, is the containers they come in. Wooden Bordeaux boxes make ideal storage crates. And frankly, any wines that won't be ready to drink for five to ten years are better off boxed and stashed away; you'll be less tempted to drink a wine before its time if it's inaccessible. For that reason, storing wines off the premises, with, say, a retailer who offers such a service or in a temperature-controlled warehouse has obvious advantages. For current drinking, however, you'll certainly want a large sturdy rack with individual slots for odd bottles, so that you can put your hands on the bottle you want without disturbing others.

And that brings us to our cardinal rule for beginning collectors of all types: *Don't buy more wine than you plan to drink.* To beginning collectors that may seem laughable advice. But few collectors, even those who only buy a few cases of a wine they like, give much thought to *when* they're going to get around to uncorking all the bottles they're so eagerly acquiring. The hunger for more, always more, vinous experience, feeds the acquisitive itch—that ravening desire to have endless bottles to hoard and pat and plan their glorious sacrifice at the dinner table. No true wine lover thinks he can be *overexposed* to wine. Thus, in many instances acquisition eventually outstrips a wine lover's consumption (and that of his guests), which is why estates are the sources of a significant share of the offerings at wine auctions. Few connoisseurs determine their needs as neatly as André Simon did; he is said to have died with only two bottles of wine left in his cellar.

COPING WITH STORAGE

In summer a wine lover's fancy darkly turns to thoughts like: *Is the heat ruining my wines?* This disturbing notion occurs to practically anyone who has a few bottles of something special set aside under conditions far different than the cool, damp, cobwebbed cellars extolled as the ideal by many wine authorities.

Take a friend of ours who never fretted about the niceties of storing wine. Like many wine lovers, she bought bottles to drink, not gather dust. Then she uncharacteristically gave in to a momentary whim and bought a bottle of very expensive first-growth Bordeaux from a classic vintage because it was the year that she and her husband had been married. She thought it would be nice to drink it on their twenty-fifth wedding anniversary ten years hence. But once home with her prize, she was suddenly struck with the thought that putting it in the rickety wine rack on top of the refrigerator might not be ideal for long-term storage.

She understood the necessity of horizontal repose for wine bottled with corks—storing the bottle lying flat keeps the cork wet and tight, which in turn keeps air from entering the bottle and spoiling the contents. But, she wondered, what about temperature? Humidity? Was vibration a problem? She remembered allusions to "weeping bottles" and "cork weevils" in the wine books she'd dipped into and wondered if her purchase had been a mistake.

For her the solution was simple: squirrel the bottle away on its side in the fruit cellar—an area of their turn-of-the-century home they'd never previously thought of using for wine.

For those without access to a deep, naturally cool cellar, however, there is no simple solution to the problem of proper wine storage, yet it can't be ignored. Why? Because the conditions under which a wine is stored affect its quality in the glass when it is finally consumed.

It's long been known that with time, wines in bottles change, losing certain characteristics associated with youth—freshness or fruitiness, for example—which is why the vast majority of the world's wines are best consumed young. Certain fine wines, however, improve in bottle, gaining desirable characteristics—a complex bouquet, for example—that more than make up for loss of freshness.

Storage is most critical in the case of fine, expensive wines that require years to mature, because there's more to gain—and lose— in terms of quality. Besides, when the wine is expensive, it's foolish not to ensure that you'll get all the potential quality out of it when you consume it. But it's important to realize as well that *all* wines benefit from proper storage conditions and suffer from poor ones. Even a jug wine will begin to fade in flavor if stored in a hot place for a few months.

Curiously enough, while a good deal of wine lore exists concerning the ideal conditions for storing wine, only in recent years has any of it been substantiated by scientific research. One man responsible for such confirmation is Professor Vernon Singleton of the Department of Enology and Viticulture at the University of California at Davis. For over two decades he has been studying the effects of aging on wine. When we spoke with him by phone, he explained that the rate at which the various chemical changes—such as oxidation, precipitation of tannin, and evolution of esters—responsible for the development of the wine's quality occur depends on temperature. Singleton described the following as a "good rule of thumb": Chemical reaction rates *double* with each 18 degrees Fahrenheit (10 degrees centigrade) increase in temperature. In other words, a wine stored at 75 degrees Fahrenheit will age twice as fast as a wine stored at 57 degrees.

The idea that you could speed up the aging process and thus drink wines that normally require lengthy aging sooner rather than later sounds appealing. Why wait twenty years to enjoy your '75 Bordeaux if they can be just as good in ten years? But will they be just as good?

"You can probably cut aging time in half," Professor Singleton told us. "But the problem with accelerating the process is that you run the danger of missing the wine's zenith of quality." Cool storage is better because it ensures that the wine's aging curve is extended over a longer period of time, which means a lengthy "plateau" of maturity and a *gradual* descent into deterioration. Warm storage conditions result in a sharp, exaggerated curve of development—and that means a precipitous downhill slide once the wine has reached maturity. If you don't catch the wine at its peak, you'll find it "over the hill" in short order.

More importantly, there is a point beyond which a wine's maturation cannot be accelerated without deleterious effects on its quality. "I would consider seventy degrees Fahrenheit about the maximum I'd recommend for home storage," Singleton allowed, adding that "under sixty-eight degrees would be safer, particularly for fruity white wines." We've found, to our sorrow, that within a year or two whites stored at temperatures in the eighties end up tasting flat and lifeless, while reds often develop an unpleasant cooked taste.

Some wine enthusiasts will argue that you can get away with hotter temperatures than 70 degrees, and we've had a few bottles that, considering the way they were kept, should have been vinegary ghosts and instead were defiantly superb. But storage over 70 degrees is always a gamble. We've had far more bottles of prematurely decrepit wines—wines that had lost their vibrancy by stewing through several hot summers.

Steadiness of temperature is another important consideration. Daily ups and downs on the Fahrenheit scale will turn the sturdiest Cabernet into a tired, flat wine within months. Scientists now know that fluctuations in temperature—unless very gradual—affect the internal pressure inside wine bottles and result in shifting (and "weeping") corks. This allows air to enter and excessive oxidation—and eventually, spoilage—to occur.

Steady, cool temperature is only half the battle. It isn't enough for your cellar to be cool; it should also be moist. The effect of humidity on a wine collection is often ignored, even though it can be critical. The problem is that its effects are subtle and are enhanced or diminished by variations in temperature.

What happens in very dry conditions is that the top of the cork dries out (even when the bottle is stored on its side), eventually breaking the essential seal between the cork and glass that prevents spoilage. If a dry environment is combined with daily fluctuations in temperature that change the internal pressure in the bottle, moving the cork and also endangering the seal, the stage is set for actual evaporation of wine. Wines held for a decade or more in a dry apartment will show startling amounts of ullage—excessive space between the cork and the level of the wine when the bottle is stood up—and the telltale dead, flat taste of prematurely oxidized wines.

A cool but excessively damp environment, even though it can encourage mold to grow and labels to disintegrate, is actually superior to an equally cool but dry environment when it comes to the conservation of wine. Any grand old wines that prove to be drinkable after a century or more invariably come from a damp cellar.

The lesson in all this? Keep a hydrometer as well as a thermometer by your wines and monitor the changes. (We use a $6 Taylor Humidiguide from our local hardware store.) Lacking any hard evidence on ideal humidity levels, we'd guess that 65 to 85 percent relative humidity is a good range. If you have a basement cellar you can always add a few basins of water during the winter or even get a dehumidifier if your labels start deteriorating from too much moisture. Anyone relying on mechanical means to control the temperature of his wines should be certain that humidity levels are satisfactory as well. According to other authorities, light and vibration exacerbate a wine's chemical breakdown, although cork weevils fortunately don't seem to be a problem on this side of the Atlantic.

The ideal, obviously, is to store wine where it can rest undisturbed at an unvarying temperature of around 55 degrees and high humidity, in total darkness. In other words, a sort of vinous time capsule.

But wine enthusiasts without such ideal storage conditions— even those living in studio apartments—shouldn't think there's no point in laying away a few cases.

Short of having a cool basement corner or fruit cellar that can be pressed into use, an interior closet is probably your best bet for wine storage, as it offers darkness and a place to keep the wine undisturbed. Resist the temptation to make your bottles of wine part of your decor. Choose a closet away from stairs (too much vibration). Avoid hot-water pipes and exterior walls, both of which can cause sudden changes in temperature. Check the temperature and its steadiness with a minimum-maximum thermometer; this will show you the highest and lowest temperatures reached since you last set it. There should be no more than a few degrees variance during any twenty-four hour period, though a slow rise and fall of temperature in a wider range from summer to winter is tolerable.

If the temperature in your closet exceeds 70 degrees or fluctuates excessively, it doesn't make sense to try to store *large* quantities of fine wine for very long. Concentrate instead on buying wines that you can enjoy within a year or two and that don't have to be aged to be at their best—sparkling wines, Beaujolais, and lighter Burgundies, *petits châteaux* from Bordeaux, most California wines, almost all white wines.

We know wine enthusiasts with a passion for collecting and aging fine wine but without proper storage facilities who resort to all sorts of strategies, from imposing on friends and relatives with cool basements to renting corners of fur vaults.

If you don't have trustworthy, teetotaling relatives with an empty fruit cellar, you can, as more and more enthusiasts are doing, turn to a temperature-controlled storage unit. Thanks to the miracle of modern technology, the steady, damp chill of a château's subterranean vault can be re-created in such unlikely spots as a beachfront condominium in South Florida—albeit at a price. From our unscientific survey of users of the various units available—which store from 72 to nearly 2,000 bottles—we'd say they appear to do what they claim to do—store wine under optimum temperature and humidity conditions.

Unfortunately, buying and operating these temperature-controlled units can run into money, and for this reason we'd say they're for the passionate collector of expensive wine, not the average consumer. One typical unit costs $2,000 and stores 200 bottles. That's an initial investment of $10 *per bottle*. Some smaller-capacity units are even less economical—one costs $2,500 and holds only 100 bottles—that's *$25* per bottle. (The largest-capacity units offer the lowest per-bottle storage cost—down to about $5 apiece.) Many wine lovers would simply prefer to spend their dollars on more or better wine.

Often consumers who purchase these units don't realize that start-up costs are just the beginning, only gradually discovering that the hidden costs of running them can be very high. It may cost over a dollar per bottle per year to operate one of these units in some parts of the United States where electricity rates are steep—such as New York City. (Converting refrigerators or pressing air-conditioned rooms into service won't result in significantly lower operating costs, and such makeshift solutions often don't work properly—air conditioners freeze over, for instance, and refrigerators vibrate.

Consumers who own these units have told us that the small size of most of them is another drawback. Here's an example: Take one unit on the market that costs $2,500 and holds 100 bottles—just enough space to store, say, a case of each of the eight first-growths of Bordeaux from the excellent '85 vintage now on the market. Let's suppose a collector then closes the door for the fifteen years the wines need for proper maturation. At the end of that time, he would have to figure the wine cost at roughly $40 per bottle (for storage), in addition to the initial price of the wine. Furthermore, he wouldn't have had any space for storing other wines during the years spent waiting for these Bordeaux to mature. Buy a bigger unit? Certainly, if your collection or collecting ambitions warrant it. The cost of temperature-controlled storage is well worth it for any substantial, particularly valuable wine collection. It's essential, after all, to protect the value of your investment, and the cost of keeping it cool may be small in relation to the value of the wines.

INVESTING IN WINE

. . . 1947 Cheval Blanc, $4,000 a case . . . 1929 Mouton in jeroboam, $5,800 . . . 1979 Pétrus, $1,500 a case, up $100 from last month . . .

If there were such a thing as a ticker tape for the fine-wine market, it would probably read just like that, a litany of dizzying figures documenting the extraordinary rise in the price of certain fine wines, not just rare wines at auction but recent vintages as well. It's no wonder that some retailers have started to sound more like aggressive stockbrokers peddling hot issues than merchants advising on wines for your next dinner party. *Wine is a hot collectible* is the not-so-subtle pitch; one retailer took out a full-page ad in *The New York Times* to offer 1961 Lafite for $3,600 a case. The very same wine, the ad hammered home, would have cost you a mere $50 a dozen in 1964. Figures like these are giving many wine amateurs the idea that collecting wine might be a very profitable hobby indeed.

We tried out some of our thoughts on investing in the grape on John Train, president of Train, Smith, Investment Counsel, in his New York office. Train, the author of several books on investment and an expert on collectibles, began by dismissing the idea of amateurs buying wine for resale at a profit with the air of someone used to deflating overoptimistic financial schemes.

But, we pointed out, obviously there are profits to be made in various aspects of the wine trade, so why aren't there profits to be made by investing in fine wines, buying at retail for the purpose of eventual resale? "Let's be precise," Train insisted. "What we're talking about is wine *speculation,* not *investment.* An investment offers you a return out of an ascertainable cash flow— an investment in a business, for example. A speculation is when you put your money on something and hope it will go up."

And, we conceded, wine prices haven't always advanced steadily in the past two decades. The pace-setting red Bordeaux in particular have had impressive ups—but also downs. Train went over to his files. "I remember in the early seventies—this was before the big slide in wine prices in 1973–1974—I used to walk past a retail wine shop on Seventy-second Street that actually displayed for months a sign in the window that said: 'IT'S A FACT—WINE PRICES ALWAYS GO UP!' I couldn't resist taking a picture. . . ." Train leafed through a folder and paused. "Yes, here it is," he said, tapping it with his finger. He closed the drawer. "A few months later wine prices fell dramatically." We remember well, in fact, that during the 1973–1974 period, 1970 Château Mouton-Rothschild was offered at $13 a bottle.

Of course, a knowledgeable collector, anticipating at that point the eventual recovery of the Bordeaux market, would have done well with that particular wine—it's now over $100 a bottle retail.

That knowledgeable people can make profits in wine is something of which Train is well aware. With several partners, he bought Château Malescasse, a *cru bourgeois* estate in the Haut-Médoc, in 1970, "when it was a buyer's market." He went on to explain, "My partners and I developed it to a point that when it was sold in 1979 the investment paid off nicely—we roughly tripled our money. I must admit, however, that if I hadn't been in the investment business and owed it to my colleagues to do well for them financially, I never would have sold. Wine," he added, "is a way of life." It struck us that for many interested in wine, the act of *collecting* it has become a way of life, and for many more, an aspiration.

But for Train—who has spent a great deal of time analyzing the price history of "collectibles"—collecting should not be confused with investing, much less speculation. Collecting offers personal satisfactions, but very rarely financial rewards. "You can only become a great collector," he said, "when you're passionately interested in something and buy it when it's affordable." And, he went on to say, the same possessive passion that motivates your collecting also prevents you from selling. Not surprisingly, his advice on collecting modern art (it applies equally well to wine) is: "Buy what you love and want to keep, and not what you hope to sell to somebody else."

We've long maintained that it only makes sense to lay down wine for future pleasure. If you buy fine wine when good vintages first come on the market, you can select while wines are relatively cheap and available and enjoy them years later at the peak of their maturity. For some collectors it adds a certain frisson to be drinking a scarce, twenty-year-old wine whose original cost was a small fraction of its current price tag. For others, however, those hoarded bottles now worth hundreds apiece begin to take on a value quite removed from vinous considerations.

But had we laid the wine-as-profitable-collectible question to rest? What about the wine collector who has made some shrewd—or excessive—purchases? Why wouldn't it make sense for him to cash in, if only to finance further purchases? And if that's reasonable, we wondered, then why wouldn't it be reasonable to purchase wine with the initial intention of selling some of it eventually, with the goal of using such profits to build a wine collection?

The idea of developing a wine cellar "by its own bootstraps" is an attractive one. But Train was skeptical of an amateur's ability to pick wines that would appreciate significantly in value. "Looking with hindsight at certain wines that have risen spectacularly is like interviewing a number of people who live to be a hundred—you might come to think there were a lot of them, instead of one in a million."

True enough, we admitted; it's easy today to look back and say the 1961 Bordeaux were absurdly cheap in the midsixties, and that if you had bought them then, you would be able to sell them now at a fabulous profit. But was that so apparent back then? In fact, it wasn't. Many who remembered the prices of the 1950s regarded the '61s as overpriced—and didn't buy.

Now it's become clear—as it wasn't to many people then—that what has been sharpening the scissors of supply and demand for certain classic wines is an ever-growing, worldwide interest in fine wine, and the existence of certain factors—vintage-to-vintage variation, legal constraints on yields, and so on—that limit production and/or exacerbate scarcity and cause prices to rise.

Consider the factor of constant consumption. Wine is a collectible with a difference: To enjoy it you have to consume it. There is no way you can have your Pétrus and drink it, too. This creates a dilemma that will continue to affect auction prices for all older wines. Every time someone pulls the cork on a '47 Cheval Blanc, the number of bottles extant dwindles. At the same time, the number of people who want to sample famous wines from legendary vintages constantly grows. With a dwindling supply and an ever-increasing demand, prices inevitably climb.

But for every fine wine? Those wines that are of intense interest today may not be the focus of intense interest tomorrow. Yet, on analysis, we think that the wines that have so far commanded top prices from collectors seem to share certain characteristics: They are individual wines of specific character and hence in limited supply; they are not overly esoteric wines but have a clearly defined image and reputation; they last and improve with age.

With these thoughts in mind, we continued our discussion at The Four Seasons over a lunch of grilled pompano and a bottle of the magnificent '76 Laville-Haut-Brion. The only honest way, we all agreed, to test the hypothesis that a knowledgeable collector could purchase wines today whose prices might rise significantly in the future would be to develop a portfolio of selections and keep track of their shifts in value. Train pointed out, however, that the problem with a hypothetical wine account is that on paper everything works as it can only in a fictional world: The desired wines are always available, purchased at the lowest possible cost and sold at the peak; bottles are never damaged or broken; storage is no problem—a file folder will do.

In reality, wine collecting has considerable practical difficulties: Wine bottles are fragile and so are their contents; corks can be unreliable; labels get torn off; an auction purchase arrives with a bottle missing; and proper storage conditions—essential for the conservation of fine wine—can be costly. And perhaps the most significant stumbling block for the collector who hopes to cash in is that wine, ironically, is *not* a very liquid asset. Virtually the only legal means for individuals in the United States without retail or wholesale licenses to dispose of wine is through wine auctions, which are held only infrequently in this country. By the end of lunch, we all came to the conclusion that, in our professional capacities as investment counselor and wine critics, we'd have to regard wine speculation as financially foolhardy.

In our strictly private capacities as wine lovers, however, we were still intrigued and decided to indulge in a modest experiment: The three of us would constitute "The Wine Syndicate," Train adding his financial acumen to the Walkers' wine expertise. We would actually buy some wines we thought would rise in value (basing our choices on a serious analysis of wine and market factors), see what happened, and report with ruthless accuracy on the results—broken bottles, cost of storage, profit or loss, and so on. We agreed not to purchase larger quantities of wine than we would be happy to end up drinking ourselves. "Liquidations" of our purchases would take place at auction (for a cash gain, we hoped) or at table (a dollar debit, but a pleasure profit).

Most important of all, we needed a buying strategy. "In my business," Train had said earlier, "you spend your time figuring out what makes sense and what no one else is doing." Exactly. Most people's idea of what to buy in wine, as in anything else, is what everyone else is buying, not stopping to consider that the time to have bought the wines now in greatest demand—Lafite, Pétrus, etc.—was *before* they became the vinous equivalent of "glamour stocks," fashionable and priced accordingly. Fashion is an element that can't be ignored, however, as the price a wine fetches in the open market is only partially determined by its taste qualities. Reputation, scarcity, and the changing patterns of taste in collecting and consumption all play a role in conferring cachet on certain wines and a negative image on others.

Thus, in selecting wines for The Wine Syndicate, we followed Train's general dictum: "Investment opportunity consists of the difference between perception and reality." That meant concentrating on those wines that not only would repay cellaring in tasting terms ("the reality") but also were generally underappreciated ("the perception") and hence undervalued in the marketplace ("the opportunity"). Between two undervalued wines of equal merit, we would choose the one most likely to be revalued upward in the marketplace—become fashionable—more quickly.

In looking for wine investment opportunities, we were looking for wines that had the potential of becoming collectibles because more and more people would want them.

Some undervalued wines, despite their quality, are unlikely ever to become collectibles because they are simply too obscure (like Eastern European wines), or too hard to understand (like many German wines), or they may just have an unexciting image (like Portuguese reds). None of this prevents these wines from having devoted fans willing to seek them out, master their complexities, and serve them with pride. But they are likely to remain specialists' wines.

Consider, on the other hand, classified-growth Bordeaux. They have a centuries-old reputation and a track record of quality. Their relative availability, simple nomenclature, and built-in classifications make them easy to find, easy to know, and easy to collect. No wonder there's a worldwide cult of claret.

While we thought it still possible to do well, in investment terms, with red Bordeaux, it hardly qualified as an undiscovered category. We were dubious of the advice offered by many wine merchants that Bordeaux is always a great investment. Such advice seems to be based on the "greater fool" theory—that no matter how much you pay for Bordeaux, someone out there will be willing to take it off your hands for even more. But that scenario depends on ever-swelling numbers of new, well-heeled converts to fine wine—perhaps a questionable assumption, given that wine is a luxury, not a necessity.

But what about speculating in wines that *may* become classics? Here, too, advice from retail quarters has been anything but sage. During the mid-1970s, when California wines were making headlines by topping French wines in blind tastings, California Cabernet Sauvignons, particularly from the much-talked-about '74 vintage, were touted as liquid gold. Today, many of those wines haven't lived up to early expectations. Part of the problem was that there was no way to know how these bottlings from brand-new wineries would age. (As many have found out, banking on wines with little previous history is risky.) As a consequence, only a few—such as the '74 Heitz Cellars "Martha's Vineyard"—have proven good investments. Many of the others have maintained elevated prices only at charity auctions, where high bids may have little to do with actual quality or demand. California collectors now choose their Cabernets very carefully or simply ignore the investment angle.

Obviously, we had to look for wines that last. If a wine is too short-lived, not enough time elapses between its first appearance on the market and its decline in taste quality for supply and demand forces to have an effect.

The ability to age well eliminated from consideration any wines that wouldn't keep and improve in the bottle, no matter how fashionable or soon-to-be-fashionable. For example, we saw no sense in stockpiling Champagne (unless we planned to auction it off to the English, who have a taste for faded fizz).

Naturally, we considered only those whites—mostly sweet—that can be counted on to last a decade or more in the bottle. Sauternes were the obvious choice in this category, not only because they appeared undervalued but because they last at least as long as clarets and are well-established, classic wines. We were on the lookout for the odd bargain case of wine from an older vintage, but initially we purchased wines still generally available in New York in February of 1982. By the fall of that year, the Syndicate's portfolio consisted of the following case lot purchases:

First, "blue chips": red Bordeaux. We picked Château Margaux '78 and '79, at that time relatively undervalued for a first-growth at $420 and $310 per case respectively. We added '78 Château Pichon-Lalande at $200, '78 Château Léoville-Las-Cases at $210, '78 Château Prieuré-Lichine at $99, '78 Château Beychevelle at $156 and the '75 at $270.

Second, "growth stocks": Sauternes, Barsac, and Vintage Port. Classic dessert wines were still out of fashion and undervalued, but we detected signs of renewed interest. Our choices: '75 Château Climens at $255, '75 Château Coutet at $144 and the '71 at $192; in Port, the '77 Taylor-Fladgate at $225, '77 Warre at $144 and the '63 at $350.

Third, "speculative issues": California Cabernet Sauvignon. Picking tomorrow's classic labels from the welter of offerings is like trying to pick which solar-energy stock will be the Xerox of the future. We settled on the '78 Clos du Val ($130) and the '78 Stag's Leap Wine Cellars Lot #2 ($175) on the basis of aging potential and reputation.

We doubted our selection constituted *investment* advice—the dollar gain of our selections was purely speculative. We were confident, however, that such wines represented first-class wine-making and good value for the price, and if well-stored, would be magnificent drinking in ten to fifteen years.

As for the rest, only time would tell.

ANNALS OF THE WINE SYNDICATE

By the beginning of 1983 the wine trade was nervous. We heard a great deal of talk about the "dollar-to-franc ratio," the "coming shakeout in California wine," the "end of the wine boom," and other notions that seemed to suggest the bottom was about to drop out of the wine market. True enough, we saw a good many French wines at very competitive prices, and growth in wine consumption slowed down. There was talk that the California wine industry in particular would be hit hard as a result.

Those developments spelled stable or even declining wine prices in 1983 for all but the very finest wines. But we saw no evidence of any softening at the top of the wine pyramid; the prices of the finest Burgundies, top California Cabernets, and Bordeaux *crus classés,* for example, continued to show the upward pressure of sustained demand.

This was clear later on when we were able to review The Wine Syndicate's acquisitions. In fact, the value of the Syndicate's holdings increased some 23 percent in nine months, which illustrated that certain fine wines were still showing a significant upward trend.

We concluded that even the "worst-case scenario"—falling wine prices brought about by a growing European wine lake and panic dumping by large corporations stuck with huge amounts of unsold and costly inventory—would be unlikely to affect the prices of recent top Bordeaux vintages ('75, '76, and '78) still available in retail shops.

Others in the wine trade seemed to think the possibility of a dramatic fall in prices was remote. They foresaw stable—or only slightly declining—French wine prices.

We reviewed these and other current developments with John Train over lunch. What did they mean in terms of investing in wine? Since we were encouraged by the fact that some very fine wines continued to increase in price, we resolved to look for more undervalued fine wines in scarce supply. One area that intrigued us was dry white Bordeaux; there are only a handful of châteaux that produce substantial white wines intended for long aging, and at their best these wines rival the great white Burgundies. They had yet to become as fashionable or expensive, but there were signs of increased interest among collectors. We decided to add an undeniably classic Graves, the 1978 Château Laville-Haut-Brion ($324 a case, but already rising in price).

We finished lunch with some cheese and a second glass of the Stag's Leap Wine Cellars' marvelous 1978 Cabernet Sauvignon, and we felt pleased that the Syndicate had salted away a case of the even finer Lot #2, as well as some Clos du Val Cabernet Sauvignon from the same vintage. These two wineries, we felt, were among the small, fine California wine producers that could survive the widely predicted shakeout among California wineries.

A year later, in January 1984, the wine market was awash with bargains. We'd been told by the wine trade for at least a year that the bottom had been reached and that wine prices were sure to climb. But for a variety of reasons, prices of most European wines continued to represent remarkable values for the consumer, as did some California wines. 1981 Château Pichon-Lalande was $10 a bottle; Sterling Vineyards Merlot, $7.50.

The big question for The Wine Syndicate in 1984 was, how long would these bargain prices last? That depended on how long the factors that drove prices down—among them the flattening of growth in U.S. wine consumption, the strength of the dollar in comparison with European currencies, and the size of stocks of unsold wine in Europe and California—continued to exert pressure. Then there were the effects of the 1983 vintage, which looked promising in Europe but less so in California.

We suspected those price levels wouldn't hold much longer. If you looked at the very top end of the market and the prices paid for the finest European and California bottlings, you would almost have thought the above factors were *not* at work. Strictly from an investment point of view, many fine wines from both areas seemed virtually immune to the ups and downs of the market as a whole. Back in mid-1982, when we purchased the experimental portfolio of fine wines, we set out to test the thesis of whether carefully selected fine wines, purchased at retail, would appreciate significantly in price. Our particular selections *all* rose significantly, and some other choices would have done equally well. For example, The Wine Syndicate initially invested heavily in 1978 Bordeaux, which was then very attractively priced. When we decided to diversify our holdings, we "liquidated" five cases of wine (four cases of 1978 Bordeaux second-growths and a case of '78 Clos du Val Cabernet Sauvignon), trading them for credit at the store where they had been purchased and stored, for a paper profit of 23 percent in twelve months (not bad), and bought three cases of '82 futures (Lafite, Mouton, and Ducru-Beaucaillou), which in the case of the Lafite, rose sharply in price. It remained to be seen if we would have done better to have held on to our '78s instead. (The Château Pichon-Lalande rose about 30 percent over the same time period.)

The British wine trade was waxing enthusiastic over the '82 vintage, and some in the Bordeaux trade went so far as to term the wines "perfection." That sort of talk whipped many American wine lovers, eager to be bedazzled by visions of ultimate wines, into a buying frenzy. According to one trade source, an unheard of 40 percent of the '82 Bordeaux crop had already been presold as futures (normally only 10 percent is sold in this fashion). Certain châteaux with small productions, such as Pétrus, were said to be unavailable or even oversold.

We noted, however, that the classic '77 Vintage Ports from top houses such as Taylor, Fonseca, Graham, or Warre were still available at around $20 a bottle, but we predicted they wouldn't be for much longer. If recent price increases for older vintages of Port were any indication of newly awakened interest in this classic wine, Vintage Port, long underappreciated in America, wouldn't continue to be ignored by collectors and drinkers in the future. As an experiment, The Wine Syndicate sold off some '63 Vintage Port (purchased back in 1982) at Christie's auction in Chicago in October of 1983 for a 44 percent profit. Understandably, we regretted not having bought more!

By mid-1984, in fact, we realized that Vintage Port was due for a major revival. Back in 1982 we had been unsure of the potential demand in this country for this powerful fortified wine. Now that the signs were clear, the Syndicate took a major position: ten cases from the 1963, 1970, and 1977 vintages.

By the end of 1985, we had traded a portfolio that consisted largely of Bordeaux for one that was now half Vintage Port. Along the way, we drank some wonderful bottles, too. (Well, there was no reason to make it a dull, dry exercise.) After expenses and personal liquidations, we estimated the remaining twenty cases were worth, at auction, 50 percent more than the original investment three years earlier.

Apart from three cases of '82 Bordeaux purchased as futures that had doubled in value (Lafite, Mouton, and Ducru-Beaucaillou), Vintage Port proved to have been the syndicate's wisest choice. In fact, we realized then that from a purely financial point of view we should have put *all* our money on Vintage Port from the beginning. The signs were there: a classic wine, produced only in the better years by a small group of shippers, not yet discovered by the American market . . . and its keeping ability is legendary.

Our only hesitation at the time about its investment potential was that, fabulous as it is, it's a wine drunk after meals, not with them, and we wondered how strong the American demand for that sort of thing could be. We should have looked more closely at the figures. Only about 250,000 cases of Vintage Port are produced in a year when most of the Port shippers "declare" a vintage (that is, when they decide to offer a Port from a single year,

which happens only about three times a decade). That's about
the total production of the top dozen Bordeaux châteaux. Such a
small market is sensitive to even modest increases in demand, and
the surge in Vintage Port prices has been dramatic.

Prices for remaining '63s (a very great vintage) available at
retail in this country doubled in 1984/85, and a $75 price tag
became commonplace. When you consider that '63 for Vintage
Port is the equivalent of '61 in Bordeaux, it was clear prices
could go *much* higher for good vintages of these wines.

We could have made an additional investment in Vintage
Port at that point, but we decided against it. Ours was intended
to be a passive investment after all, not one that would require
frequent attention or active trading. So far, the balance of the
Syndicate's portfolio hadn't been too dissimilar from what a collector might have purchased purely for future drinking, and we
wanted to keep it that way to underscore what an amateur might
accomplish with well-chosen selections—and the passage of time.
So we decided to hold our current selections for further appreciation.

As we got nearer to the fifth anniversary of our experiment,
however, we made the painful decision to put our thesis—that
carefully selected fine wines purchased at retail would appreciate
significantly in price—to an actual test. We packed up the majority of our collection for sale, and off it went to Christie's in
Chicago for auction November 8, 1986. When Michael Broadbent, the wine auctioneer, banged down the hammer on the last
of seventeen lots listed as "the property of a wine-collecting syndicate," the three of us felt reasonably smug. Every parcel sold
for more than we had paid; some went for double our original
cost.

So, even after paying commissions, temperature-controlled
warehouse storage, delivery and insurance charges, the three
of us still recovered our total capital outlay of $7,500. Along the
way we drank some lovely bottles (1971 Château Coutet, etc.)
for which we had paid $588, and we were still sitting on three
cases of 1982 Bordeaux (Château Mouton-Rothschild, Lafite-

Rothschild, and Ducru-Beaucaillou), then worth around $2,800, and had a cash balance of $362.95. In all, our syndicate had shown a 50 percent gain on its purchases.

A spectacular investment? Not really. During the same five-year period we would have earned a better overall return in a good mutual fund or even in tax-exempt bonds. But the original goal, of course, wasn't purely financial. What we really wanted to determine—by actually buying, developing, and selling a wine cellar—was whether the price appreciation of well-chosen wines could, at least in part, pay for consumption.

Clearly it can. But we still think the ultimate hedge is to do as we did and buy only those wines you'd be happy to drink yourself.

6

Wine at the Table

WINE WITH FOOD IN FRANCE

The view of the Eiffel Tower at sunset from our table at Morot-Gaudry on the Rue de la Cavalerie was dramatic and impressive, as was the wine list. After quickly choosing the *menu suggestion,* we took our time savoring the various wine possibilities and discussing them with the sommelier before selecting the '62 La Mission Haut-Brion (superb, as it turned out). "And a half-bottle of the Bollinger to start," we added, feeling the evening called for effervescence.

The sommelier looked thoughtful. "May I suggest a wine to follow the Champagne? You see, there is the salmon course to consider. . . ." His recommendation was a 1979 Savennières (a dry Loire white made from Chenin Blanc). The sip before the salmon arrived was a disappointment—a pleasant but unexciting wine, we decided. But our opinion shifted as we drank it with food: It seemed to gain in depth because its flavorful tang perfectly complemented the richness of the salmon.

The wine didn't change; our perception of it did. That experience and several similar ones in restaurants on a recent trip to France brought home to us once again the importance of evalu-

ating wines in the presence of food. It's not surprising that we
should be thinking about this in France, as the French have a
long tradition of drinking wine with their meals. For them, finding suitable wines to go with particular dishes has become a
highly developed art. Again, we wondered whether the way wines
are often evaluated and judged—on their own or against other
wines—while necessary for any objective analysis, doesn't miss
the larger aspect of *appreciating* wine. Wine, after all, is intended
to accompany food. No matter how good or bad a wine tastes on
its own, it's how that wine tastes with food that counts, because
that's the way we consume virtually all wines.

At another fine Parisian restaurant, l'Olympe, the sommelier
suggested an inexpensive Bourgogne-Passe-Tout-Grains (a very
light red blend of Pinot Noir and Gamay) to go with the first
course. It was not a wine we would have picked for its individual
merits. Yet he was thinking of the food the wine was to go
with—baked oysters—and the fact that we had ordered a 1971
Mazis-Chambertin (Faiveley) to accompany the breast of duck.
Served chilled, his choice was delightful with the oysters and a
fine prelude to a great Burgundy.

Additional lessons in the ways in which wines seem different
with food were in store for us at Restaurant Paul Bocuse in Lyon,
where we joined a group of journalists at an elaborate nine-
course dinner hosted by Moët & Chandon. We began with magnums of Dom Pérignon Rosé 1969 and caviar and ended hours
later finding room—somehow—for just one more Lyonnaise chocolate. The dinner wines, chosen by Georges Duboeuf, the respected
Beaujolais shipper, included his own first-rate 1979 Pouilly-Fuissé.
But we were puzzled that Duboeuf had picked a still immature
wine, a 1969 Côte Rôtie "La Mouline" (E. Guigal), for the
main course. We tried this superb, concentrated wine without
food and found its mouth-coating tannin excessive. After tasting
it with the rich *canard de Bresse à la broche,* however, another
wine-with-food principle emerged: Wines that seem imbalanced
on their own—very acidic or tannic, for example—may harmo-
nize with a dish that needs just the accent or contrast the taste
elements of that wine provide.

Then there was the dessert wine, a 1949 Château Gilette. This pale, Cognac-colored Sauternes, with its faint nose and dry fruity flavor, seemed quite unimpressive until we tasted it alongside something called "Dessert du Printemps." The Gilette's low sugar level and monotone flavor showed off Bocuse's stunning selection of unusual fruit sorbets marvelously. One more wine-with-food principle: The best wine and food combination isn't necessarily a great wine with a great dish, even at a grand dinner.

When we drink wine *with* food we enjoy a wider range of tastes and types of wine precisely *because* they go well with certain foods. Although we try to keep the ultimate destiny of wines in mind when evaluating them on their own, it takes direct experimentation—trial and error at the dinner table—to discover just which wines and which dishes together make satisfying combinations. We hope it won't take us centuries of experience with our own American wines—oaky Chardonnays, fruity Zinfandels, tannic Petite Sirahs, and all the rest—to arrive at the kind of felicitous food matchings the French have found for their wines.

WINE WITH FOOD IN ITALY

One of the great pleasures of eating and drinking in Italy is the ease and naturalness with which wine and food are enjoyed together. As you travel, you become aware that you're in a country where wine is omnipresent. Everywhere you look there seem to be vines growing; wine flows without comment (few countries have a higher per capita consumption), unless comment is called for, and it is a constant delight to find that wines are so often served with foods that complement them, and vice versa.

We've always thought that the best way to understand the

wines of a region is to taste them on their home ground, and during a recent trip to the classic wine regions of Tuscany (the home of Chianti and Brunello) and Piedmont (famed for Barolo and Barbaresco), we decided that this is particularly true for Italian wines. In these traditional wine regions, where the local cuisine and the winemaking are centuries old and long intertwined, there is a natural affinity between the two, so much so that one comes to believe that it isn't possible to understand either completely in isolation. How, when, and with what the people of the region enjoy their wine makes one appreciate the individualities of the wine in a way that no grasp of its technical aspects—no matter how detailed—will reveal.

Critics of Italian wine sometimes say that the Italians are casual about wine; it would be more accurate to say that they have a sense of proportion about it—they don't regard it as something to be created for its own sake, but as an accompaniment to food. It's not surprising, therefore, that Italian wines often show their best in the natural context of dining.

Even when talking about wine with Italian winemakers, we noticed that this sense of proportion prevails. Certainly there were the technical questions in the cellars, samplings from vat and barrel, thoughtful assessments before spitting into the drains, followed by scribbling in notebooks. But more often the "serious" wine talk waited for the table when the wine's merits could be meditated upon in its proper setting, as its various aspects were revealed in the course of a meal and against different foods.

In fact, when looking over our notes from our trip, we realized that our most memorable wine experiences couldn't be summarized in the notes we'd taken on the bottles tasted. Oftentimes, the occasion and the accompanying food contributed as much to our overall appreciation of the wine as drinking it did.

Tuscany and Piedmont have a number of fine restaurants with excellent cellars of regional wines, and a leisurely lunch or dinner at several of them is one of the best ways to experience the local wines in their traditional context and enjoy the Italian approach to wine and food.

We spent one Sunday afternoon high in the Tuscan hills not

far from Siena with friends at a remarkable and elegant restaurant, Fattoria La Chiusa, in the tiny town of Montefollonico. The unhurried pace and the Italian predilection for letting the meal design itself around the occasion and simply develop from course to course encouraged us to try a series of local but very unusual wines paired with imaginative variations of traditional Tuscan dishes.

The first wine was an experimental blend of Trebbiano and Sangiovese, made into a white as pale as mineral water, and rather neutral—but a suitably subtle opening to what was to come from the kitchen and the cellar, which was to culminate in a classic pairing of roast veal and a sturdy 1968 Costanti Brunello di Montalcino.

Afterwards, in our reluctance to break the mood, we drifted outside to the tables in the courtyard to enjoy the warm late-afternoon sun, watch the children play, and fall into conversation with fellow diners. At that point, the proprietor produced his own startling, sweet, fragrant, pink-hued wine made from a grape known locally as the Fragola, or "strawberry," which turned out to be Clinton, a native North American Labrusca variety. How the grape got to Italy is obscure, but it continues to be made into wine and enjoyed. If Italians can't find the right dish for a wine, they can find the right occasion for drinking it.

In Siena itself we had a simple lunch of first-rate *cannelloni* and *nodino di vitello* at an outside table at a modest restaurant on the Piazza del Campo, Al Mangia. The waiter, seeing that we still had half a bottle left of the light but flavorful '73 Barbi Brunello di Montalcino, insisted on bringing us a chunk of a local Sienese cheese, an aged Pecorino, "for the wine." The match was inspired, in fact better than either of the components: To our taste, the Barbi Brunellos can be somewhat coarse and lack finesse, and the Pecorino could hardly be described as an elegant cheese. But the combination was so savory, so perfect, that we were happy to linger over the last glassfuls and crumbs on our plates and watch the sun steal across the facade of the Palazzo Pubblico.

In Piedmont, we had more wine-with-food lessons in store for us. We'd come early to watch the sunset before having dinner at the Belvedere in the hilltop town of La Morra with its views over the vineyard-covered hills surrounding Alba, the source of Barolo. Soon after darkness fell, the restaurant became crowded with boisterous groups for whom tables were pushed together and who began enjoying rich Piedmontese fare and the heady local reds with infectious gusto, sharing dishes, bottles, and opinions. We joined in, and over filling dishes such as spinach flan with *fonduta e tartufi* and *risotto al Barolo,* we began to understand the Piedmontese tradition of a progression of reds, building in intensity of flavor from soft, fruity Dolcetto to a striking Barbera, which prepared the palate for the splendidly pungent Barolo that was the crowning wine of everyone's meal.

We had a chance to consider the Piedmontese approach to their wines from another perspective at a lunch at La Contea in neighboring Neive in the Barbaresco hills. This small restaurant, with its series of tiny rooms with fading prints and softly crackling fires, had the ambience of a prosperous farmer's home. The door to the kitchen was in constant motion as dish after brilliant dish emerged, competing for superlatives in our notes with a succession of perfectly chosen northern Italian wines. They culminated in a magnificent '75 Barolo Riserva Speciale Bussia di Monforte d'Alba (Bruno Giacosa), served with a marvelously rich roast veal. Again we were reminded that the classic Piedmontese reds show best against the background of Piedmontese cooking, which is about as far from *nuova cucina* as one can get. Tasted alone, or against insubstantial or delicate dishes, or even too soon in a meal, their marked pungency and power can often seem merely coarse and clumsy.

On the long flight home, we had ample time for reflection and wondered how that Barolo would have shown in the comparative tastings we'd had of Piedmontese reds in New York. In those tastings we'd found that much of the touted complexity of the wines consisted merely of roughness and rustic flavors due to excessive time in wood and high levels of volatile acidity. But would the Barolos we had thought technically "cleaner" and more polished in style have the character, the sheer gusto to stand up to the dishes Barolo is classically paired with? Could it even be argued that wines so intimately associated with their local cuisine—as in fact many Italian wines are—can't be expected to show particularly well except in the company of the right foods? If so, we wondered what this implies about the usual comparative tasting assessments of Italian wines—and whether they don't miss something essential about the wines.

FISH WINES:

DO THEY HAVE TO BE WHITE?

Always serve white wine with fish. Wine lovers who know little else about matching wine with food have heard this dictum and follow it religiously. To order red wine with fish has been thought almost a social blunder. We remember a James Bond movie in which 007 realizes as he is being strangled by the villain that he had been a fool to turn his back on someone who'd ordered Chianti with fish.

Until recently, when we began to research the question of what wines go best with various fish dishes, we'd never doubted the general validity of the white-wine-with-fish rule, in spite of the fact that it covered an awful lot of culinary territory and ignored some delicious exceptions (such as bouillabaisse with Bandol rosé). But dozens of experimental wine/fish pairings later, we have to report that our original belief that fish on the plate calls for white wine in the glass has been irreparably undermined: we now think that for some fish dishes, the best match is a red wine.

Gastronomically speaking, such a notion is hardly revolutionary (Parisians think nothing of drinking red wine with fish, as anyone who's dined at Le Bernardin knows). But many connoisseurs are dubious of the combination. A perusal of our wine book library revealed little support for our newfound contention, and in fact, much weighty opposition. The late André Simon flatly asserted that no red wine tasted good with fish. Well, we admit that it is easier to go awry with a red than a white when it comes to the fish course. Few white wine/fish combinations are actually unpleasant, while tannic reds in particular can taste peculiarly metallic after a bite of something finny. The trick, obviously, is to pick your red carefully.

Before the oyster-and-Chablis loyalists rise up in indignant protest, we hasten to concede that shellfish, by and large, call for the clean, crisp contrast of cold white wine, whether it's the savory single-note flavor of Muscadet against steamed clams or the mouth-filling richness of a California Chardonnay pointing up the flavor of cold cracked crab (a classic combination if there ever was one). But even with shellfish, it's possible to think red, and that brings us to the first of our principles for successful fish and wine matching:

Which wine one chooses depends more on the dish than the fish. You can't determine a suitable wine match merely by knowing the kind of fish. You have to know what's been done to it. Has it been grilled or poached? Simply broiled with a squeeze of lemon or highly seasoned, elaborately garnished, smothered in a cream sauce? Though it's important to know whether a fish is mild in flavor (tilefish, for example) or strong (such as mackerel), what really tells you that the accompanying wine should be delicate or forceful is the flavor of the total dish. Take shellfish: spicy, breaded baked clams marry happily with a dry, characterful rosé; Crab Imperial, with its rich cheese topping, can be enjoyed with a fine red—as we discovered recently when dining out. Our guest wanted calf's liver, so we ordered a '76 Château Lynch-Bages. To our surprise, we found that claret and crab (well, *that* dish anyway) sounds far odder than it tastes, and neither dish nor drink suffered by being consumed together.

With simply prepared delicate fish, stay with light white wines.

Sole *sans* sauce, for example, would be overpowered by a great Graves. Flounder, broiled red snapper, and other mild-flavored fish call for equally delicate but crisp whites, such as a German Riesling.

With flavorful, fatty fish, serve rich, assertive whites or light reds. We found bluefish, for example, requires an aggressive white (Sicilian, perhaps) or a light red (such as Italian Merlot) served slightly cool.

Swordfish and tuna, depending on their preparation, mate very well with either big whites or lean reds. Grilled medallions of tuna seem ideally matched with flavorful California Sauvignon Blanc, but at The Four Seasons' fourth annual Bordeaux dinner, we encountered medallions of tuna served with a red wine and tarragon sauce, this time served with a quartet of '81 red Bordeaux. The wines' youthful acerbity contrasted successfully with the intensity of the dish.

Salmon, too, can sing with red or white. At Lavin's in New York, we tried broiled baby coho with a range of top-class California wines and found the fish (with a mild fennel sauce) a fine match with a surprisingly wide range of wine flavors. Further experimentation at our own table convinced us that salmon's fatty, flavorful meat can either be complemented by round, rich whites (especially California Chardonnay) or contrasted with intense, fruity-sharp whites such as Vouvray or—for a different sort of contrast—low to moderately tannic reds such as Chinon. When served with a *beurre rouge* sauce, salmon is definitely a red wine dish. And Salmon Livornese, with its olive and caper garnish, needs a firm young red (lighter Bordeaux or Tuscan red).

Among the unexpected happy combinations we've enjoyed are smoked trout and Gewürztraminer and sushi with off-dry California Chenin Blanc. We've yet to try other seemingly odd couples suggested to us—turbot with sauce mousseline and Sauternes, mature Bordeaux and crayfish, Lake Garda trout and Valpolicella—but after all, who would want to rush a research project like that?

RED WINE, RED MEAT

Red meat calls for red wine. This piece of gustatory advice is endlessly repeated, rarely disputed, and hardly ever analyzed. Doubtless that's because this combination is successfully put to the test at mealtimes every day all over the world. So we decided to look a little deeper into some of the intricacies of this universally accepted food-and-wine match. To keep our investigation within reasonable bounds, we pinned down the meat end to beef—beef in its simplest, most unadorned form, broiled steak. (Any beef dish requiring more culinary ingenuity, we concluded, would merely confuse the issue.)

Requiring a wine list equal to the scope of our inquiry, we headed for our favorite steak house—Sparks, on East 46th Street in New York. Joining us in our research were Texas wine collector Dr. Marvin Overton and his wife, Sue, and on another occasion, poet and wine lover Daniel Halpern. At each session, the participants faced a row of wineglasses and a piece of steak tender and flavorsome enough to bring out the carnivore in all but the most hopeless vegetarian.

We were able to dismiss the question of whether white wine can be drunk with steak in a matter of minutes. Sure you can drink anything with anything, in a *physical* sense. But white wine flavors don't mesh with the taste of beef, even if in specific instances (we tried Chardonnay with the prime sirloin) they don't actually clash. In our view, with steak a white wine is reduced to the role of mere lubricant. As an aside, we ought to point out that a powerful, oaky Chardonnay will mate surprisingly well with rare baby lamb chops. But let's get back to beef.

Almost any dry red wine would probably accompany steak

reasonably well—provided you had only one choice on the table. When you try several distinctly different reds against steak, not surprisingly, you begin to notice distinct differences in how they contrast with, compete with, or complement the flavor and texture of the meat. Unlike cheese, which enhances reds and makes them taste richer, the savory flavors of a good steak can make a thin wine taste thinner. As Daniel Halpern pointed out at the end of one lunch, steak can be a tough partner. "The flavor of beef seems to spread apart the flavors of a wine—separate its components."

We'd tried several reds: a 1978 Côte Rôtie (André Drevon), a 1971 Borgogno Barolo Riserva, and a 1974 Hanzell Pinot Noir. The youthful awkwardness of the woody, powerful, almost plummy Rhône obscured its basic compatibility with the steak, while the Barolo—despite its maturity and fine, expansive flavors—seemed to coexist rather than interact with it. We thought the Barolo required a spicier dish (steak *au poivre?*). The Pinot Noir was superb, powerful but elegant, and its flavor was clearly in harmony with the beef. But to all of us it seemed too refined for the monochromatic richness of the sirloin—"like Catherine Deneuve playing opposite John Wayne," Halpern observed.

The classic match for beef is said to be Burgundy, particularly substantial specimens such as Corton or Chambertin, and clearly there *is* something about the meaty character of fine Pinot Noir that is synergistically complementary to the flavors of beef. But the seared flavors of broiled steak can overpower a light Burgundy, as we discovered with the Overtons, with whom we shared a light but well-balanced 1976 Beaune Premier Cru (Louis Latour). The tastes married well, but the subtleties of the wine were lost. Perhaps something that you sink your teeth into with gusto requires an equally fleshy wine—in other words, a bigger Burgundy. We found the Beaune went better with a trial dish of medallions of beef with mushrooms.

The least appealing match of the lunch, we all agreed, was the 1975 Clos du Val Cabernet Sauvignon. A fine wine in other contexts, it came off as a weedy, thin thing when it followed a bite of steak. We found this interesting, considering that the typically herbaceous, sometimes olive-y character of Cabernet Sauvignon—and Bordeaux—has a special affinity for more intensely flavored meats such as lamb and game.

But two other wines proved unexpectedly good as steak wines. A 1978 Ridge York Creek Zinfandel was marvelous. As Marvin Overton put it, "This Zinfandel's got what it takes to stand up to steak. I'd say it's an all-American match." We'd thought that the Zinfandel might be too fruity for steak, but it was clear that its spicy intensity explained the success of the pairing. So we tried another characterful, but this time straightforward, California wine: the 1978 Petite Sirah from Stag's Leap Wine Cellars—and discovered another outstanding combination. As Dr. Overton pointed out, the thick-textured Petite Sirah seemed to fall somewhere between the Burgundy and the Zinfandel, sharing some of the warmth of the former and the spice of the latter. Sue Overton summed up the consensus of the table: "If I were serving a fancy prime rib, I'd serve a fine Burgundy. But for charcoal-broiled steak, I'd pick a Zinfandel or Petite Sirah every time."

GAME WINES

Not long ago, game was a pretty exotic item on restaurant menus and—save in countrified settings where it was a seasonal treat—not often served at home. Now that's all changed. Having grazed to boredom on such trendy staples as range-fed chicken and mesquite-grilled salmon, today's adventurous eater can prowl the culinary frontier for all manner of game dishes, from breast of pheasant to civet of wild boar.

Those for whom eating doesn't become dining unless there's wine on the table should raise a glass to game's new popularity.

Let's face it, many contemporary food trends—Cajun, Southwest, Third World—lead to recipes liberally laced with exotic and incendiary spices. Whatever their gustatory value, too many of the dishes are flat-out wine killers. Game, by contrast, not only accommodates wine, it showcases it.

Yet people often pick the wrong wine for game dishes. Powerhouse reds of tooth-staining intensity invariably are recommended for all sorts of game preparations. Like the equally misleading notion that Chinese cuisine always calls for Gewürztraminer, such advice ignores the spectrum of different tastes and the variety of wine types needed to match them. This oversimplified rule of thumb also encourages the unwary to do silly things like smother a delicate quail dish with a big and brawny Barolo.

In an effort to clarify what goes with what, we offer a checklist of reminders, some hints on splendid combinations we've enjoyed, and some cautionary notes.

There's a wide range of flavors in game, and one type of wine won't match them all. Wild duck, especially if grilled, works best with a thicker-textured wine, such as a California Merlot (say, Jaeger-Inglewood) or Pomerol (Château Le Gay, for example). And wild boar, with its succulent taste that suggests a cross between pork and mutton, takes a more aggressive wine yet, such as a rich Rhône or Syrah. Dove, on the other hand, doesn't require such a concentrated wine. A deep, earthy Burgundy (we're thinking here of the 1985 Domaine Dujac Gevrey-Chambertin Les Combottes) perfectly echoes the bird's sweetly rich flavor.

Bear in mind that with few exceptions, the game on restaurant menus or in butcher shops in this country isn't truly wild but is raised on game preserves and ranches. It is a more consistent product than what comes from the woods and fields, though typically less intense in flavor. Sauces aside, farm-raised rabbits or pheasants can be chicken-mild and hence successfully matched with a suitably rich white, such as a top-class oak-aged California Chardonnay.

By contrast, the game that is served in European restaurants is generally wild, and its intensity is sometimes accentuated by its being hung (aged, essentially) to tenderize it. The strong, pungent, gamey flavor that results is best matched with meaty, gutsy reds. In Scotland we've dined on that classic game bird grouse, which had been hung in the traditional manner for a week, and found it perfectly suited to the direct, pointed flavors of a 1985 Côtes du Rhône.

Hanging game, however, is not a universal practice in Europe, particularly outside the British Isles, and many wild game dishes are flavorsome but subtle, tailor-made for pairing with the complex taste of older clarets. This is particularly true of game birds. At L'Escargot restaurant in London, we took the advice of wine author Jancis Robinson and her husband, Nick Lander, and reveled in the brilliant match of savory breast of wood pigeon with a splendid 1964 Clos Fourtet St.-Emilion.

Wild venison, whether from deer or antelope of any species, *can* be as mild as game-ranched versions. All have quite similar flavors, recalling the taste of mutton or lamb, or even the sweetness of beef. Rich, deeply fruity reds are the answer, notably California Cabernet Sauvignons, Rhônes such as Gigondas, and northern Italian reds such as Barolo and Barbaresco.

Types of preparations, marinades, sauces, and accompanying garnishes can all turn game dishes in particular vinous directions. Last winter, Bordeaux proved a happy partner for a roast wild Canada goose stuffed with dried fruit. But an Alsace Vendange Tardive Gewürztraminer was even better, a brilliant match. Its powerful, dry, spicy style with the characteristic bitter note in the finish stood up to the fruity richness of the dish better than the red.

Wild game can vary tremendously in quality, depending on the time of year, the game's diet, age, condition, and how expertly it was field-dressed and handled. We've had venison as tender as veal and thus perfectly matched by a delicate Oregon Pinot Noir, and venison—destined by its toughness for the stewpot—that needed a hearty, no-nonsense Zinfandel. On the other hand, if you've actually managed to bring the entrée home from the field instead of the butcher's, such perseverance calls for a certain largesse in the choice of wine—what else are you saving the '79 Château Ausone for?

BREAD AND WINE

When we stepped into La Contea, a tiny restaurant in Neive, it-self barely more than a crossroads in Italy's Piedmontese hills, we thought at first we'd intruded into a private home and hesitated at the open door. But at that moment the proprietor emerged from the kitchen with an armful of hot breadsticks, a little thicker than fireplace matches and just as long. He gestured us to a table and wordlessly made us welcome by unwrapping the bread with a flick of his wrist. Fanned out in the center of the worn, polished wood table, the bread was a gesture of hospitality that needed no translation. We snapped the sticks into manageable lengths and nibbled on them while our host uncorked the first in a series of the region's classic reds—Dolcetto, Barbaresco, Barolo—for us to sample. The crunch of that fresh, flavorsome bread and the first taste of the wine, all fruit and scent and grapy intensity, made the long, tiring drive through the Barbaresco hills recede, and we gave ourselves over to the pleasant anticipation of the meal to come.

We'd spent the morning in the company of Angelo Gaja, the iconoclastic master winemaker of Barbaresco, whose superlative wines are as suave and sleek as any French bottlings but com-pletely Italian in flavor. We tasted many wines that day and with that meal, but somehow it is the emphatic Gaja reds that we re-member whenever the smell of fresh breadsticks brings back the memory of that visit.

It intrigues us that the essence of that splendid meal was al-ready there in the beginning moments with the oven-warm bread and the deep, generous wine. The bread gave substance; the wine gave style. As we think about it, it's not really so remarkable.

Most Western cuisines—certainly French and Italian—would be unthinkable without bread and wine. Bread, of course, is a staple; you could survive on it if you had to. Wine certainly isn't a staple in that sense; what makes it seem a necessity is that the addition of a simple glass of it to a meal transforms mere eating into dining. In fact, there are several pairings of classic breads and wines that seem almost obvious in their rightness once they're mentioned.

But it is strange that these two pillars of Western gastronomy are rarely thought of as ideal partners. Partly it's because there is little dramatic interaction of flavors, few arresting combinations or startling clashes. That's not to say that bread and wine are indifferent to each other. Even the plainest of breads has a basic affinity to wine, which is why it is so frequently offered as a palate refresher at wine tastings: a bite of bread neutralizes the flavor of a just-tasted wine without prejudicing the palate's impression of the next wine, the way cheese certainly would. With bread at hand one can always retaste a wine afresh.

Some breads and wines pair very effectively. Consider a particularly modern combination: San Francisco sourdough bread and California Chardonnay. The taste of just-baked sourdough, its tang and chewy texture, so perfectly sets off the almost buttery body and effusive ripeness of a chilled, top-class Chardonnay that the addition of, say, cold cracked crab or Sonoma *chèvre* to bring out further harmonies between the two seems almost superfluous. Sourdough bread—made by using a "mother" starter dough— may not be a purely American invention, but the San Francisco version is unrivaled in flavor. And with their vibrant balance of ripe fruitiness, crisp acidity, and subtle nuances of oak, who can dispute that today's Chardonnays are worthy, albeit fleshier, cousins to the white Burgundies of France?

(The pack leader of the moment for top-class Chardonnay is Sonoma-Cutrer, of which the 1985 "Les Pierres" designation is a prime example. But in truth, so many brilliant state-of-the-art bottlings are being produced these days that at least two dozen other producers could be named as exemplars of what is now indisputably this country's finest dry white.)

Admittedly, bread and wine are most effective in tandem with other foods. The right wine and the right bread, paired with meat or fish or cheese, can offer a splendid variety of tastes and textures. On many occasions, that's meal enough to satisfy both stomach and soul. We recall a picnic on the banks of the Dordogne in southwestern France one spring day that consisted of a chilled bottle of Beaujolais and a *ficelle*—that long, even skinnier version of the classic French *baguette*—that we picked up at the *boulangerie* along the way. One more stop for a wedge of *pâté de campagne,* and we had all the essentials. What remains strongest in the memory is the scent of the bread torn off in chunks and the taste of the cellar-cool, grapy wine while we watched the sunshine dance on the rushing river, swollen with spring rains of the week before. Perhaps our sense of how perfect the bread and wine were was partly a case of "a loaf of bread, a jug of wine, and thou," but the charm of such a simple combination of tastes was inherent in our choices. Beaujolais, after all, is a wine that might have been preordained to go with picnics and bistro fare. It is all lightness and grapes, dry and fruity-tart—not a wine to study and admire so much as to quaff for its sheer deliciousness. That particular Beaujolais *cru* bottling was from a now much-too-old vintage, but at two years of age it was then just right.

And the bread. Oh, we know that there are some gastronomic critics who complain that even the bread in France is no longer what it used to be, but these are the same people who like to claim that you can't get a good meal in Paris anymore, or some such nonsense. The standard loaf enjoyed by the average Frenchman is still superior to most American efforts to duplicate it, simply because the French still stick to the classic recipe of flour, water, yeast, and salt (as, for that matter, do the Italians). Sugar, which is a much overused ingredient in American recipes in general, even those with gourmet pretensions, results in breads that begin to taste suspiciously like cakes—hence fit merely to serve with coffee or tea. There's nothing wrong with that, so long as one intends to snack instead of dine. Sharp, savory breads stimulate the appetite; sweeter breads cap it, which is why they belong (if they belong at all) at the end of a meal. Now that this gastronomic principle is more widely understood, fewer of us are still subjected to silly little sweet loaves served on miniature cutting boards and other pseudobreads that used to be mainstays of the American restaurant scene.

At the other end of the bread spectrum are those weighty loaves that give meaning to the phrase "staff of life." Take a classic brown peasant bread such as Pain Poilane—still made in Paris, and flown over to the United States to satisfy those who will settle for nothing less. A fat, dark, heavy, disc-shaped loaf crusty with character, it is truly a bread to sink one's teeth into. Buttress it, or a similarly worthy dark bread, with a simple, hearty dish (a soup, a stew, a cassoulet) and an equally substantial wine (red, of course), and one has a meal that would satisfy anyone hungering for genuine flavor. French cuisine, for all its refinements, has its roots in such solid fare as this.

Of course, there are dozens of French wines that would make a perfect partner for *pain de campagne*. We'd pick a flavorful red from that country's Rhône Valley: Hermitage, Cornas, Châteauneuf-du-Pape, Côte Rôtie. Take the Côte Rôtie of Robert Jasmin, as exemplified in the vintage of 1983: a red with power and elegance and a flavor penetrating enough to stand up to wild game, strong cheese, and highly seasoned foods. It's a taste that will make you understand the origin of Côte Rôtie—literally, the roasted slope—and what fuels the fashion for fine Rhône wines.

Sourdough and Chardonnay, *baguette* and Beaujolais, country breads and country wines—the list could obviously be much longer. There are even combinations that come to mind for the end of a meal, ideal for lingering over the last of the bread and wine.

A meal grand enough to call for a dessert wine might have a confection to go with the wine, but hardly a bread. There is one exception, however, and that is Vintage Port, the ultimate in a dark, dramatic, deeply fruity wine. The ideal accompaniment is a nut bread—not a cake, really, but a rich, dense, and nutty loaf. The example we recall as near perfect is the walnut bread that used to be served with the cheese plate at The Four Seasons, nutty enough to show off the fruitiness of a great Port, yet dry and savory enough to convey a crumble of sharp, salty Stilton, Port's classic contrast.

Vintage Port, long an English favorite, has recently shed its club-chair-and-monocle image to be rediscovered for the grand wine it is. True Port, of course, is from Oporto, Portugal, and Vintage Port, the finest of all, gets the connoisseur's attention. Although really at its best twenty or more years old, it is by no means unpleasant at ten. The vintages of the 1980s are really too young to show their best, as is the classic '77 vintage. But the lighter '75s are drinking well, and the '70s from top houses such as Taylor-Fladgate are already splendid and will be even better in the years to come.

Obviously, this sort of pairing could open up a whole new area of gastronomic investigation. Think of the matches worth savoring: raisin bread and Riesling, rye and Gewürztraminer, potato bread and Zinfandel . . .

GREENS, SPICE, AND WINE

Why is it, we wonder, that there is no dearth of advice about what wines are appropriate to serve with meat or fish dishes, and yet hardly any about what goes best with vegetables and salads and spicy foods?

Let's tackle the vegetable kingdom first. Perhaps it's because we always think of meals as dominated by their main course and think, sensibly enough, that the wine ought to be paired with that. But who doesn't commonly serve vegetables along with the main dish? In our search for practical, down-to-earth guidance for the herbivorous wine enthusiast, we were thrown back on our own devices. We quickly discovered that testing vegetables, both raw and cooked, for their friendliness to various wines was largely an excursion into terra incognita with few guideposts along the way. As a working principle, we looked for wines that either complemented the flavor of vegetables or contrasted with them, hoping to find some combinations that seemed to enhance both the dish and the drink.

Bottles at the ready, we first tackled asparagus and artichokes, a pair often cited for their antiwine tendencies. Frankly, we found asparagus was less of a problem than artichokes. Steamed asparagus with melted butter proved tolerant of assertive reds such as Côtes du Rhône. But boiled whole artichokes, with their sweet, penetrating flavor—no matter whether dipped in melted butter, served vinaigrette or with hollandaise—jarred with every wine type we tried them with.

Just as a chicken can be transformed from a white wine dish to a red wine dish by the addition of a rich sauce, so too vegetables can be made wine-friendly by the use of, say, cheese sauces. But not wanting to confuse the issue unduly, we then confined our investigations to raw, steamed, and braised vegetables. We decided that young, tannic Cabernets or Bordeaux have the acerbic, olive-y flavor to stand up to broccoli, mild peppers, and cauliflower.

Among the squash family, baked butternut squash posed difficulties; it made several dry wines like Sauvignon Blanc taste unpleasantly metallic. But a mildly sweet wine, such as Chenin Blanc, proved amicable.

And salads, which are traditionally thought to be extremely wine-hostile? One wine lover we know regards his best bottles with such reverence that the salad course, when it's not banned altogether from his dinner parties, is offered almost apologetically, as a concession to those who have an inexplicable interest in solid as well as liquid fare. But he regards this as a risky business: a wine neophyte might inadvertently alternate a forkful of dressed lettuce with a sip of Pétrus without interposing the obligatory bite of bread, thereby ruining his appreciation of the wine, not to mention his pretensions to connoisseurship.

In our view, the green salad danger is highly exaggerated. Admittedly, salads can clash unpleasantly with wine. We used to think this was due entirely to the use of vinegar in the dressing, but in fact a bite of the more aggressive raw greens used in a tossed salad will give a follow-up glass of red wine a decidedly grim, gripping flavor. It may have something to do with the wine's tannin, because with the exception of a fresh, sappy young Beaujolais, whites pose less of a problem than reds, particularly if they are crisply acidic and not overly subtle (California Sauvignon Blanc, for example). Emphasis on milder greens—butter lettuce instead of escarole—and the addition of more wine-complementary elements such as chèvre, will "tune" the salad toward wine, as will a minimal use of vinegar.

But spicy foods are another matter. As anyone knows who's tried to serve wine with an intensely flavored, highly seasoned dish—say, vindaloo curry—an overdose of spice can be fatal to a fine wine. To be precise, the subtleties of wine are lost on a palate whose taste buds have just been numbed. Certainly, no wine can stand up to any dish that makes your eyes water, your scalp tingle, or your voice disappear. (Reach for a large cool lager instead.) But even dishes with a mild amount of zip can interfere with your appreciation of fine wine. Wine-compatible cuisine needn't be bland, but some spices, such as ginger, pose a particular problem: their penetrating character seems to dominate the relatively low-key flavors of wine. Other spices, like paprika, are more wine-friendly. A dish such as chicken paprikash, while noticeably spicy, doesn't cancel out the lively fruit of a young Zinfandel or Cabernet Sauvignon. With most spices, we find the amount is critical; pepper is fine until it reaches palate-punishing levels. At that point, all that you'll be able to notice about a wine is its wetness.

The usual wine-matching advice is to fight spice with spice and serve Gewürztraminer. It does work, so long as the intensity of the wine matches the intensity of the dish. Lightly spicy California Gewürztraminer can stand up to lightly spicy Southwest dishes, but full-throttle Cajun cooking calls for Vendange Tardive

Gewürztraminer from Alsace. Now there's nothing wrong with relying on Gewürztraminer, but like the habit of always serving rosé when you can't make up your mind between red and white, it lacks imagination. It isn't always necessary to set out an assertive wine to do battle with a potent dish. On many occasions we'd just as soon forgo gladitorial gastronomy, serve a mild-mannered wine, and let the food have center stage. For not-too-fiery dishes, a fruity-sweet, inexpensive wine with few subtleties to lose, such as a not-too-cloying California white Zinfandel, happily plays the vinous equivalent of background music and nicely assuages mildly tingled taste buds.

When all other choices fail (or pale), as they might do in the face of Texas chili, serve an inexpensive sparkling wine. We got that idea from our friend Nika Hazelton, the well-known cookbook author, who likes to give Champagne-and-chili parties. The pairing, as we can attest, is offbeat and fun, ideal for a crowd, and it makes gastronomic sense. The wine's effervescence refreshes the palate and cuts across the spices, and it's obviously not necessary to spend big bucks on the label. The old saw that you can serve Champagne with everything is doubtless based on the fact that while the flavors may not always mesh, the presence of bubbles provides a contrast (if only physical) with any dish.

MATCHING AMERICAN WINES
WITH FOOD

Champagne and caviar . . . Chablis and oysters . . . Riesling and trout . . . Bordeaux and lamb . . . Port and Stilton . . .
To a wine and food lover, these combinations go together like

bacon and eggs, bread and butter, coffee with cream. They—and several others—are *the* classic wine and food matches because they've worked so well for so many people for so long. They've also become classics because they go beyond the limitations of the occasional heaven-sent perfect match of a particular dish and a particular bottle of wine. We remember, for example, drinking a strikingly earthy, pungent Cabernet with smoked duck at a restaurant. We were never able to get that delicious combination to work with any other birds or bottles. But classic matches work within a wider range of flavor variations in both the food and the wine, and differences don't cancel out the general affinity of the taste combination.

Since Americans are using European grape varieties to make wines designed to rival their classic counterparts, we wondered whether these American wines would work in these long-hallowed combinations—could they handle the liquid role in these tabletop duets?

We decided to put the question to the test, using American wines as stand-ins for the European bottlings in these long-accepted pairings. Herewith a report on our research. In brief, we found that some classic combinations do work in an American mode and some don't, and along the way, we also discovered some potential classic American combinations.

We started with caviar and Champagne/sparkling wine. First-rate caviar—say, fresh beluga malassol—is so subtle, rich, and intense that only the finest Champagnes seem equal to it. To us, even the best American sparkling wines come off as flat, simple, and tinny in such a match. If serving an American wine, the solution is to choose a less dramatic caviar—salmon roe, for example.

We've found California Chardonnay a sorry substitute for Chablis when it comes to what to serve with oysters on the half-shell. Admittedly, oysters demand sharply acidic, bone-dry wines without much apparent fruit. There is a reason why wedges of lemon appear on oyster trays, and if the accompanying wine doesn't provide the right touch of asperity, one has to lean on the lemon. We find virtually all California Chardonnays too soft, rich, and fruity to provide ideal pairing with oysters. Northwest and New York State Chardonnays offer more "cut," but we've yet to come across an American equivalent to Chablis, with its particular depth, tang, and acidity. On the other hand, a tart Seyval Blanc is a fair stand-in for Muscadet, which the French regard as the universal workhorse white for shellfish.

But California Chardonnay is our preferred choice for an All-American classic match: Chardonnay and cold cracked crab. We've found that the richness and especially the buttery, fat texture of first-class California examples make them unsurpassed accompaniments to these sweet-fleshed crustaceans.

The much-beloved combination of Riesling and trout seems to work just as well with a delicate East or West Coast Riesling as it does with a Mosel. The trick is finding an example that has the attractive balance between fruit and acidity that a good German wine does. We had better luck with the lighter, more acidic East Coast examples.

Probably the single most successful American stand-in for European wine in a classic match is California Cabernet Sauvignon instead of Bordeaux as an accompaniment to lamb or game birds. We've proved this to our satisfaction on any number of occasions. What's more, the combination works with modest examples, such as Louis M. Martini, as well as with magisterial ones, such as Robert Mondavi's Reserve.

There are few wine and food combinations as satisfying as a standing rib roast and a bottle of good Burgundy. California and Oregon Pinot Noir, provided they have the meaty, complex flavors that make Burgundy so complementary to beef, work equally well.

One of our favorite classic matches is the exquisite sweet/savory contrast of Sauternes and Roquefort cheese. But when we tried sweet, botrytised California Sauvignon Blanc/Semillon blends and Sauternes with Roquefort after dinner, we found the California examples too simple, direct, and sweet to provide the same piquant contrast to the cheese.

On the other hand, differences in flavor between at least one California Port-type wine, Ficklin Tinta, and a Vintage Port didn't seem to matter when it came to doing justice to a Stilton. Despite its more obvious, fruity character, the California example was as satisfying with the cheese as the classic European bottling.

COUNTRY WINES

It's curious how many of the most memorable wine experiences don't involve great wines. Like many wine enthusiasts who've traveled in various wine regions, we have often come home with tasting notes on grand important bottlings, but found that the wines whose taste remained most vivid were modest country wines we simply didn't think worth taking a note on at the time.

There was the evening in the little Piedmontese *ristorante* where the proprietor frowned on our efforts to organize a series of wine and food combinations into a dinner. He wondered aloud how we could know what we'd feel like having halfway through the meal, and strongly suggested that we leave it all to him.

Soon we were delving into a soul-satisfying risotto and a wonderfully purple, vibrant, grapy Dolcetto from an unlabeled bottle—the local red that turned out to be on everyone else's table, too. We never did get the particulars on that wine, but then and now it seemed a detail irrelevant to our enjoyment. It also firmly eclipsed in our memory the big-deal Barolo we thought we ought to order next, although we must have a note on its pedigree and state of development somewhere.

Please don't misunderstand; we haven't lost our enthusiasm for *vino fino*. It's just that we've come to recognize that a love of country wine is perfectly compatible with a passion for fine, classic wine.

In a sense, both are special occasion wines because both demand a certain moment, a certain setting, a certain dish. Country
wines are for when you feel like embracing a wine instead of
having a tête-à-tête with it. Let's face it: nuzzling-and-guzzling,
as opposed to sniffing-and-studying, is what most of us want to
do with wine most often. We're always ready to enter into a
séance with a *cru classé,* but frankly, if left to our own devices,
we don't choose to do it that often (well, maybe on weekends).
Most of the time we're looking for substance behind the label,
something that delivers the goods to the palate without our having to ponder its evolution and nose out nuances—or check our
bank balance.

But why are we talking about *country* wines? Aren't there
legions of bottles and jugs that would fit the bill? Well, yes and
no. We want the wines we drink to have character, personality,
vibrancy. In our view that eliminates anonymous, overly neutral
blends from a variety of regions. Good as they are, they're more
a product of the cellar than the vineyard.

A good country wine, on the other hand, is an authentic
product of its region, with a taste marked by its soil, climate, and
winemaking traditions. It doesn't pretend to be the greatest
wine—but it's an honest one. We agree with Steven Spurrier,
who defines country wine in his *Concise Guide to French Country Wines* as "a wine which is drunk by locals and tourists in the
place where it is made, and has certain defined regional characteristics and is not too sophisticated or expensive."

France and Italy in particular produce hundreds of these wines,
many of which show up on the tables of travelers in carafes, not
bottles. Unfortunately, there are far fewer examples to be found
in new, high-tech wine areas such as California, where sleek,
sophisticated products have largely overrun the simpler, heartier
local wines made by many of the pioneering winemaking fami-
lies. A few, fortunately, still remain. Most require a trip to the
winery to find them—but not because they don't "travel well."

This business about country wines not being up to the rigors
of shipping needs to be laid to rest. Except for a few very delicate
low-alcohol wines that would lose their principal appeal—fresh-

ness—if sent halfway around the world, country wines can go as far as any without ill effects. What happens when a country wine goes on a journey is really something else. The story usually goes like this. Couple abroad discovers delicious wine in small trattoria, made down the road by the proprietor's cousin. Visit to cobwebbed cellar and more enthusiastic sampling results in trunk loaded with cases of said wine, which, after much travail and red tape, is brought back home and served with great fanfare to guests who are polite enough not to say they think it no more exciting than the $4.99 wine they bought last week. Couple decides, sadly, that the wine seems to have lost something along the way—in short, it didn't travel well.

In reality, the wine travels; the atmosphere doesn't. But that's not necessarily fatal to re-creating the enjoyment the wine afforded where it was discovered, so long as the approach to it doesn't change. A country wine can't be put in the sort of spotlight you'd normally reserve for opening a carefully hoarded *grand cru* Burgundy. It's unlikely that the wine that was quaffed with gusto on your travels will stand up to sudden scrutiny at home. In absolute terms, fine, classic wines remain clearly superior (as any blind tasting would show).

At the dinner table, however, the superiority of better wines isn't always so clearcut. It's often the meal as well as the moment that can make a country wine gleam in the glass. As accompaniment to hearty dishes, country wines are often preferable to overly refined wines for a paradoxical-sounding reason: their coarseness, which in another context would be regarded as a shortcoming, coupled with their direct, gutsy flavors stand up to flavorsome foods in a way no merely subtle wine can. Take cheese, for example. All but the mildest varieties are far too pungent and overpowering for fine wine, but they meet their match with something slightly rustic. It's a revelation to discover that with the right dish a wine that won't shine on its own can come into near-greatness. (This doesn't mean, we hasten to add, that for every wine in the world—no matter what its limitations— there exists a dish that will redeem it.)

Another example: We once tasted a perfectly ordinary, slightly

green, *vinho verde* in a little Portuguese restaurant before dig-
ging into our bacalao (salt cod) and found it merely pleasant.
But later in the meal, the wine seemed heaven-sent, falling on
our spice-stimulated palates like spring rain on parched ground.
Then there was the lunch in Italy where the rough-hewn *rosso
d'Assisi,* brought to the table in a pitcher, perfectly echoed the
earthiness of the pasta and mushrooms, its faintly bitter bite
adding just the right amount of spice.

But enough traveler's tales. The point is that with some foods—
many foods—what's needed is guts, not elegance. Once that's
conceded, it's clear that country wines aren't what you drink in
a pinch when you can't get something better. They're a staple of
the table, like good bread, and their modest prices make getting
to know them a doubly delightful hobby.

Some (but not all) country wines can only be tasted on their
home ground. Many attractive, authentic country wines are, like
fine wines, the products of small estates and aren't as widely
available as commercial blends. Many praiseworthy country
wines, however, are bottled by local cooperatives, and these are
more likely to be seen on retail shelves here.

Unfortunately, because the fine wines of Italy, Spain, and
Portugal are often modest in cost, there is little incentive to im-
port mere country wines. By contrast, some Swiss wines, which
would otherwise qualify, are too expensive.

The French, who have always understood that the best wine
to serve with dinner isn't always the "best" wine, know when a
country wine is called for. We once had a stunning cassoulet
prepared by Arnaud Briand, then the chef of New York's Café
43. It was the sort of deeply satisfying dish most of our mothers
never made but should have.

We thought our choice of a 1979 Côte Rôtie (Paul Jaboulet
Aîné) would prove sufficiently hearty, but in fact, next to the
cassoulet, that substantial Rhône was hopelessly elegant, its refinements lost in a welter of penetrating flavors and richness. We
should have picked a really hearty, even blunt, wine, something
with foursquare solidity and directness of flavor, such as the

sturdy reds from the southwest of France—Cahors, Madiran, Côtes de Buzet.

Even famous French wine regions have their quaffing wines. Four refreshing whites we look for are Aligoté (from Burgundy), Entre-Deux-Mers (from Bordeaux), Pinot Gris (from Alsace), and Gros Plant (from the Loire). We are also unabashed fans of Dolcetto, that delightful red from Italy. From California, apart from the odd Carignane, we look for Zinfandel, particularly from Amador County, a stronghold of country-style red.

Above all, don't ignore the possibility of worthwhile local wine. With vineyards in nearly every state, there may well be a decent *vin de pays* made down the road (Oregon Pinot Gris, Maryland Seyval, Hudson Valley *nouveau*-style reds, New England Chardonnay, just to name a few.)

The other day we discovered a Merlot from Long Island, as charming a light red as any Chinon or Bourgeuil from the Loire—just the right "little local country wine" to offer traveling Europeans who think we lack such rustic pleasures on this continent.

WINES FOR DESSERT

By now the following is an all-too-familiar exchange: One of our dinner guests, offered a dessert wine after the main course, waves away the glass and the very idea with an arch comment like, "I'll pass, thanks. I don't care for liquid sweets." But a few minutes later, as the other guests are inhaling the spurned wine's fragrance with fond sighs, cooing over its nectarlike flavor and vying for refills, we invariably hear a request from that same guest for "just a drop to satisfy my curiosity," quickly followed by, "Say, that's really lovely . . . could I, um, have a little more?"

We've had so many reruns of that scene that recently we decided not to tell guests when there's a dessert wine on the menu. We just pour it.

It's ironic that fine sweet wines meet with such resistance in the abstract, considering that in reality they're usually the biggest hit with the palate. Mind you, we're not talking about wines that barely meet the technical definition of sweet—those that show 1 or 2 percent residual sugar by volume when measured in a lab and are better described as "fruity" or "off-dry." And we're not talking about high-alcohol fortified wines (sherry, Madeira, Port), which, fine as they can be, constitute a different breed altogether. We're talking about those wines that are out-and-out luscious, unctuous, and honeyed—not just noticeably sweet, but *dessert* sweet. Special as this category is in the world of table wines, it is remarkably diverse in scents, flavors, and textures, taking in the classic Sauternes of France, German Auslese, late-harvest Rieslings from California and Australia, *sélections des grains nobles* from Alsace, bunches of Muscats and scores of others, all distinguished by their relative rarity and the fact that even the beginning wine lover can instantly appreciate their qualities. (Years ago our first taste of France's greatest reds made us wonder if we were missing something, but when we first tasted Château d'Yquem, greatest of the Sauternes—it was the 1962— we had no trouble recognizing its nectar-of-the-gods greatness.)

Knowing that, we hardly ever give a dinner party, whatever the season or menu, that doesn't end with a dessert wine. Initial misgivings notwithstanding, we find that all our guests revel in them. Besides, uncorking a fine sweet wine turns the dessert course into a true grand finale. While it's true that not every sweet wine is a bottled masterpiece, some of the world's greatest, most complex, and intriguing wines are sweet—praised by connoisseurs and coveted by collectors.

Is serving a sweet wine with dessert Edwardian overkill? It all depends on the dessert and the wine. Just as all desserts aren't heavy and sugary, not all dessert wines are syrupy, alcoholic, and overly rich. It's not a question of calories—a fine Sauternes has about as many calories as a glass of milk—so much as it is a question of balancing the richness of the dessert and the wine.

Serving a powerful dessert wine (Muscat de Frontignan at 18 percent alcohol) with Aunt Sophie's killer black-bottom pie would probably be a bit much, but a glass of chilled Moscato d'Asti (only 7 percent alcohol and mildly sweet) alongside a dish of fresh raspberries hardly constitutes a Diamond Jim Brady menu.

There is some truth to the claim that it's difficult to match desserts and sweet wines. Extremely sugary, intense desserts flatten most dessert wines. (We once attended a disastrous Sauternes and confection tasting where, after the first bite of a sugary éclair, the wines all tasted sharp and tinny.) The key is to ensure that the dessert isn't sweeter than the wine. When we're not familiar with a particular combination and think the dish might overpower the wine, we simply serve the dessert wine a few minutes before the dessert so that it can be appreciated on its own.

When it comes to menu planning, it's important to know the relative intensity of fine sweet wines—how they differ in alcohol levels, sugar content, acidity, and flavor. We find it convenient to think of dessert wines as falling into four groups: Sauternes, Rieslings, Muscats, and everything else.

Sauternes are classic choices. These golden, heady, and powerful (as you might expect with alcohol levels of 14 percent or more) wines from Bordeaux have sufficient acidity to balance their rich textures and honeyed flavors. Sauternes are ideal to end a grand dinner with and will stand up to rich, sophisticated desserts—floating islands, charlotte russes, and the like. But when matching Sauternes to a dessert, make sure that the dessert is not overly sugary. We've found light custards, lemon soufflés, pound and almond cakes, and berry tarts also work very well. We also often serve a Sauternes by itself *as* the dessert, throwing its lusciousness into relief by accompanying it with wedges of Roquefort cheese. The sweetness and intensity of the wine contrasts wonderfully with the salty, biting character of the cheese.

Château d'Yquem, greatest of the Sauternes, is the ultimate expression of the style, with a perfumed scent that suggests tropical fruit, vanilla, toffee, and layers of unctuous flavors to match. Unfortunately, it has now reached so high a price ($100 a bottle) that its use is confined to state occasions or fits of largesse. All recent vintages have been superb, and an older top Yquem vintage, the perfectly balanced '71, for example, will leave you staring dreamily into the bottom of your glass. Nearly as exalted are the other top Sauternes châteaux such as Suduiraut, Guiraud, Climens, and Coutet; smaller stars such as Nairac are not to be ignored either. These last three châteaux are in the commune of Barsac, whose wines are lighter and more acidic than most Sauternes, trading richness for elegance.

Rieslings, late-harvest and otherwise, reach top form as dessert wines in Germany, California, and a few other New World locations. Alcohol levels are modest—7 percent to 11 percent—and the concentration can achieve honeylike intensity at the Trockenbeerenauslese and "Individual Bunch Selected" levels. Acidity runs high, which keeps the best-balanced examples from a cloying sweetness. Floral scents and ripe apricot flavors predominate, and so these stylish wines are particularly good with lighter desserts such as mild fruit tarts.

The German names are legion—in theory virtually any Rhine or Mosel estate might produce (given the right conditions) a nectar-of-the-gods Auslese. The greatest examples, say, the 1976 Bernkasteler Doctor Beerenauslese of Dr. Thanisch, can put you into a swoon from a single sip or for that matter, from just the thought of the tariff: that particular bottling is now somewhere in the $300 range. At a far more affordable level, an Auslese from a top producer such as Dr. Bürklin-Wolf will demonstrate why these classic flowery, low-alcohol wines are so supremely elegant, and for wines so sweet, remarkably refreshing.

Not to be outdone, Chateau St. Jean and Joseph Phelps in California have led the state in producing extraordinary late-harvest Rieslings that are fully the equal of the best of Germany—and about half the price.

Muscats represent the essence of ripe grape flavors. In weight and substance, they vary from delicious, delicate, frivolous, and slightly effervescent Italian versions to fragrant-floral examples (such as Robert Pecota's) to far deeper, more concentrated versions such as the slightly fortified Muscat de Beaumes-de-Venise from the Rhône Valley in France. Lighter versions go with melon or fresh berries; the highly perfumed Muscat de Beaumes-de-Venise can stand up to vanilla ice cream.

Others not to be overlooked are the rare sweet wines from the Loire (actually late-harvest Chenin Blancs), such as the honey-and-lemon-scented Moulin Touchais, which is brighter and more lemony than typical Sauternes, and the unusual *sélections des grains nobles* wines from Alsace, especially the Gewürztraminers, which are all clover and sweet spice. All of these medium-weight wines would pair well with mild nut cakes and soufflés.

In picking a dessert wine, consider the entire menu and occasion. A winter-weight entrée and a fine Bordeaux would nicely lead up to a substantial Sauternes. A roast chicken and Beaujolais lunch would appropriately wind up with a light Riesling and fresh berries.

Remember that fresh, strongly flavored citrus fruits, used in some fruit salads, for example, are too acidic to be complementary to dessert wines, and that chocolate in many forms is too bitter or sugary to pair with anything but sweet red wines (Port, for instance). When in doubt, choose a mild dessert—hazelnut torte, for example—to showcase the wine.

Dessert wines are best served lightly chilled but not stone-cold (which flattens the flavor) in small tulip-shaped glasses to concentrate the bouquet. A bottle will comfortably serve six to eight people. Incidentally, dessert wines keep well once opened, for a day or two anyway.

But you won't have any left over.

GARDEN WINES

We can picture the scene perfectly: It's a bright midsummer day. . . . In the dappled shade of a grapevine-covered arbor, amidst a profusion of blooming flowers, there is a long table set with cold salads, soft cheeses, charcuterie, crusty breads, bowls of ripe fruit—and several tall, cool green bottles, beaded with condensation, already uncorked. There's the right mix of friends, and as the afternoon slips by at a languid pace, we all slowly sip pale refreshing wines that invite glass after glass, wines as simple and scented as garden flowers, as succulent as ripe peaches, as evocative to smell as wild thyme plucked from a sunny herb border and rubbed between the palms. We call them garden wines.

There's something about drinking (and dining) al fresco that appeals to us all, especially when climate denies us the opportunity for months at a time. Our own garden is a favorite outdoor setting for afternoon get-togethers from the first spring daffodils to fall's chrysanthemums. But the mood can be reproduced in a variety of settings, from Alpine meadow to city terrace.

We're less willing to take a laissez-faire attitude on the subject of garden wines—and not because we think that many wines are poor choices. But there are definite types of wines so perfectly suited to open-air summer sipping and dining that we think they never taste better than when drunk in such a setting. California and Pacific Northwest Chenin Blancs and Rieslings, German Mosels, Loire whites, various Muscats, and certain rosés and reds come to mind—but we're getting ahead of ourselves.

Just what makes an ideal garden wine? First of all, it has to match the occasion as well as the food. When we're entertaining outdoors, we want the wine to play a secondary role, not dominate the scene the way the weighty reds and whites of the winter table (Cabernet, Chardonnay, Burgundy, Barolo, and Bordeaux) tend to do. Foolishly, we once served a Clos de Vougeot to guests at a picnic. It went marvelously with the food but was too grand and serious for the occasion, provoking a woefully inappropriate amount of winetalk. In retrospect, a light, frivolously forgettable Beaujolais would have been just the wine the dish and the moment needed. Garden wines ought to be simply delicious, not too complex, so that they will fit in with the casual feeling of a table under the trees. We're looking more for lightness than depth, more for charm than character. Choosing wine by the setting may sound overprecious, but half the fun (and all the appreciation) of wine lies in such nuances.

We want wines that are, well, close to the grape in style: tart, ripely fruity, fragrant. Outdoors, but especially in a garden, wines are in their natural setting and have to fit in with the smell of roses or freshly cut grass. They should be a part of the pleasant confusion of the senses. The ideal garden wines are those that are always described in images of flowers, fruits, herbs—smells of violets or sage or honeysuckle, tastes of cherries or peaches or green apples.

Garden wines are at their best only for a single season, making them, in vinous terms, annuals, not perennials. Although light, fruity, and perfumed wines are deservedly popular, they're often ignored by wine lovers, in part because most don't last more than a year or two without fading—hardly the stuff of serious cellars.

But let's get down to specifics. The choice of off-dry or dry, white, rosé, or red will depend on what you're eating—or not eating, if you just want something to sip with the sunset.

To us, the only reds that fit the bill are those light reds with little tannin that can be chilled without tasting metallic. Our favorites are reds from the Loire such as Anjou Rouge, Chinon, and Bourgueil, which are made from the fragrant Cabernet Franc grape and taste like soft, summertime versions of Bordeaux. But these bottlings are hard to find, so let's not ignore the obvious: Beaujolais—particularly if it's from the *crus* of Fleurie, St.-Amour, Chiroubles, and Chénas. Cold roast chicken couldn't ask for a better companion.

Dishes such as *salade niçoise,* smoked turkey, and herbed potato salad need good, dry, flavorful rosés—those from Provence, say, or California's best, the rosés of Cabernet Sauvignon.

But in most cases, the choice will be white. We think California Chardonnays and white Burgundies are generally too oaky, rich, and heavy, but a Mâcon or Pouilly-Fuissé has the requisite lightness of character if you must have a Chardonnay of some sort. Bone-dry Sauvignon Blancs from California and Sancerres from the Loire can compete in aroma with an herb garden. To us, they're the ideal choices with pasta salads, tangy chèvres, and cold vegetable dishes.

But in general, for dry whites we'd prefer wines made from the Chenin Blanc grape, whose scent and flavor suggest tree-ripened fruit—a very dry, savory Savennières from the Loire with grilled salmon, an off-dry but crisply acidic Vouvray or Pacific Northwest Chenin Blanc with perch, pike, or snapper.

Fruity-tart wines with a small amount of residual sugar balanced by vibrant acidity, such as Rieslings from the Mosel, are excellent for sipping on their own. Despite their delicacy, they are a perfect choice with freshly caught trout. To many people, any good Riesling, with its expansive floral aroma, is a quintessential garden wine, but for that honor we'd pick the wine whose sheer grapiness is a perfect echo of most soft fruits, from kiwi to berries: Muscats from Italy or California. For sipping with fruit or with a mild dessert, they're exquisite. The lighter ones are all perfume and lingering flavor and so perfectly sum up a garden in full bloom that a glass seems to bring sunshine indoors.

Come to think of it, that's not a bad choice for a rainy day.

BRINGING WINES TO FRIENDS

Arriving on your dinner-host's doorstep with a bottle of wine in hand used to be a simple and thoughtful gesture. It still is, under most circumstances. It seems to us, in fact, that showing up with wine is appreciated at any sort of get-together that's sufficiently casual, particularly in summer. But more on that later.

These days we've noticed that people are giving considerable thought and planning to the dinners they give and the wines they pour at those dinners. As long as people are enjoying them-selves, we see nothing wrong with that, but it's clear that sophis-tication and informality sometimes clash. When the host or hostess has carefully chosen the wine and matched it perfectly with the food, a guest bearing an unasked-for bottle wrapped in a brown paper bag is not applauded the way he once was. It's awkward for the host to have to decide if he's obliged by the gesture to serve the wine, particularly if it doesn't fit in with the meal as planned.

According to one school of wine etiquette, showing up for dinner with a wine you weren't asked to bring is akin to bringing a bag of snacks to the dinner table—the implication is that what you will be served won't be good enough. A bottle of wine, it follows, should be brought only as a gift for the host and hostess to enjoy by themselves at a later time.

We have to admit this attitude makes sense. Generally, we don't bring wines to dinner parties, except by prearrangement, and don't expect guests to bring wines to ours. If someone brings us a bottle, we either serve it as an aperitif or alongside another wine we intended to serve—if appropriate—or put it aside with the proviso that the bearer will be invited back to share it on another occasion.

Whenever we have bent this rule, we have done so for admittedly self-serving motives, and we haven't always been successful. We recall a few years back being invited to dinner at another couple's home where the husband, a first-rate cook, was known for his imaginative menus and unimaginative selection of wines. He thought nothing of spending days in the kitchen preparing the food but gave no more thought to the beverage than to pick up a couple of bottles of something inexpensive on his final shopping expedition. From previous experience, we did not look forward to washing down our food with his choice, which usually varied from cotton-candy-sweet whites to raspingly rough reds. We decided to bring something we wanted to drink—a mature Cabernet Sauvignon, as we recall. After the expected exclamations of delight that we came with such a gift, it was—you guessed correctly—whisked away with promises that they would save it for their anniversary. Having got the comeuppance we deserved, we drank our crackling rosé without a murmur.

Since then, we have come to the conclusion that we have a better time if we leave our wine pretensions at home, and besides, we recognize our limitations in the art of manipulating hosts and hostesses.

There are those, however, who are willing to take desperate measures when faced with the prospect of an entire dinner party laced with lesser lubricant. Consider a friend of ours, whom we usually refer to as the Artful Guest. He has an uncanny ability to make parsimonious hosts think it was their idea to serve him the best bottle in their cellar. If the pickings appear slim, however, he will resort to taking his own. He assures us that the secret of bringing your own wine to drink at someone else's dinner is to make your snobbish gesture appear flattering.

Arrive late, the Artful Guest advises, with the potation of your choice, and after dramatically displaying the label and receiving the obligatory expressions of gratitude, announce loudly, "There's no one else I'd rather share it with than you," and—without relinquishing your grip on the bottle—magnanimously demand corkscrew and glasses. If this isn't sufficient, he assures us that even the strongest-willed host can be overcome by the rude strategem of arriving with wine already in a decanter. "Too much sediment in these old clarets," explain portentously, "to transport them safely," and then follow with a glance at your watch and a blurted "Hmpf! Hope it holds until the cheese course."

But we can't leave the subject without conceding that vinous contributions are always in order at informal summer events such as barbecues, boating parties, and picnics. Certainly if you're invited to spend a weekend in the country or at the shore, arriving with wines is never out of place since thirsty guests can make startling inroads into a summer's wine supply. A glimpse of several promising bottles peeking out of a beach bag tends to ameliorate the sinking sensation your host may feel at the sight of you and the amount of your luggage, which, even for a weekend, can look ominously as if you're prepared to stay well past Labor Day.

WHEN WINING IS DINING

We recently attended a private wine dinner where what can only be described as a barrage of great wines were served. Despite the impressive array of bottles, however, it was not a memorable evening. Considerable thought had been lavished on the choices of wine, food, and guests—and little else. The dinner proceeded at a snail's pace, and so many bottles and glasses were on the table at once that mix-ups were inevitable and frequent. As the evening dragged on, several guests visibly wilted under what seemed to be an interminable discussion of the wines, and the host became grumpy. The whole event seemed disorganized and yet at the same time too formal and stiff.

By contrast, a week later we had an impromptu Italian wine dinner at a friend's house, where, with the main course of osso buco and fennel salad, we compared a California and an Italian Barbera. The wines were less grand, but the evening was certainly more fun.

What made one evening so entertaining and the other seem to last an eternity? A wine-tasting dinner sounds enticing, but we've noticed that they are not so easy to host and can be a chore to attend if they don't work well. Yet when they do, they *are* the most memorable of meals. Having been hosts and guests at quite a few, we've observed that a successful wine dinner requires adequate planning, reasonable pacing, and artful management of winetalk. It isn't as hard as it sounds—the secret is to keep it uncomplicated, natural, and fun.

A wine dinner is a curious hybrid of a wine tasting and a dinner party. The menu is planned around the wines, and the wines will, presumably, be discussed off and on during the meal. This entails serving unusual or at least interesting wines, not usually but sometimes blind, and often side by side with similar wines. Of course such dinners needn't be elaborate, nor do the wines have to be expensive.

In planning a wine dinner, the first major decision is picking the wines. We have found that wines that have some relation to each other or can be meaningfully compared are more interesting to taste and talk about than a succession of unrelated wines, no matter how great. A simple dinner might be centered on a comparison of two wines from California—say, a pair of Sauvignon Blancs from two different producers. A more elaborate meal might contrast differences in style between a California Chardonnay and a Puligny-Montrachet of the same year with the fish course, and a California Cabernet Sauvignon and a Médoc of the same vintage with the main course. We're fond of five-wine dinners for six people—an aperitif/first-course wine, followed by a pair of reds with the main course, something special with the cheese, and a dessert wine.

During a lengthy dinner, we've found that guests will drink as much as a bottle of wine apiece with little effect—not so surprising when you consider it's being consumed with food over a period of several hours. Since a bottle will serve six to eight people one glass each, you can count on an enthusiastic party of six doing justice to five or six bottles. Eight wines are about the practical limit that can be tried in the context of a meal, and more than three wines to compare at any one course is usually confusing and unwieldy.

Unless the theme of the dinner is to see how different wines go with various dishes—say, a Gewürztraminer, a Riesling, and a Chenin Blanc with Chinese cuisine—it's best to underplay the food rather than risk serving a dish that overpowers a delicate wine. A common mistake is serving cheeses that are too powerful and pungent for the reds. Stick with fresh, mild cheeses, such as triple crèmes, young chèvres, and Wensleydale.

In choosing the variety and number of wines to serve, pacing is a vital consideration: A series of grand bottles leaves a less focused impression than a series of wines that build to a climax with one outstanding and properly showcased wine. A friend once asked our advice on planning a wine dinner for six around a bottle of 1959 Château Mouton-Rothschild she'd been given. Once we found we were to be invited, our enthusiasm picked up considerably, and we suggested the following vinous sequence: for openers, a crisp white Graves with the baked oysters, and with the main dish—roast leg of lamb—a 1970 Château Lynch-Bages. A younger, less powerful, and less complex wine, it proved a perfect foil for the '59 Mouton, which followed with the cheeses. Had the Mouton not been preceded by a smaller scale Médoc, its finesse and power would not have stood out so clearly. (Of course, a lesser, more recent vintage of Mouton—'76, perhaps—would have set off the '59 just as well.)

When serving a series of wines such as the ones above, it's important to give your guests some idea of what to expect in the way of wines and courses at the beginning of the evening. Once when we failed to do so, we were taken to task by our friend the Artful Guest. He protested that we were robbing him of the pleasures of anticipation. Later, he confessed that his real interest was in knowing what was coming so he "could pace himself." We've since decided that most guests are happier to have some idea of how many courses and wines they're facing—for both reasons. And if there will be quite a few courses and wines, it's important that they follow each other smoothly so that guests don't lose enthusiasm before the meal is half over. We think it helps if wine dinners start soon after all the guests have gathered. For that reason, we keep the aperitifs simple and the time for predinner socializing relatively short. We serve one or at the most two glasses of something light and crisply acidic—say a Pinot Gris from Alsace, or if we're going all out, brut Champagne. We save any comparisons or real vinous treats for the table.

It's easy to say that the wines you choose will be the center of the meal; it's quite another to make them the focus of discussion. Frankly, it's often difficult to put together guests who will all be equally interested in discussing what's in their glasses. Even those with a professional interest in wine are liable to find a dinner of nonstop winetalk heavy going. One solution is simply to get most of the winetalk over with in the beginning. This is an approach that can be used by anyone who, like us, might want to hold formal or informal wine tastings—such as a group of friends interested in trying a number of Cabernets from the latest vintage. We often try to take advantage of having a dozen just-opened bottles of wine on hand by inviting any tasters in attendance to stay on for a simple meal, to which we ask additional guests. Since the wines have already been discussed in detail, it's possible to avoid the longueurs occasioned by lengthy pauses for sniffing and swirling and gurgling, note-taking at the table, and extended vinous disagreements. After a recent sampling of current California Chardonnays with a couple of keen enthusiasts, we asked additional guests to a meal of bay scallops accompanied by the wines we'd been tasting. We simply put some of the better bottles in the center of the table, along with an empty pitcher for guests to dump wines they didn't want to finish, and provided each guest with several glasses. Another solution is to focus the

wine discussion on one particular topic, such as which of a pair
of wines goes better with the food.

At many wine dinners, the best way to ensure that the winetalk is neither forced nor interminable is to create natural breaks
in the meal for it to occur. We were taught a lesson in this regard
by the Artful Guest on one of the few occasions he played the
Artful Host. The company was "mixed"—enthusiastic and not-
so-enthusiastic about wine. He cleverly served the aperitif blind
and asked us all for our opinions on his latest discovery, thereby
immediately starting a conversation about the wine. (It turned
out to be an inexpensive but appealing Argentinean Chardonnay.) The main dinner wine was a modest but very attractive
'78 Côtes du Rhône, which went particularly well with the *boeuf
en daube*. When he commented that it was a mere stalking horse
for the thoroughbred bottle to follow, everyone's interest was
heightened.

After the plates were cleared away, he unveiled the vinous
climax of the evening, a 1969 Côte Rôtie. He opened and decanted it at the table, making perhaps just a little bit too much
fuss with the cork and candle, but the insertion of this ceremony
unquestionably served to rivet everyone's attention on the wine.
The eagerness with which we awaited a glass of this nectar was
fed by the Artful Host's recounting of how exquisite previous
bottles of this wine had been, although we noted he took care to
insert the thought that he had experienced "some variation from
bottle to bottle." This qualification only served to augment the
sense of drama as we each inhaled the pungent bouquet and
savored the full depths of the wine. He collected the ensuing
praise from the knowledgeable and the naïve alike. Then, just at
the moment when talk of the Côte Rôtie seemed to falter, he
produced an assortment of cheeses, and the conversation swung
back to the more usual mix of politics, movie gossip, and real
estate. Later we reflected on just how much enjoyment he had
engineered for us all—with mostly modest but well-presented
bottles.

Inspired by his example, we spent the drive home contemplat-
ing how we might set the stage to sacrifice our only remaining

bottle of 1970 Ridge Occidental Zinfandel. Let's see . . . could we open with a *white* Zinfandel . . . ?

ON SERVING THE BEST BOTTLES

For a wine lover, one of the greatest pleasures of giving a dinner party is the opportunity to share some good wines with friends. Partly, we're sure, it's the good talk wine engenders. It's also the toasts, spoken or unspoken, that lifting a glass together symbolizes, for wine definitely adds a touch of ceremony to gathering around a table. And when the wine itself is special, something further is added, acknowledged openly or tacitly by everyone who shares in the taste. There are plenty of wine lovers who demur on this last point, however, maintaining that it's clearly a waste to serve wines that really deserve comment and discussion to a group only mildly interested in matters gastronomic or who regard the very idea of winetalk as silly.

We used to hold that point of view and thought we were squandering our better bottles if we served them to neophytes. But gradually the churlishness inherent in applying such a draconian rule became apparent. We remember serving a magnum of 1969 Bonnes Mares (Domaine Dujac) to sophisticated but not particularly wine-knowledgeable friends. We expected it to be good, but we weren't prepared for it to be utterly magnificent. The uncharitable thought *we've overdone it* initially crossed our minds, but our guests rose to the occasion. Their surprise and delight at the greatness of the Burgundy was so genuine that we felt not only that they deserved every drop, but that we couldn't have served it to a more appreciative audience.

But we continued to regard serving a fine wine to a crowd a

matter of, well, casting pearls before swine, until another incident convinced us otherwise. Some years back we drank part of a case of a deliciously fruity Pomerol from the rapidly maturing 1976 vintage, then put a half-dozen bottles into long-term storage and promptly forgot about them for several years until we had some wines shipped back to us. Fearing the wine would be long past its best, we unwisely tried a bottle immediately after its long journey. Oh, it wasn't that bad, really, but it seemed such a shadow of its former splendid self that we relegated the rest to a corner of our cellar. Months later we were asked to contribute some modest red to a potluck buffet. We brought the remainder of the Pomerol. It turned out to have recovered from its travels and then some. It was all roses, crushed cherries, and velvet, and simply delicious. The guests were wowed, and we gained an instant reputation for largesse—quite undeserved, of course, as the wine was far better than our intentions. Later we sheepishly admitted to ourselves how salutary it was to be reminded that it's never a waste to pour something that will please your guests—no matter how numerous.

Since then, we've taken particular delight in sharing fine wines with guests who may not have had the unusual vintages or bottlings we've picked for the meal. It's wonderful when it works, when just the right vinous note is achieved—and that means wines that suit the dishes as well as the interests of your guests, so that the wines contribute subtly but unmistakably to the success of the occasion. But picking wines that are an appropriate match for the food, the moment, the mood, and the company isn't easy. It's the wine lover's equivalent of the writer's struggle to find *le mot juste,* and frankly, we haven't always been equal to the challenge. But in the process we've learned what *not* to do, and why.

An example: Some friends stopped over in the afternoon with friends of theirs in tow. We opened what we regarded as a delightful, flowery Rhine, thinking it a perfect choice for casual but elegant sipping. "I don't know anything about wine," said one young woman, accepting a glass. Curious to have a fresh opinion, we incautiously asked what she thought of the wine. "It smells like floor wax," she replied. We hastily produced an alternative.

Then there was the guest who later admitted that he thought the twenty-five-year-old Rioja we proudly poured simply stank. We realized he'd probably never had a really old red, just as the young woman had clearly never before encountered a mature Rheingau. Those experiences, among others, led us to formulate our first maxim of sharing wines: *Don't expect fine wines to seem fine to people unfamiliar with the taste.*

But our most uncomfortable wine-sharing experience involved wine served in an unmarked decanter. A few years back, a friend brought a man to one of our dinner parties who appeared quite knowledgeable about wine, but who was somewhat overbearing in talking about his wine collection and his favorite claret, Château Latour. We were pleased, nonetheless, because by coincidence we had planned to serve a '71 Latour with the cheese as a surprise, and in due course we produced the unmarked decanter. Without prompting, and before we'd even finished pouring the other guests' glasses, he pronounced it "Definitely Bordeaux." Lulled by this display of expertise, we unwisely asked what he thought of the wine. Unfortunately, he took this question as a challenge to identify it and insisted on trying to guess. "Well, it's not a first-growth, that's for sure," he concluded. "Certainly not Latour," he added gratuitously.

We were in a quandary. To reveal the wine's identity would have been tempting—he deserved deflation—but cruel. What hosts would insult their guests? Fortunately, one of us had the inspiration to claim it was a '75 Cos d'Estournel, an empty bottle of which still stood in the kitchen from the previous evening's meal, should anyone ask to look at the bottle. "Cos . . . Cos . . . ," mused the wine bore out loud. "I *was* thinking along those lines. . . ." Later, after the guests had gone, we formulated our second maxim: *Don't serve mystery wines to strangers.*

Every wine-loving host wants to serve wines that will delight his guests, and that requires gauging their level of wine sophistication and interest. However, when trying to second-guess the reaction of guests to the bottles on the table, it's easy to be over-clever and assume that even the knowledgeable drinker knows more than he does. You may go to all the trouble of serving a highly regarded, superscarce debut bottling from the latest California winery to a West Coast wine enthusiast only to discover that he or she has never heard of it and has no idea it's anything special. This puts you in the awkward position of explaining to your guests how perfect your choice was. Hence, our last maxim: *Find a subtle way to let your guests know what they're about to appreciate.*

Our friend the Artful Host has contrived a sly way to ensure no guest of his misreads the worth of his vinous offerings: He lets them choose. The Artful Host is far too canny to let guests (particularly knowledgeable ones) run amok in his cellar, so he offers airernatives. For openers, he may proffer two Champagnes and let a guest pick. Naturally, the guest asks about the differences, which the Artful Host is only too glad to expound upon, confessing that he found himself unable to decide which of the two equally superb bottlings—the racy, stylish Blanc de Blancs or the deeper, richer, classic cuvée—would have suited his guest's discriminating palate better. Having made the selection, the guest not only is prepared to appreciate what's served but having been a party to the decision, is in fact committed to liking it!

But let's suppose you're thinking of uncorking the last two bottles of that super Burgundy you bought years ago or that extravagant bottle of Château d'Yquem you've just splurged on. You want to underscore a special occasion—a holiday gathering, anniversary, or birthday—or maybe just to create one. How can you ensure that your grand bottle, not to mention your generous gesture, is appreciated?

Remember that anticipation is half the fun of drinking a great wine. The British connoisseur Maurice Healy once complained that "the average host bids you to dinner and without a word of warning, sets you drinking Lafite 1864 or something like that. The result is that he robs you and the wine of a great deal of your due. If you are going to drink a great wine, you should be told you are going to drink a great wine." Average host, indeed!

Although it's hard to imagine anyone serving prephylloxera claret today without calling a press conference, Healy's point is still valid, which brings us to another caution: *Don't serve a wine with too much fanfare.* Years ago, we once primed our dinner guests much too thoroughly, sharing every detail of the great wines to be served. When the doorbell rang on the evening of the dinner party, we opened the door to discover our first guest on his knees with an empty wineglass raised reverentially. Obviously, despite our overdone preliminaries, he'd kept his sense of humor intact, which helped us regain ours. Between underplaying it and overplaying it, there's a thin line for a host to tread if he wants to keep it all fun.

You can, however, *titillate your guests with the name of a special bottle you plan to open.* Take the useful stratagem employed by the Artful Host. Some hosts dangle other guests' names as bait for a dinner; he dangles the names of wines. "I have a magnum of 1967 Château Trotanoy that needs drinking up," he'll say. "Care to be in on the kill?" Knowing what the main gastronomic event will be gives guests who may not have heard of the wine a chance to find out what's so special about it before they arrive—in this particular case that Château Trotanoy is considered second only to Château Pétrus in Pomerol, that it made a splendid '67, etc. The hint is sufficient to prime everyone's palate and makes it unnecessary for the Artful Host to lecture us on the merits of what we're drinking. (Let's face it, no matter how charmingly a host does it, a lecture is deadly. It suggests that his guests are unknowledgeable or don't have the taste to discover the wine's quality on their own.)

Don't be too clever about matching vintages and birthday or anniversary dates is our last hint. Remember that a great year for people was not always a great year for wine. If you do serve a wine from a guest's birth year, don't make the mistake of dramatizing how old the wine is and how amazing it is that it's still alive, or you'll find yourself apologizing to the guest you intended to treat.

If you're serving an antique with your fingers crossed, have a backup bottle—just in case it turns out to have a bouquet of old boots. It's risky opening older wines on such occasions, but if the bottle is a disappointment, you can always tell your guest that they've clearly held up much better than the wine.

HOW TO WAFFLE ON WINE

When we first started writing about wine, it wasn't so hard to keep ahead of our readers, but today many of them are frighteningly well-informed. What's worse, an ominous number of them, knowing that we presume to advise others on matters of taste, will put us through our paces when they have the chance. Even well-intentioned acquaintances will put us on the spot in restaurants by handing over the wine list and announcing loudly that the bottle will doubtless be brilliant now that the choice is in expert professional hands.

Ah, but the worst is being asked to comment on the wine at a dinner, particularly if it's served anonymously. Innocents must think they're giving us an opportunity to astound the other guests with our expertise. Not-so-innocent types must secretly hope we'll amuse the party by making fools of ourselves. Alas, it's much easier to do the latter than the former.

When we can't wiggle out of such situations, we resort to a few tricks of the trade, which we now reveal here. They're extremely useful for anyone who wishes to preserve or create an image of wine expertise.

If you're asked to guess a wine—you know, when the unmarked decanter is put down in front of you by a smirking host and all the eyes of the guests fall upon you—remember, all's fair. Stay alert. Listen for the unintentional hint and watch for possible clues. The naïve host will wrap a napkin around a bottle and think he has disguised it when all it takes is one glimpse at the telltale slope of the bottle's shoulders to get you safely past the critical question of "Bordeaux or Burgundy?" If you're lucky, you may get a peek at a remnant of the neck foil or even a corner of the label, which will give your critical powers an amazing boost.

Along that line, a visit to the bathroom—via the kitchen—can reduce the possibilities to a manageable few if there's a just-opened bottle in evidence. But that maneuver can backfire if your host has the sort of low, caddish sense of humor that motivates him to leave enticing but entirely false clues around—such as bottles left over from the previous night, corks from entirely different wines, and the like.

Personally, we think it's much safer to put up a smoke screen of winetalk designed to dazzle your audience and make them forget their original mean mission of trying to get you to come out and say authoritatively exactly what that wine in your glass is. The following parlor tricks are equally effective when the bottle is sitting in front of you and you have no idea what to say about it. When cornered, the grand masters of the wine waffle adopt one of three classic approaches.

The French tactic, for openers, consists in raising one eyebrow in appreciation of the color and letting the eyelids flutter while sniffing long and lovingly. Take a sip, gurgling it through pursed lips. Swallow, pause, and follow with a stream of Franglais: "Hmm . . . good depth . . . what the French call *fond* . . . some *nervosité* . . . *mais un peu passé, n'est-ce pas?*" Wind up by describing it as definitely masculine or feminine, and hope that someone at the table will rise to the bait and deflect the conversation away from the wine into semantic/political issues. Whatever you do, don't pronounce the wine *typique*. Some smart aleck will surely ask you what the wine is typical of.

The California approach lies in browbeating your companions with pseudoscience. When questioned on the wine, complain about the lack of proper facilities for analysis. Ask for more light. Sniff through a favored nostril. Then gargle the wine, working it around the mouth as if rinsing the gums. Swallow and time the persistence of flavor by your watch. Describe the olfactory and gustatory sensations in terms an ear-nose-and-throat specialist would use. Expain how the odoriferous compounds excite the nasal receptors and how hard tannins interface with the soft palate. Speak of phenolics, extract levels, and an exotic defect or two. If you're lucky, no one will ask you if the Chardonnay has been kept in oak.

The English method is even better, particularly if you're served a wine blind. Begin by sniffing the wine with sharp snorts. Swallow, and then smack your lips appreciatively. Pronounce the wine "flavory, but a bit short." Point out that it would definitely appeal to certain palates, indirectly planting the suggestion that it might not be up to your sophisticated standards. Then abruptly sniff the wine again and look concerned. Ask how long it has been in your host's cellar. Whatever the answer, nod knowingly. Hint darkly that one never knows what wines like this have been through once they leave their home ground. Expand on that theme with a few horror stories of great wines reduced to a confusing shadow of themselves by summertime shipping and primitive storage conditions.

You'll have given yourself a wonderful out. When you're finally forced to offer a guess and barring luck, get it wrong, you can gaze sadly at the glass and mutter, "What a pity. It's not at all like the bottle I had last year."

7

A Different Perspective

PRESSING BUSINESS:

MAKING OUR OWN WINE

It's a common complaint among winemakers that journalists who've never picked a bunch of grapes in their lives nevertheless show not the slightest hesitation in telling winemakers how they ought to make their wines. A wine that typically represents a season of sweat in the vineyard, a harvest of sleepless nights, and months of patient nurturing in the cellar may just as typically be dismissed by a wine pundit with a curt comment like: "Overoaked, overoxidized, and overambitious."

If you're so smart, many winemakers would like to tell the wine critics, let's see *you* produce a wine that will make the world sit up and take notice.

Well, we can empathize with that reaction—and wonder if, along with other wine critics, we haven't been guilty of dispensing winemaking advice from time to time without a real understanding of what's involved. So when a phone call came in the spring of 1982 inviting us to try our hand at making wine, we couldn't resist the opportunity to see firsthand what it's like.

It would be a chance to put some of our pet theories about California wine to the test, because the caller was Tor Kenward from Beringer Vineyards in the Napa Valley, and he was inviting us to make a barrel of Chardonnay from scratch—pick the grapes, crush them, ferment the wine, age it, bottle it, keep it—and live with the results.

Kenward, Beringer's spokesperson, is an experienced amateur winemaker. With him and Myron Nightingale, then Beringer's winemaker, available for consultation, we had hopes of turning out something very drinkable. We'd be picking from one of Beringer's best Chardonnay vineyards, and considering the sort of wines Nightingale had been turning out from those grapes in recent vintages, we felt confident. Beringer is one of Napa Valley's pioneering wineries (founded in 1876) and owns some 1,800 acres of vineyards in Napa and Sonoma. Since its resurgence as a quality winery in the 1970s, it has continued to keep pace, as a taste of its Private Reserve Chardonnay and Cabernet Sauvignon will attest.

The agreed date of our visit—the third week of September— appeared to be premature. A long, cool growing season, which is excellent for grape quality, had delayed ripening and hence the harvest. "The sugar levels just aren't up there yet," Kenward told us by long-distance phone. "Can you wait and come a week later?" We couldn't, but we weren't concerned. A standing complaint of ours was that the alcohol levels of California Chardonnays were often excessively high. We'd pick at lower sugar levels and trade power for elegance. At least, that was our theory when we boarded the New York to San Francisco flight. When we landed and saw the headlines about rain, doubts arose. We hurried up to the Napa Valley.

"We've had two days of heavy rains in the valley that got everyone worried," Kenward explained to us over dinner at the Napa Valley's Auberge du Soleil. "But as you can see, we've got clear weather now." Indeed, the sunset was as stunning as the food, and we talked winemaking options while comparing a California Chardonnay with a Puligny-Montrachet. None of that overoaked, butterball Chardonnay style for us, we declared. We wanted a real thoroughbred—elegant, lean, long in the finish. It should have the vibrancy that comes with high acidity—what the French call *nervosité*. While conceding that we could choose winemaking options (such as the type of yeast, the use of barrel fermentation, skin contact, etc.), Kenward reminded us that most of the decisions that would affect the wine we would produce had already been made in the vineyard—and not by the vineyardist, but by nature.

The overconfidence of dinner-table theorizing was quickly checked by a firsthand inspection of the grapes the next morning. We went by truck to Beringer's Gamble vineyard (an all too appropriate name in 1982), east of Yountville, and walked down the rows. Our shoes sank into the earth, still damp from two days of rain. Our hearts sank, too, as we inspected the grapes. Some clusters were perfect, but others would turn out to be a sticky mess of rotten grapes when one reached behind to give an exploratory heft. The normally unruffled Kenward looked worried. "If only we had some wind to dry the grapes," he muttered. Instead, the lingering humid conditions were allowing grape molds—botrytis and bunch rot—to spread ominously.

It is one thing to look at harvest conditions with the detachment of a reporter. It is another to realize that the grapes in front of you are what you'll be making *your* wine out of. But the sun was shining; and wasn't this California, the new frontier of wine? We'd triumph over nature by sheer sweat and rigorous selection of bunches. It had been a near-perfect season so far, hadn't it?

We squeezed the juice of a few berries on Kenward's pocket refractometer to check sugar levels and squinted through it at the sky, reading the sugar content marked off on the scale by a dark blue horizontal line—a level that both literally and figuratively sets the horizon of a winemaker's ambitions. Without the proper ripeness—a percent of sugar level, expressed technically in degrees Brix—the resulting wine would be a thin, weedy, inconsequential mouthful. Twenty-two degrees, the refractometer told us. That meant a wine with roughly 12½ percent alcohol—certainly no monster by California standards. Well, we wanted elegance, didn't we? We decided to take some bunches back for a more detailed analysis in Beringer's lab. If the figures were encouraging, we'd pick tomorrow.

Before dinner, we had the technical specs: 22.5 percent sugar, 0.98 percent total acidity, and a pH of 2.95. In plain English, we were in the ballpark. But numbers don't make wine—grapes do. Only the finished wine would tell us about the quality we would achieve. In terms of style, we were getting exactly what we claimed we wanted—a low-alcohol, high-acid Chardonnay. But we wondered about the botrytis. Over dinner with Myron Nightingale, we asked him what he thought about the rains, the rot, pH levels, the sugar/acid balance, and so on. Nightingale, who had worked forty California harvests, didn't mince words. "Hell, a couple of days of rain and everybody in the valley starts screaming and yelling and pushing the panic button. We had early rains back in '57, and there were some fine Chardonnays from that year."

But there was more rain forecast in forty-eight hours, and we had appointments to keep. What did he think about picking tomorrow? Nightingale pushed a glass aside and leaned on the table. "I wouldn't get out there much before ten o'clock. Give the sun a chance to give the sugar a boost." He sat back and winked. "And don't forget to wear a hat. It gets hot out there."

As it turned out, we didn't start picking grapes before eleven-fifteen. Several dozen lug boxes—small crates that hold about fifty pounds of grapes each—got misplaced, and we spent an hour or so chasing them down. It was another reminder—by then we had caught on—that winemaking is not a cut-and-dried procedure. Despite the advances, it remains as much of a seat-of-the-pants craft as a science.

Nightingale was right: It gets hot out there. We were thankful for our straw farmer's hats. Grape-picking is dirty, sticky, backbreaking work. We declined the offer of the traditional but wicked-looking razor-sharp grape knives, grateful that we'd borrowed a couple of pairs of needle-nosed grape shears as finger insurance. Even so, we had to tangle with the luxuriant foliage of the California vine to clip off the compact, juicy clusters; and with all the stooping involved in filling the boxes—not to mention dragging them, lifting and piling them on the truck—our backs soon noticed the effect. We reassured ourselves that all this effort was worthwhile by stopping to chew a berry now and then to see if it tasted any different from the last one. Nearly two hours and a six-pack of sparkling mineral water later, three of us had loaded up the back of the pickup truck with twenty boxes—that's half a ton—of individual-bunch-selected Chardonnay and were bumping north on Highway 29 to Beringer.

According to the textbooks, we probably should have pressed the grapes immediately. Instead, we took an hour off for a much needed break and lunch, punctuated by a few inspirational samples of Beringer's latest wines. We then got back into the rhythm of the harvest, rolled up our sleeves, and started the laborious but immensely satisfying process of dumping the contents of each lug box into the hopper of a small, noisy stemmer-crusher—a machine that removes most of the stems and breaks up the bunches of grapes.

The operation became trickier as the lug boxes got progressively heavier and the floor slippery with grape juice. But our enthusiasm mounted as the damp cellar air grew thick with the scent of crushed grapes, and we eagerly took turns pressing the grapes batch by batch through a small, slat-sided basket press—and watched the cloudy sweet juice stream through the sides and funnel directly into two 30-gallon Limousin barrels for fermentation. Following California practice, we sulfured the must and added a cultured yeast to ensure a rapid, clean fermentation.

We had the pleasure of discussing a sample of our own still-fermenting, semisweet juice the next morning, drawn directly from one of the quietly burbling little barrels. Some winemakers argue that fermenting directly in a barrel adds a subtle flavor to Chardonnay that can't be achieved by simply aging finished wine in oak. We'd have to wait and see; when a wine's in its infancy, it's hard to predict its future. But we thought it was possible to discern in the near-wine the lineaments of a promising Chardonnay. At that moment, we understood in a very personal way how a winemaker could love a wine even if it could never win a prize: It's his child, after all.

During the months that followed, we made all the technical decisions that shape the wine in the cellar—whether to put it through malolactic fermentation to lower acidity (no), how much oak to give it (five months), whether to clarify it by fining (yes, with bentonite), how much sulfur (minimal), and so on, by phone, based on samples Kenward sent us.

Now, after nine months in the cellar, the wine was finished. Everything on the bottling line was ready: the two 15-gallon wicker-wrapped glass demijohns of our own oak-aged Chardonnay, stacks of sterilized bottles, the hand corker, capsules, handwritten labels, cartons—all laid out in a corner of Beringer Vineyards' old stone cellar near the wide doorway that revealed a bright Napa Valley spring day. We'd finally reached the point anticipated by every winemaker, professional or amateur, when there's nothing left to do with your wine but bottle it. Now you live with it. If you're a commercial winemaker, you hope it's good enough to sell; if you're an amateur winemaker, you hope you like it and that it's good enough to serve to your friends.

At the time of the crush, we'd been as bubbly as the newly fermenting wine; from picking to crushing to final fermentation there's something immensely satisfying about hands-on participation in all the processes of winemaking. It's at once atavistic and technical, intellectual and sensual—in short, the sort of experience that is magnetically attractive to a great many people, which is why so many Americans abandon perfectly sound careers or comfortable retirements to sink their fortune into making wine. What they get are such dubious pleasures as pruning in sleet or sleeping on cots by fermenting tanks during the crush to monitor the temperature. Yet making one's own wine, we've learned, is also the secret dream of many wine consumers.

Feeling very pleased with the progress of our personal product, we indulged ourselves in one last "cask sample" on the bottling line. It wouldn't hurt, we thought, to see if it tasted any different

than it had the day before. We stood in the sunny doorway with
Kenward.

"Nice wine. Real tart," he commented. We agreed, rolling the
wine thoughtfully around in our mouths. All things considered, it
tasted just the way we thought it ought to taste at that point—
meaning we were making allowances for its awkward youth.
Kenward passed on some encouraging reactions to the wine from
some of the cellar staff.

Had Myron Nightingale tasted it?

"Yes," said Kenward, agitating his glass vigorously, "but he
didn't say anything."

Nothing at all?

"No, but he did give it the high sign." Tor smiled, making a
thumbs-up fist.

We clinked our glasses, drained them, and with the assistance
of several Beringer personnel who volunteered some much appreciated help, we began bottling the 1982 McCoy-Walker Napa
Valley "Gamble Ranch" Chardonnay. Our bottling line was not
the sort of gleaming, computerized state-of-the-art setup where
bottles whirl around conveyor belts like soldiers in perfect step.
No, we passed the bottles from person to person; and the process
of filling one bottle with wine from a gurgling siphon, of driving
in a cork, of smoothing on the label, and of topping it with a foil
capsule took a good five minutes.

A tour group passed through, slowing down as it filed past our
noisy little endeavor with its cacophony of squirts, thumps, and
slaps (not to mention oops and ouches). We noticed a look of
concern pass over a few visitors' faces at the sight of us fumbling
with the hand corker in what was clearly the amateur's corner.
Fortunately they'd disappeared before we discovered that in order to finish filling the two giant Salmanazar bottles that had
been set aside, we had to uncork several bottles we'd just filled.
But that was mere detail, and despite the makeshift look, we uti-
lized up-to-date quality controls—blowing out the bottles with
nitrogen, handling the corks with rubber gloves (well, when we
remembered). Soon everything was boxed and after a suitable settling period would be ready to ship.

But what about the *taste?* Did it turn out the way we expected? We'd had great plans for this wine. Like most winemakers—amateur or professional—we had an idea for the kind of wine we wanted to make. It would be lower in alcohol, higher in acid than most California Chardonnays. It would be similar in flavor, we hoped, to one of our favorite types of wine—Chablis (French, that is). When our wine was in its infancy in barrel, it had all those funny little stinks and quirky flavors of a wine that—to borrow a phrase from winemaker Mary Ann Graff—is "still in diapers." Back then it had been easy to interpret the tasting impressions we got as promising portents. A hint of pineapple? A mineral note? A whiff of spearmint? A lemony finish? From such signs we extrapolated an impressive bottle a few years hence. But after bottling, our confidence gradually began to slip. The samples we tried weren't exactly music in the mouth. The wine seemed to sing a single note when what we really wanted was a chord. So we scaled down our expectations; maybe our coltish young wine wouldn't turn out to be a thoroughbred after all. It seemed potentially less like *cru* Chablis and more like a mean little Mâcon. . . .

Kenward was aghast at our disloyal thoughts. "Give it time. It's only been in the bottle two months!" he reminded us when we talked by phone.

It's true—it takes time for Chardonnay to develop in the bottle. We decided not to try it for several months. Then, in the late fall, we tried another. It had, well, bloomed! Oh, it hadn't turned into anything that would bring home the *gold,* you understand, but it had real Chardonnay character and a long, crisp finish.

In an effort to be scrupulously objective about our own wine, we'd forgotten our favorite wine dictum—that ultimately wine is for enjoyment, not analysis. And here in front of us was something unusually rewarding—our own wine that we'd made with our own hands on our own table. With a bowl of steamed mussels and some sourdough bread to mop up the broth, what more could we want from a glass of wine?

INDEX